The Best of the Grapevine

VOLUME THREE

OTHER BOOKS PUBLISHED BY THE AA GRAPEVINE, INC.

The Best of the Grapevine
The Best of the Grapevine 2
The Language of the Heart: Bill W.'s Grapevine Writings
The Home Group: Heartbeat of AA

IN SPANISH:
El Lenguaje del Corazón

Copyright ©1998 by The AA Grapevine, Inc.
All rights reserved
First printing 2002
ISBN 0-933685-40-8
Printed in the United States of America

The AA Grapevine, Inc.
Box 1980, Grand Central Station
New York, New York 10163-1980

—THE—
—BEST—
—OF THE—
GRAPEVINE

Volume 3

Jocelyn L. Monsma

┌─Registered Social Worker─┐
└──Registration #1404──┘

1411 A - 2nd Street S.W.
Calgary, Alberta T2R 0W7
T 403 290-1805

THE AA GRAPEVINE, INC.

NEW YORK

Alcoholics Anonymous® is a fellowship
of men and women who share
their experience, strength and hope
with each other that they may solve
their common problem and help others
to recover from alcoholism.

The only requirement for membership
is a desire to stop drinking.
There are no dues or fees for
AA membership; we are self-supporting
through our own contributions.
AA is not allied with any sect,
denomination, politics, organization or
institution; does not wish to engage in
any controversy, neither endorses
nor opposes any causes.
Our primary purpose is to stay sober
and help other alcoholics
to achieve sobriety.

CONTENTS

Contents

SECTION FOUR
Overcoming Adversity

SECTION FIVE
Interviews

SECTION SIX
Is AA Changing?

Contents

Contents

SECTION TEN
Old-Timers Corner

These sixty-eight articles, selected from ten years of publication in the AA Grapevine, reflect the varied interests, the range of recovery tools, and the broad spirituality of a diverse group of AA members. Offering personal stories, shared experience from around the world, and interviews with people who have helped shape the course of AA history, this volume is a powerful testimony to the strength, durability, and accessibility of the AA message. We hope it will give our readers a sense of the excitement and growth of AA as it has been expressed in the pages of the Grapevine over the past decade.

The Editors

Stories

MORE PRECIOUS THAN LIFE
SEPTEMBER 1987

Sometimes, when I least expect it, I wonder how it would be to go out there again. I find myself looking into one of the many new bars that have sprung up in my neighborhood, watching the young and attractive new generation of drinkers having a wonderful time. What does a wine cooler taste like, anyway? It has been so long since I've had a drink that maybe, just maybe, it would be different. Maybe, after seven or so years, the old body hasn't got an alcoholic cell left in it. Haven't I learned to be responsible and moderate in most areas of my life? God knows I've learned the pitfalls of unrestrained boozing. I'm an expert on how bad drinking can get, so who is better qualified to do it right? Right?

The fact of the matter is I never wanted to be a responsible drinker; I always got a thrill out of living on the edge; I courted disaster as surely as I courted pleasure, and if I went *out there* again it would be to embrace chaos.

I think of these things when I think of Cliff. "Cliff" and I had a lot in common. We both started drinking in the nineteen-fifties; we both became Bowery derelicts; we both had a long and hard time getting sober once we were introduced to AA: it took Cliff seventeen years to get a year of sobriety; it took me eight years to get that first year. Cliff finally got sober during the period I was still in and out: sober for a few months, then drunk for a few weeks — a deadly pattern that seemed endless and hopeless to me.

Before Cliff was back three months, he was working hard at the hospitality table; at almost every meeting he stayed late to do the mopping-up. We tend to view the progress of one who has been a chronic slipper with a skeptical, if not jaundiced, eye, but after about six months, the group began to think there was something different about Cliff this time: he appeared both more serious and, somehow, more relaxed; he raised his hand frequently and said really good things — there seemed to be a new honesty this time, a real commitment.

When he was seven months sober, Cliff announced that he'd gotten a good, full-time job with the city — the first real job he'd had in many years. Some of us thought that Cliff would slack off on meetings now, and, we asked ourselves, how would he handle the infamous "payday syndrome"? So many drunks do fine as long as they are broke but when the first big payday comes along, they are *gone* — down the road and out of sight! Cliff couldn't have handled this better: when his first check day arrived, he asked another AA member to accompany him while he cashed it, paid off a few debts, and opened a small account at the bank. He went to at least as many meetings, if not more, as he had before.

Even before Cliff had his first anniversary, he spoke frequently at hospitals, jails, and rehabs. He had a quiet, serious strength that newcomers, chronic slippers, and hard cases responded to. By the time he was a year and a half sober, he had half a dozen sponsees. He continued to live in a welfare hotel by the river that housed drunks, drug addicts, and psychotics; he brought many of these men to their first AA meetings, and some of them got well. When Cliff got a year of sobriety, I felt a tiny glimmer of hope for myself — not a lot, mind you, but at least *something*.

It was quite clear to our group that Cliff had a special quality; even old-timers began to defer to him. By the time he had two and a half years, Cliff seemed as solid as anyone our group had produced. He had had many jobs within the group and we elected him to be one of the three members on our beginner's panel; at the same time he became our group chairman by acclamation.

This was a very busy year for Cliff; besides his growing prestige within the group, he had become a supervisor at his job, he got a girl friend, found an apartment, was moving out of the welfare hotel, and had made a down-payment on a brand-new car. I'm sure some of the more cautious types thought Cliff was moving too fast, but I don't recall hearing it at the time — only afterward.

I'd just come back from one of my many slips when it happened. It was a Monday night and I noticed that somebody was sitting in for Cliff on the beginner's panel. At the break between meetings, nobody knew what had happened to Cliff. He hadn't called anyone to say he wasn't going to be there, and no one could call him because he hadn't yet connected a phone at his new apartment. The next day somebody called his job, but he hadn't been heard from since Friday.

By Wednesday we all knew Cliff was drinking; the atmosphere at the meeting that night was so thick with gloom and foreboding it was like walking in on a wake.

The next few weeks were an agony for the group. Several members who were close to Cliff tried to get him to sign himself into a detox. I don't remember now if they were successful or not, but if he did go, he didn't stay long because there was little letup in his drinking. He came to several meetings during this time, and sat in the rear, his back against the wall. He didn't say much to anybody and it was very awkward and difficult for most of us to approach him. It was as if he was saying, "I'm here, but nothing you can say or do will make a damn bit of difference."

I, who had so closely identified with Cliff, lost much of what little hope I had for my own recovery. If Cliff, with all his strength, couldn't make it after nearly three years of steady and solid sobriety — what hope had I?

We tried to understand why Cliff had gone out. There were many theories: he'd moved too fast; there was too much happening in his life all at once — too much change; his ego got him drunk and was preventing him from coming back; he hadn't talked enough about what was *really* going on; his sponsor should have seen the warning signs; he'd relied too much on his own strength and not on his Higher Power; had he diligently been doing the Steps?

It's normal for us to do this kind of postmortem. If we know why someone has gone back out, we feel we can take measures so it won't happen to us. I was sure Cliff would come back, sadder but wiser, counting his days again. Both of us had gone out and come back so many times, what was the big deal?

On Cliff's last day, a member of the group saw him sitting in his new car parked a couple of blocks from the river; he was drinking from a fifth of whiskey. Afterward a witness told police he'd seen the speeding car smash through the barrier and go careening out onto the abandoned pier and into the river.

Cliff ended his life ten years ago. I know several men, sober today, who were taken to their first meeting by Cliff; another man, who is a former sponsee, has been sober for over eleven years. Cliff had a legacy for me also, but I didn't see it until I'd been sober for almost as long as he was when he got drunk and killed himself.

Two years after Cliff died, I finally threw in the sponge. I'd been getting used to sobriety on the installment plan for over seven years and one morning when I awoke I knew it was over: I'd been drunk and I'd been sober, and I finally realized that sober was better — not a very dramatic revelation, but that was how it was for me.

By the time I had three years of sobriety, my life had changed completely: I'd started doing the things I had dreamed of doing; my life had gained the breadth and depth I couldn't have imagined three years before; there were loved and loving people in my life. It occurred to me, at that time, that I had built up an equity of sobriety that I could not easily bear to lose; I could not envision myself starting over again. Sobriety had become *more precious than life* — than any life that was *not* sober! That was Cliff's legacy to me: sobriety is precious! A fact I didn't know until I *had* some.

I don't know what went on in Cliff's head that last day. He'd been drinking for nearly a month; his decision to end it all was not rational. But I can understand his despair at losing the gift that had turned his life around so. It's easy to say that it was pride that prevented him from starting over again — but what power did he have over pride in the state he was in? All he knew was that he didn't want to live if it meant living the life of a drinking drunk. He had tasted the sweet fruits of sobriety.

R. K., New York, New York

THE STRANGER

SEPTEMBER 1989

Outside, on the other side of the window, the late August rain came down in a steady mist. The gray day was cold and damp. Inside, the warm air rising from the radiator vent smelled of dust. I'd been in treatment for two weeks and increasingly felt I'd made a mistake in committing myself to the hospital. It seemed to me that I was very different from the twenty-five other veterans with whom I was being treated for alcohol and drug addiction.

I caused no trouble, but simply coasted passively through each day, becoming more and more detached from my surroundings. I felt the old familiar feeling of separation as the bell jar descended, shutting out the world. My counselor sensed my withdrawal and confronted me, pressing for an explanation. I answered that I felt like a fox in a chicken coop. Her pupils opened wide for a moment, and then her whole demeanor became defensive. I left the interview knowing from her reaction what I had long suspected — that I was different from other men. I also knew that there was something wrong with me, but I didn't know what.

I wondered again if all the killing in Vietnam had changed me in some fundamental and irreversible way. I knew I'd lost my innocence and my capacity for joy. I knew that the experiences of war had changed me to the point that all of my illusions about society — our myths and beliefs — had been permanently shattered. I suspected also that I had been too long a soldier, lived too long in a state of emergency after emergency, felt too many times the warm blood of others flow out of their bodies while they cried out because of the wound that was killing them. I knew from my reading that these were the reasons why I was bored with the experiences of a normal life, why my subconscious was forever unexpectedly throwing up memories of the war, and why I was burdened with guilt and a sense of futurelessness.

I had felt my old familiar depression returning as I left my encounter with the counselor earlier that morning. Now, sitting on the edge of my bed, staring out the window, I told myself that there was nothing to be done, that I might as well stay in the hospital and finish the treatment. I resisted the thought of suicide once again, and told myself that I would embrace it when the time came.

That night I attended the compulsory Monday night AA meeting on the first floor of the old wing of the hospital. As I walked to the meeting, I reflected on the fact that I was half finished with the treatment, and that the lectures and films, although interesting, had not touched me. I began to worry about my chances of staying sober once I left treatment. In the auditorium, I found a seat well in the back — alone. I'd been there the week before, sat in much the same seat, and listened to the same drunkalogs. It all seemed so irrelevant, so miserable, so pathetic. I wasn't like that. I slid down in the seat, quit listening, and began to remember other times and places.

I sat like that for the first hour, consciously drifting in and out of my memories, when I began to hear a voice. It was a quiet voice, but it was also profound in tone and strong in its emotional force. It came from the stranger who now stood at the podium. He was a big blond man with huge hands and the face of a policeman — a policeman who, always seeing people at their worst, had lost faith in human beings. He was dressed like an ordinary merchant seaman and spoke with difficulty, his eyes cast down, his manner one of suppressed anger and embarrassment. It was obvious from his speech that he hadn't been well educated. He used no philosophical generalizations, employed no humor, told no ego tales. He talked about his life simply and told us about alcohol, how it had defeated and humiliated him, and how at last he had admitted his powerlessness and sought help. He spoke slowly, pausing between statements, staring into the nothingness of the front row as he struggled to master his emotions. Now and then he would stop his narrative, hunch his shoulders forward in response to the pain he so obviously felt, and struggle to gain control of his emotions. When he looked directly at me for the first time, I felt myself blush with a deep sense of shame.

He said, "All of my life I have felt different than other men, but I did not know why. All of my life I have known something was wrong with me, but I did not know what." I could hear my heart beating, and I began to take quiet deep breaths to get control of my own emotions. The bell jar lifted, and I became acutely aware of every nuance of his speech and manner. His words were at once so personal and so painful that without warning I found myself identifying with his experiences as if they were my own. He said, "Now I know what's wrong with me. I am an alcoholic." He paused again and stared into the space in front of the podium. Then he began to talk about his recovery and about his long road back from the edge of suicide. When he talked about his feelings, he talked about my feelings, about feelings I had! He had never been to war, was not even a veteran. And yet when he talked, he gave voice to my thoughts. He talked about his troubled youth, his depression, his hopelessness, his inability to stick with anything. I had thought myself unique, but here was another like myself — but he had been sober for five years. He thanked us for listening and sat down.

He was not the last speaker. While the others spoke, I kept going over in my mind what the stranger had said. After the meeting ended I went up to where he was sitting. He sat alone in the front row, slumped down in the seat, staring straight ahead, absorbed in his own thoughts. He looked up at me when he sensed my presence, and I could see in his eyes that it had been difficult for him to confess himself to us. His look at me was at once wary and hostile. I knew that look too. Here was a man I'd never seen before in my life, and yet I felt I knew him as well as I knew myself. I spoke and said that he had helped me.

At once his manner changed. He jumped out of his seat, smiled broadly, grasped my hand, asked my name and how long I had been in treatment. His hand was calloused and strong. He stood close to me as he asked me about myself. I could smell the clean smell of laundry soap in his cotton clothes. He didn't let go of my hand and laughed when I spoke about myself as if we both shared some kind of secret. Seeing him laugh I realized he was younger than I thought. He must have had some kind of job where he did hard physical labor. He obviously had just showered and shaved before coming to the meeting. Then he let go of my hand, wrapped his big arm around my shoulders, and led me off into a corner of the large room where we were even more alone.

He seemed to know all about me and kept asking questions that caused me to open up to him in a way I later could not understand. He smiled as I talked, locking his eyes into my eyes. As the words rushed out of me, he encouraged me with nods and smiles; sometimes he would laugh out loud and punch me in the arm or thump me on the shoulder. At one point he said, "Why, shoot! You're a stubborn and hard-headed SOB just like me." Without knowing the precise moment when the change occurred, while talking with this stranger, I stopped feeling sorry for myself and for the first time began to hope that maybe I might make it after all.

I don't remember how long we talked. I do know that we were the last ones to leave the auditorium. He walked me to the elevator and said goodbye. I never saw him again. I never even knew his name, but he changed my life. The next day, treatment began to work for me, and in the years that followed I met others like him in various AA meetings throughout the city. One such man became my sponsor and set my steps on the long road back from the brink.

R. A., Woodinville, Washington

A LONG WAY DOWN

JULY 1994

My name is Nell. I'm an ex-inmate, a recovering alcoholic, and a member of Alcoholics Anonymous. I've been sober since December 7, 1984. That's the longest I've stayed sober since I was a teenager. I was introduced to AA while incarcerated and finally found a glimmer of hope that I'd never known before. I also found understanding, unconditional love, hope, and real friends.

I never felt like I fit in anyplace. My dad abused alcohol and was my drinking buddy. There was a lot of fighting and turmoil between my parents. I was abused terribly, and I wanted to die beginning very young.

I was born the fifth of nine children. The first child died before fifteen months of age. No medical attention was sought by my family. I was the oldest daughter, and I was placed in the mother role at the age of eight when my youngest sister was born. My mom had addictions other than alcohol and was a very sick person.

I was made to go to church, and what I seemed to hear about was a punishing God. I begged God to let me die. I felt different, looked different, and was treated as different. I asked many times if I was adopted. I didn't understand why I was ever born.

I never got to be a child and play as other children did. Lots of responsibilities, work, punishment, and abuse of all kinds were what my life consisted of. I lived in fear but I was never allowed to express my feelings. I learned early on to keep my mouth shut and stuff my feelings. I was never believed, it seemed, so I learned early not to trust anyone. I was incested severely by the time I was eight years old. It continued longer, much longer.

My mom didn't want alcohol in the house, so my dad made me hide his moonshine for him. I'd sneak around and drink out of his bottle. Alcohol gave me courage and made me feel like the adult I was forced to be. I ran away several times and was beaten unmercifully when I was found. I couldn't feel safe anywhere or with anyone. I continued to want to die.

I ran away at fifteen years old and married a man twenty years my senior — one of my dad's drinking buddies. I found myself worse off. That marriage was a real nightmare which seemed endless and hopeless. I finally managed to escape that situation — two daughters later.

My first serious suicide attempt (one among many) was at sixteen years of age. My husband abused alcohol and was constantly drunk. It was like living in a concentration camp. I was beaten and tied up in the nude off and on for at least a year. I passed out from pain several times. My husband sold my body to buy booze. I begged God to ease my pain. My husband poured booze down my throat to quiet me. That was the only relief I had.

Drinking, suicide attempts, abuse, and getting in trouble with the law were a way of life for me all those years. When I finally left my husband, he said he'd kill me if and when he found me. I believed him and hid for years in fear.

I felt so empty, dirty, worthless — a nobody with a hole in my gut. I was always looking for something to fill that emptiness. Booze eased my pain, but only temporarily.

My life consisted of shoplifting, stealing, lying, hot checks, and daily drinking. I got into another relationship and had two more daughters. I was institutionalized in jails and mental hospitals countless times. Everyone who said they loved me hurt me; so I was real confused and afraid of love. I never found a gleam of happiness, love, or hope. By the time I was incarcerated the last time, I'd attempted suicide at least twenty-two times, been in jail at least thirty-nine times, and had been in and out of various hospitals. I'd tried everything. I couldn't die and didn't know how to live. Nor did I want to.

That day in December 1984, I came to in my own vomit and a pool of blood. I was sick and tired of being sick and tired. I finally had that moment of clarity we talk about. Taking a big risk, I called my parole officer pleading in desperation for her to help me. I could have been sent back to prison that day. I'd been drinking since my release the previous December.

My parole officer suggested I go to a halfway house. I was beaten down to complete demoralization so I went where she suggested, leaving behind every material thing I owned. I was penniless with only the clothes on my back. I was bankrupt in every area of my life.

AA meetings were being brought into the halfway house from outside. The first time they were announced I didn't hesitate to attend. I knew my life was unmanageable and I was powerless over alcohol. I really surrendered and admitted complete defeat. For the first time in my life, I was able to see a tiny light at the end of that dark tunnel I'd been in for over forty years.

I didn't know what AA was — I thought it could teach me how to drink successfully or control my drinking — but I was willing as only the dying can be to do anything suggested. The eight-year-old girl in me began to live instead of merely exist. Somehow I knew I was finally safe. I was shown a new way of life — one I never dreamed that poor, abused, neglected child would ever have.

AAs loved me sober and loved me back to health. I was afraid of their I love you's — I wondered what they wanted from me. But they really cared, and I'd never known anyone who really cared. Somehow I trusted a tiny bit. I began to feel freedom and peace.

That empty feeling in the pit of my stomach has now been filled. It's been filled with a loving, caring, and a forgiving God of my own understanding. I'm starting to learn a little about me, and I accept myself most of the time. I've had to obtain some extra help to work through my past. That's okay. Without AA I couldn't have done it. It's been painful, but worth it.

Since coming to Alcoholics Anonymous I've always had someone to take me by the hand and assure me that "this too shall pass." I want all there is in recovery. I started with a sponsor, working the Twelve Steps and Twelve Traditions, and applying the principles of the program in my life. I call my sponsor or another alcoholic daily, go to at least one meeting, read the literature, write daily, and thank my Higher Power for another day of sobriety. I'm involved in my home group and go to lots of service meetings, as well as sponsoring other people. It's very important for me to go into jails and prisons and work with inmates and ex-inmates. I seek in prayer and meditation to improve my conscious contact with God, and I make a lot of gratitude lists.

My life is full today. I have all I need and most of what I want. I'm learning to be a mother, a friend, a grandmother, and a sister. My friends are a close-knit support group, and they're as near as the telephone. I have my own apartment, thanks to God and my AA friends. At first I found it hard to accept these gifts because of my pride and ego. I didn't know how I could ever pay it back. My friends told me to "pass it on." I can never find the words to express the depth of gratitude for my newfound happiness and freedom. I'm even learning how to have fun and not take life too seriously.

There are still lots of life's problems. I have a grandson in jail and a granddaughter who attempted suicide and is in treatment for emotional problems. I recently fell and broke my wrist (lots of pain). But no matter what there is today, nothing is so bad that a drink won't make worse.

I never knew I had choices. Today I have choices.

Nell S., Arlington, Texas

HE GAVE ME THE SHIRT OFF HIS BACK
DECEMBER 1994

Before I had my last drink in July 1986, it was necessary for me to try every form of self-deception and experimentation that the Big Book refers to. I found myself in and out of Alcoholics Anonymous for about eight years. I became familiar with the program and could recite large portions of the Big Book from memory. Even so, I kept right on drinking. My unsuccessful attempts at the AA way of life led me to believe I was doomed to a miserable future of drinking that surely would end in tragedy.

I openly balked when the Promises were read, and thought that I'd have to be a simpleton like the others for the Steps to work for me. Then one night, much to my surprise, I was in a meeting with my hand raised. It had been a very difficult day for me and I was overcome with a feeling of guilt for a decision I had recently made.

To the group I expressed my desire to ride my newly purchased motorcycle at full speed on the highway and lay it down. I went on to give the reasons for my wish to die. Following a nearly fatal accident I had been in only six months earlier, I promised my dear mother I'd never ride again. It was she who had nursed me back to health, and I felt that the least I could do to repay her was keep my promise. Now, I had just gone out and bought a new motorcycle. Coupled with the unbearable guilt this had brought on was the pitiful and incomprehensible demoralization that my attempts at controlled drinking had produced. So, now my dilemma was twofold: I was unable to imagine life with or without alcohol, and I was unable to imagine life with or without a motorcycle. Truly, I was at the jumping-off place and wished for the end.

After I had finished talking, a man named Lee shared. He said he could identify with me because he'd seen an accident similar to the one I had described. He went on to tell of the night he was at an AA meeting and heard a nightmarish collision on the highway just outside. He left the meeting so that he could tend to the victims of the crash. On arriving at the scene, he found a motorcycle which had become united with the car it had struck. Some distance away lay the body of a young man, face down in a pool of blood. The meeting was in a hospital, and a doctor also came rushing to the scene. The doctor rolled the body over to check for vital signs and, after finding a faint heartbeat, rushed back to the hospital to get more help. Due to the seriousness of the injuries, the young man was going to have to be transported to a trauma center nearby. Lee stayed with the man until the ambulance arrived.

As Lee told his story, the entire meeting listened intently. Indeed, you could have heard a pin drop. The love of Lee for the victim could be felt by all.

While Lee waited for the ambulance, he took off his T-shirt and placed it under the young man's head. He then held him and began to pray. He pleaded with God to spare the young man's life. Finally the paramedics arrived and whisked the youth off to the trauma center where he remained in critical condition for several days.

I was hardly prepared for what was about to happen. Lee ended his story by saying that not only did the victim live today, he was actually in the meeting that night. He slowly turned until he was facing me, raised his arm, and pointed directly at me: "It's a miracle, my friend, because you're sitting right there."

A chill ran up my spine. I still had the bloodstained T-shirt, and now, in an AA meeting, I was to meet the man who had placed it under my head. I don't remember anything that was said afterwards, but at the end of the meeting, I could hardly stand. When I did, you can be sure I embraced Lee with the fervor of a man well in the grips of a miracle. Suddenly I wanted to live!

Since this was not the first but the third near-fatal accident I'd been in, I came to believe that God had spared me for a reason. I realized that I am on this Earth according to his schedule, not my own. When the time comes for me to die, I will die — and not a moment before then. And if I'm to live, the only way is to do it sober. Armed with this conviction, I decided to live my life to the best of my ability.

I returned home that night, opened the Big Book, and began reading. Although I had read it many times, the words now became meaningful, and had a clarity like never before. I figured out why I'd been unsuccessful with sobriety in the past. The answer was on page fifty-eight: "Those who do not recover are people who cannot or will not completely give themselves to this simple program. . . ." My problem was not that I could not, because I knew I could; my problem was that I would not. After this discovery, I commenced to follow the program as outlined in the Big Book, and for the first time in my life, I completely gave myself to this simple program.

Today I am pursuing the life of sobriety with the same eagerness I drank with. As a result of practicing the AA principles in all my affairs, I've found a life I never knew existed. I'm so overwhelmed with gratitude that there's no room for a bad day. Not only am I an active member of Alcoholics Anonymous, I'm an active member of the community as well. At last, I'm a man among men, a worker among workers, back in the mainstream of life. At twenty-seven, I have the brightest future imaginable, and it is all a result of what I found within the Fellowship of AA, the Big Book, and the love of a man who cushioned my head with the shirt off his back.

W. P., Costa Mesa, California

≈

MY NAME IS JOHN AND I'M AN ALCOHOLIC
NOVEMBER 1996

I was born eighty-six years ago in a tough neighborhood known as the Brick Bottom section of Somerville, Massachusetts. We were very poor. I had a wonderful mother, four little brothers, and a little sister. We were born one right after the other; we were just like steps. My mother would say to us, "Your father's a good man when he's not drinking." My father was a rugged, powerful drinker; he was really trouble. When he'd come home on one of his binges, I'd take my little brothers and my sister upstairs to the attic until everything quieted down. It used to take four or five cops to get him out of the house and he always went the hard way. They'd beat the life out of him and my mother used to jump in and say "You're hurting him." I never could figure that out.

My mother didn't last very long; she died in her early thirties. I never saw a big, strong man like my father cry so much. He really went to pieces and then I knew that he had loved my mother, and today I know that he was an alcoholic. After she died, he did the best he could; he calmed down and took care of us. He remarried and our life began to get pretty good, but it didn't last long.

My father came home from work one day with a headache and the doctor who came to the house said he had a cerebral hemorrhage and that he wouldn't last the night. On hearing this, my stepmother dropped dead right there on the spot, and my father died during the night. I don't know where they're buried.

My sister and one brother went to California, and the others were taken in by other families. Perhaps because I was the oldest (I was fourteen then) I wound up on the street — literally.

I didn't know what to do, I was completely lost; so I drifted toward the center of town, near the Somerville Highway Department. In those days they separated the trash from the papers, so I crawled into one of the paper wagons and cried myself to sleep. The next morning I went to a restaurant in Somerville Square and said to the guy at the counter, "I'm hungry, I'd like to eat." He fed me, and after hearing what had happened to me, he let me sleep that night in his restaurant.

The next day he got me a job in a hardware store. They had a big warehouse and I loaded trucks with nails, roofing materials, and other hardware goods. I made my home in that warehouse. I used to see little kids outside riding their bicycles and I knew there had to be something different from the kind of a life I was leading. I wasn't eating right or living right. I lasted there for two years and I got real sick and ended up in the hospital. After I got better, they got me a job and a room — they were very good to me.

The new job was easier than the warehouse. There were a lot of girls there and one used to share her lunch with me. I didn't know anything about anything, but she was very kind and nice to me. We became very close and she invited me to her parent's home in Lynn for Sunday dinner. Her folks picked me up at the train station, and I had the most wonderful time. I saw more food that day than I'd ever seen in my life. I really enjoyed myself. Her mother took me aside and wanted to know all about my background, and after hearing what I had to say, basically told me I wasn't good enough for her daughter. I was very hurt; I felt awful. They wanted to give me a ride back to the train station and I refused. On the walk to the station, I thought, "What a life. I lost my mother, I lost my stepmother and my father, I lost my brothers and sister, and something good came into my life and now I've lost that too."

I quit the job. I couldn't face that girl. I was seventeen years old now and I got a job as an iron worker in construction. Soon after I started working, we all went out to a bar for lunch. The rest of the guys ordered drinks, and I ordered what they ordered — a shot and a beer. I'd never had a drink up to that point; I'd never tasted booze. That boilermaker straightened me right out; I felt so good that I didn't care what happened. It made me feel like I was part of something. I went back to work and it was always in my mind about getting another drink. I didn't drink all the time, but I was always thinking about it. I wanted to get that freedom feeling.

I was making more money than I'd ever made. I bought a little car and I was doing fine. Then this little girl from Lynn looked me up; she tracked me down. I told her that she'd be in trouble, that her mother didn't like me, and she said, "Let's get married." "Married," I said, "how do you do that?" I knew nothing about any of that. But we got into my car, drove over to New Hampshire, and were married by the justice of the peace. As sure as I'm sitting here, I thought she was supposed to go home afterwards. But she said, "No, I'm supposed to live with you." (That was sixty-seven years ago and we're still married.)

We settled in Lynn near her parents — that was a mistake. But we were going along pretty good when the Depression came

along. I got a job at Sears Roebuck changing tires. There was a little bicycle shop next door owned by Vassa S., and boy, did this
guy drink — he'd drink anything. I drank with him. I used to
swipe bicycle tires from Sears, bring them to him, and he'd sell
them. "Wait," he'd say, "I'll get some booze." He'd go across the
street and come back with a whiskey bottle filled with bay rum
shaving lotion. "This tastes funny," I'd remark. "That's good stuff,
John, drink it," he'd say. Later he played an important role in
helping me join AA.

When World War II started, I was back doing iron work, and
my business was good. I was away from home a lot and my drinking picked up; I was drinking every day. I came home on the
weekends and I drank. I tried to come home without drinking but
it never worked. I just couldn't not drink. My wife was one of
those ladies who couldn't tolerate booze. She started giving me
ultimatums; then she put restrictions on me. She'd say, "We've got
four little children and you're not going to be coming home
drinking." Things got tough. There was plenty of trouble between
me and my wife; in fact I was arrested about twenty-five or thirty
times just trying to get into my own house.

Then my wife saw an ad in the Lynn newspaper that said, "If
you drink and want to, that's your business. If you drink and can't
stop, that's our business." She called the number, and up to my
house came this guy I used to drink with — Vassa S. Another guy
was with him. They were sober, and they told me I had an illness,
that I was sick, but I couldn't buy that. They told me about their
own drinking, how sick they were, and how they recovered. They
invited me to the meeting that Vassa had started in 1944 at 10
City Hall Square. But I couldn't accept the fact that I was an alcoholic. Everybody drank on the job, I worked everyday, and I

couldn't see that I had a problem. AA was very young then and I didn't think much about it. In those days we took pledges. We'd go to a priest, say a few prayers, and promise we wouldn't drink again. That didn't work too well.

I went to my first AA meeting in 1945. Here were old men, guys who came out of the nuthouses; they all had forty-pound noses. There were no women. I went home and said to my wife, "You don't expect me to go down there. They're alcoholics, they need it. I'm not like them."

I continued to drink, and things got so rough that in 1946 I went back to AA and got sober. I still didn't believe that I was an alcoholic, but my life began getting better. I had four little girls, and in 1949 a little boy came along and joined the four girls, and life was good. I was a foreman now. We bought a big house, we both had cars, and we were getting along fine.

Time went on, and I was doing a big job in Winoosky, Vermont. Being an iron worker, I always had to go away to make a living. It was the Fourth of July, 1955. I used to fly home on weekends, but this weekend I decided to stay in Vermont. I called my wife and told her that I was going to go across Lake Champlain and relax on the beach. On the way to the ferry, I heard music coming from behind a stockade fence. I opened the gate, and there was the American Legion, having a big bash. They were drinking beer, really bending their elbows, and the thought crossed my mind that I could have one beer. Eventually, that one beer took me right to the skids. I went into a blackout and got arrested that night. Soon afterwards, I lost my job, I lost my wife, I lost the kids, I sold the car, I got put out of where I was staying, and ended up in the South End of Boston.

AA became like a memory; it went right out of my head. I

ended up in Blackstone Park, which was full of winos just like me. By now nothing except wine would stay down. I stole nickels and dimes off the newspapers along Washington Street, enough to buy a pint of wine and get back to the park and keep drinking. I used to sit on that park bench and cry my eyes out. I knew I had a wife and kids, I knew my wife was breaking her back taking care of the kids, and there I was in Blackstone Park. I tried to stop drinking and I just couldn't stop. I didn't have the power to choose to stop. Every time I tried to stop, I went into a seizure, and they had to take me to the old Washingtonian. Because of the seizures I was convinced that I couldn't live without drinking.

I was always trying to make up my mind to go to work and help my wife, and I just couldn't do it. Once I went down to the union hall and they sent me to Maine. I was working at a power plant, and we had a lot of booze. When we ran out, an engineer said if we fired up the locomotive, he'd take us to get some more. So we stole a logging train and drove it ten or fifteen miles to get more booze! It was a very serious offense, and we went to prison in Thomaston, Maine.

Later, coming out of prison, I didn't have anyplace to go, and I wound up on the Penobscot Indian Reservation. My middle name was trouble. I got in trouble there, got my leg broke, and got stabbed, then got put off the reservation with a cast and a crutch. The journey back to the South End of Boston from Maine is a story in itself. I'd go to a church, beg for a meal, get a scrip to sleep for a night at the YMCA, and drink in between. You know when you're a drunk, nobody wants to look at you. It's an awful existence. Finally, I wound up again in Blackstone Park in the South End.

I wanted to try once more to go to work so I went down to New York. I never should have done that; I was too sick. I went down there and didn't even last one day at work. I decided I was going to commit suicide. I went to the Salvation Army and told the person sitting at the desk that I was going to kill myself. I asked him if he'd write my wife a letter so she'd know that I was dead. He said, "Okay, just let me go in the back and get some paper and an envelope." Instead he called the cops. The cops came and they put me in the nuthouse. I fought them. As weak as I was, I didn't want to go to the nuthouse. When I got there they shot me with something, and I became very calm and peaceful. Eventually I liked it there. I was eating and sleeping, and I had a roof over my head. The patients were really nuts, too. This wasn't an alcoholic ward, this was a nut ward. But I didn't care.

When the time came for me to leave the nuthouse, I didn't want to leave because I didn't have anyplace to go. By this time I was in my fifties. Then I met up with a young guy half my age who was a con man. He said, "I know where we can go, John. There's a place near here, they call it the Holy Mountain. It's the Christopher's Home for Homeless Men." We went there and it was fine. We got cleaned up, but we couldn't drink there. This guy got the idea that we could steal collars and vestments, go downtown, and pass the hat — and that's what we did. We were collecting money like crazy until one day someone put a few pennies in my friend's hat, and he called the guy cheap. That was the end of posing as priests. The cops came and put us out of town. Trouble, trouble, trouble, always trouble.

This guy wanted to go home. I wanted to go home too because I felt I didn't have much longer to live. He got me a ticket to Lynn, Massachusetts. When I got there, I didn't have anywhere to go. I was restrained from my house, but I had a brother-in-law who was taking care of an apartment building, and he let me sleep in the cellar. He put a cot down next to the boiler. He didn't like me but he didn't want me to freeze to death either. One night I was lying on the cot — the room had a bare light bulb — and the light bulb was getting bigger and bigger. I thought it was going to go off like a bomb. I knew I needed a drink bad, and I went downtown and bought a jug of wine, thinking that I would go off to a side road and chug-a-lug the wine. I hoped it would kill me.

I got the jug, went off on the side road, and drank the wine, and came to in the morning lying on the grass. I heard music. "That's it," I thought, "I'm going nuts." I got up, followed the music, and came to a little church. There were some little kids running around with palms and I realized it was Palm Sunday. I went into the church and for the first time in years I asked God for help. "Let me live or let me die," I prayed. I got up, went outside, and stood on the sidewalk. That was Palm Sunday 1966 and I haven't had a drink since. The grace of God had entered my life, but I didn't know it at the time.

I was standing on the sidewalk, wondering where I was going to get a drink, and I remembered that my mother-in-law, who was now in her nineties, was in a nursing home nearby. "Maybe she'll give me a few bucks," I thought. She remembered me and said she'd give me ten dollars if I went to an AA meeting. "Where's the AA meeting?" I said. "Right next door to this nursing home," she replied. I kept my end of the bargain and went there.

When I entered the room, a guy came over and put his arm around my shoulder and said, "Are you having a problem with alcohol?" That was an understatement. I didn't have any shoes, my teeth were gone, my glasses were gone, my feet were swollen, and my scalp was full of sores. His name was Al and he took me home with him. I couldn't believe it. He cleaned me up and he wanted to put me in the Mt. Pleasant detox, but I didn't think I could stop drinking. I was convinced that if they put me in a room somewhere and closed the door, I would die. So I refused to go to the detox, but he got me medical attention. I'll never forget the doctor's name — Dr. O'Brien — he was very good to me. I had a leg that was in real bad shape and he sent me into Boston for treatment; it's not very good today either, but it's all right. If I'd continued to drink, I would have lost the leg. I don't know why I'm living today. I look back on my life and it scares me.

I stayed with Al; he did everything for me. We went to meetings together for months. He sat me right beside him. He belonged to the Green Street Group and we went on commitments together. I began to get well; I began to get back into reality.

I was still on a restraining order, and I would watch my kids from a distance. I wanted to put my arms around them and hug them. Finally I told him, "Hey, Al, it's no use. My kids are gone, I can't work, I've got a bad leg, my health is gone, and I just can't keep up. I can't get rid of that ball in my stomach. I see my kids and wife from a distance and I just can't take it." He gave me courage. He suggested that I do a Fourth and Fifth Step, try to get rid of the garbage, and begin to clear away the wreckage of the past.

A few days later I was in a meeting and I decided to get someone to talk to. After the meeting, I saw an active drunk that I knew; he was gonzo. I bought a fifth of wine, took him over to a park bench, and said, "Look, sit down, I'm going to give you this jug. You can drink it but you're going to listen to me. The minute you walk away I'm taking the jug." I did my Fifth Step with him and I got out all that garbage. I unloaded stuff with him I never thought I'd tell anyone. When I got through, he finished the jug, and I just put him on the bench and walked off. I felt better after that; I felt good. Later I teamed up with Joe H. from Malden and he really helped me with the Steps.

I continued to go to meetings with Al, and when I was eight years sober, he made an appointment for me to talk with my wife, and I returned home after being gone seventeen years. I had a lot of trouble with the kids, but my wife took me back. Two of my daughters were pretty good, but the youngest one had lots of resentment and anger.

Being sober the second time was very, very difficult, but I didn't want to go back to where I came from. I didn't want to drink — I just couldn't take that anymore. I didn't want to be in the South End living under the Dover Street bridge in the summer and then in the winter at the Pine Street Inn waiting for the van to come up and take us to Bridgewater State Hospital on voluntary commitments so we could stay warm. At Bridgewater there are graves; they have headstones without names. I didn't want any more of that.

One of my daughters was an alcoholic, and she couldn't stop drinking. She was in one detox after another. I was sitting with her on her bed one night and she put her arms around me and said, "Daddy, why can't I stop drinking?" She had an alcoholic seizure and died in my arms. It was awful. I didn't know what to do. She had a little boy, and my wife and I raised the boy. You never get over something like that.

My son went to Vietnam and when he came back he was into everything — drugs, booze — but he seemed to survive for a time. He went to college under the GI Bill and got a degree in business administration. But he'd avoid me, and then I knew he was drinking. He graduated and got a good job, but I could see how he was drinking. He got fired from one job after another.

Finally, his wife divorced him and he wound up on the street. I took him home with me and I started putting him into institutions and VA hospitals. I struggled like crazy with him. I put him in a VA hospital around Thanksgiving time. I was going to bring him home for Thanksgiving Day, so I went down there a few days ahead, and I could see he was way down, very depressed. I came home that night and later got a call to come and identify his body. He had walked out of the hospital and jumped in front of a truck. When I identified his body, I thought I was going to have a heart attack. All this time I didn't think of a drink. I thought about blowing my brains out, but not about drinking.

My wife went right out of her mind, two children gone now. I didn't sleep taking care of her; I took her to a psychiatrist for a year. One day I went with her. The psychiatrist said to her, "You know, you've been coming here for a year now and I can't seem to get to your problem." "It's him," my wife began, pointing at me. "He never was home for Christmas, he didn't see these kids graduate high school, I worked like crazy to support them." On and on she went, she let out everything that was bothering her, and everything she said was true. Afterwards she felt better. She came over to me, gave me a big hug, and we went home. On the way out the psychiatrist said to me, "I'd like to delve into your childhood." I said, "For forty dollars an hour I'll give you a story that will blow your socks off." The psychiatrist, she got a kick out of that.

I went through a lot, my sobriety didn't come easy, but my life is good today. My wife is fantastic, I love her and she loves me, we've got a grandson and his wife who are sober in AA. They asked me to speak at their group's anniversary and I was thrilled to be able to do that for them.

I'm broke but that's nothing to me. I've got some peace of mind after all these years. I'm sober over thirty years, and I'll tell you, fifteen or sixteen of those years were real rough. I didn't speak at meetings for a lot of years; I just couldn't do it. I was chasing my daughter and then my son; my wife was devastated by the loss of our two children and I just couldn't do it. Today I don't mind doing it because I like to give back some of what I got. God bless you all.

John N., Peabody, Massachusetts

DRUNK AND DISORDERLY

SEPTEMBER 1988

Act One — 1979: I screamed obscenities at the matron and rattled the door of the cell. "Let me out of here! I don't belong here. I'll kill you!"

Finally the policewoman came over to my cell. "One more word out of you, dearie, and I *will* let you out. You want to go a few rounds with me?"

Through bleary eyes I saw the stocky outline of the other woman's body. She looked formidable with her legs spread wide apart, her hands on her hips. My bravado fled. Retreating, I crumpled to the floor and crawled over to the cot in the corner. I sobbed myself to sleep on the dirty mattress.

A grinding headache woke me. The mattress was now on the floor and my face was in a small pool of vomit, blood, and God-knows-what-else. I reached up to my throbbing head and my hand came away covered with fresh blood. Dimly I recalled my rampage of the night before and me hellbent on destroying my apartment and my husband, Will, in the process. My last vision of him was him sitting on the doorstep, crying and holding his bleeding head in his hands as I was driven off, handcuffed, in the back seat of the police cruiser. It was so painful to think about that I groaned out loud.

The matron yelled over, "How's the prima donna this morning? You can call your husband to come get you. Too bad about your head. You tried to throw yourself off the cot so many times we thought we'd save you another fall and put the mattress on the floor."

The matron unlocked the cell door and grimaced at the sight of my face. She pointed me to the washroom. "You'd better clean yourself up before I take you upstairs to call your husband."

Once inside the bathroom, I stood hanging onto the sink for a minute to steady myself before I dared to look in the mirror. I had always prided myself on my youthful good looks, and I shuddered at the bruised, bloated face looking back at me. My eyes were swollen almost shut. There were several cuts on my forehead with blood congealing on one of them. I was afraid to look any closer and just cupped water in my hands and gingerly patted it to my face. I ran my hands through my matted hair and rummaged through my purse for a safety pin to try to repair my torn shirt. This was the once-proud young wife and mother who had been a den mother, active in church affairs, and vice-president of the women's club — until it became impossible to cover up my drunken escapades any longer.

A knock on the door brought me back to today. "Let's go, ma'am."

I followed her wearily up the stairs to the telephone and managed to dial my number on the third try.

A hungover Will answered. I began my familiar litany.

"Will, I'm so sorry. It will never happen again, I promise. Spending the night in jail has taught me a lesson. I've never been so humiliated." I cupped my hand around the mouthpiece and lowered my voice, "Will, honey, they really roughed me up. I'm a mess."

A half hour later Will and I were driving home. The windows of the car were open and I was gulping in the fresh air and letting the wind lift and blow my hair. Will reached over and squeezed my hand. "Laurie, it broke my heart to have to call the cops last night but I thought you were going to kill me and yourself in the process. Forgive me, baby!"

I began shaking. "Will, I'm so sorry. I must have been out of my mind. It will never happen again, I swear." My head was throbbing without letup and I thought I might throw up. "Hon?" I smiled weakly. "Would you mind stopping at the package store. Just get a pint. This headache is brutal."

"Sure, kid." He turned the wheel sharply at the next intersection and came to an abrupt stop in front of the package store. The familiar neon sign blinked down on us cheerfully. Will jumped from the car, then leaned back through the window. "I might just make that two pints. I've got a bit of a headache myself." We smiled at one another.

Act Two — five years later. The jarring ring of the telephone woke me from my sleep. I snapped on the light, adrenaline already flooding through my body as I lifted the receiver.

"This is the Danbury police station. We have your daughter, Sara, down here on a drunk and disorderly charge again." He went on, "We're willing to give her a chance to go to detox if you can talk her into it. Will you come down and see what you can do?"

Within moments I was dressed and driving the short distance to the police station. I nervously told the young officer why I was there. He opened a door behind him and gestured for me to follow him down the stairs to the lockup. Halfway down, the silence was broken by a long animal-like howl. I began trembling in anticipation of what I was going to see. In the area in front of the cell a young girl was thrashing about, flailing her arms out to grip at the matron's legs. The girl was Sara. I began to gag as the policeman reached down and pinned Sara's arms behind her. The matron quickly emptied the girl's pockets and pulled off her belt and shoes; all the while Sara was struggling to free herself. Then the two police officers dragged my daughter into the cell and slammed the door shut.

I called, "Sara!"

There was no response and I called her name again. Then she lifted her head and squinted at me, trying to focus her eyes — one of which was bruised and rapidly swelling shut. Finally she recognized me and whimpered, "Mummie, you came. Get me out of here. They've been beating me up. Take me home." The words came out slurred.

I turned my back and started towards the stairs. "Call me when you want to get better, Sara. " I could barely see through the tears.

The matron reached out and touched my shoulder as I walked by her.

"Ma'am, we ain't seen you around here for a long time."

J. L., Dietramszell, West Germany

AA Around the World

Trudge the road of happy destiny

MAKING MANUEL DRINK

JANUARY 1988

My parents always taught me not to drink alone. "Only alcoholics," they warned, "drink alone. People who drink with others are social drinkers."

I learned that lesson well. But years later, as a parish priest in a Central American country, I was faced with a dilemma. I liked to drink; in fact, I liked to drink very, very much . . . and I was alone. I staffed a one-man parish — isolated in the mountains.

To avoid being an alcoholic, I knew I had to get a drinking companion. It didn't matter that I was drinking a one-pint martini each evening, and sometimes had a second. The drinking partner would keep me from the clutches of alcoholism.

But who could accompany me in my nightly drinking bouts? I didn't want the parishioners to know that their pastor was tying one on each evening. So, in my search for a partner, I had to come up with someone who was discreet. Someone who wouldn't talk, who wouldn't tell the other people in the parish that their priest was a lush.

Finally, I came across the ideal companion. Discreet? Yes. Tightlipped? Yes. In fact, Manuel was the answer to my prayers for he was a deaf mute. No word would ever escape his lips.

He had an added benefit. Manuel couldn't hold his booze. After a single shot, Manuel passed out cold, and while his inert form accompanied me, I was free to continue drinking — without fear of becoming an alcoholic!

One night, Manuel was visiting my house, and had already passed out. I must have gone into a blackout. The next morning, I woke up in bed — badly hung over. Manuel had left. When I got myself together, I began to notice that a few odds and ends were missing. Manuel had relieved me of a pocket knife, a flashlight, a ballpoint pen, and a few other bits and pieces.

The next evening, Manuel arrived for his nightly drink. I was waiting for him, and when he was inside the house, I began to beat him up — to teach him a lesson not to steal from me. Fortunately, he was able to escape before I did him any serious damage. I drank alone that night.

The following morning, I had a rare moment of clarity, and I began to ponder on what I was doing. I was beginning to turn Manuel into an alcoholic. I had beaten him, defenseless as he was. "My God," I thought, "I came here to Central America to do good, and have stayed to do harm to myself and others."

And so it was that my Higher Power used Manuel, not to keep

me from being an alcoholic — I was already that. He used Manuel to call me back from my alcoholism. My Higher Power writes straight with crooked lines, calls to me through the wordless cry of a poor and defenseless deaf mute.

Dan J., Cochabamba, Bolivia

PEOPLE, PLACES, AND THINGS
JUNE 1991

I was born in a small, beautiful village in the hills of Nepal, but it was in Kathmandu, the capital city, where I took my first drink with some friends from school. My companions, I am sure, did not intend to turn me into an alcoholic, they just wanted to see me enjoy life. I did not refuse the request of my friends and took several sips on their behalf. In the course of time, however, I started drinking for myself. I took money from my own pocket and became a regular drinker. I began to spend my life as an alcoholic.

Back at home, my family somehow knew about my change of behavior and, as a result, they stopped their financial assistance given for my studies. Then I had a very hard time finding my food twice a day. With the worry of not getting money I intensified my drinking habit to forget the sorrow. By this time, I was a moneyless alcoholic. The friends who used to be very close to me left me alone. During the same period I was affiliated with a strong political party, but my friends within the party also started hating me as they could not persuade me to stop drinking. Finally, I had to give up the hope of their help also.

Alcohol is strictly prohibited in the Brahmin society, and

becoming desperate, I returned home. I started to control my drinking, but gradually all restraint fell away, and the time came when my family had to stop giving me anything except two meals a day. I was compelled to sell everything I could get my hands on in order to get a drink. Grains and cooking utensils were the easy articles. Later my family started to lock everything up. Viewing the dark future of my family, one of my relatives forced me to transfer ownership of my property to my children so that I would not sell that as well.

My body used to desire alcohol twenty-four hours a day. The shivering of my hands and legs, unclear vision, imbalance of the body, and headaches were the usual characteristics when I didn't drink. In the morning, I had to hold one hand with the other until I could get several glasses of liquor down my throat. Finally my wife could not stand it anymore and she and the kids took refuge in her father's house.

Once my family left me, I was free to do anything I wanted. The first thing I did was to sell off any remaining household articles. When that was done, I began selling standing crops at far below their market value just to have some money in my hands. When there were no more crops to sell, I detached the wood from my house. I did not even leave windows and doors. Once I tried to take out the wooden column on which the whole house was supported. Fortunately, I was unsuccessful in that endeavor. Exploiting the situation, my neighbors were only too happy to buy whatever I happened to be selling — always well below its worth.

One night I woke up needing a drink. I started out toward a *Raxi Pasal* (a shop that sells alcohol), but it was so dark that I fell down and broke my right arm. My neighbor helped me to the hospital where I spent three weeks. Several months later when I was coming out from another *Raxi Pasal,* I was so drunk that I could not control myself and slipped on the ground. This time my left arm was fractured. Again I had to spend three weeks in the hospital. While I was coming out from the hospital, the doctor who was attending me advised me to live "on the will of God, not on my own will." These words had a deep influence on my heart but I started drinking again. Within several months, as a result of my drinking, I lost two front teeth and fractured my backbone. I had to replace the teeth and undergo surgery for my back. There were also numerous events where I was beaten by the shopkeeper for not paying him the money I owed for my drink. This is the way I spent half my life.

Day by day, my soul, body, and brain were diverted more toward alcohol. However, I had some feelings in a remote corner of my heart that I should give up alcohol. I thought about suicide, but I remembered one of my friends saying, "Our body is a temple of God; to destroy it is a sin." Because of this message I am still alive.

After spending twenty-five years with alcohol, a significant turning point came in my life. A foreigner introduced me to AA. I started attending AA meetings regularly in Kathmandu. After staying sober for a little while, one day I met one of my old drinking friends. We visited a restaurant together where he took a glass of alcohol and I took a cup of tea. After having several drinks my friend requested me to have one too, and finally I accepted his offer. After seven days of continuous drinking, I returned to my foreign friend. Though he was disappointed that I drank, he was glad to see me again. After three and a half months, the same story repeated once again. This time the door of my friend's house was closed to me. Being desperate, that night I prayed for God to show me the way. From that day onward I started to follow the lesson of staying stopped one day at a time. I started learning that the first glass is poison for me. The Twelve Steps of AA are now the backbone of my success.

It is already more than a year, and I am in good relations with my family. I feel my body, brain, and soul are getting healthy now.

With hope and confidence I am moving ahead. Nothing is impossible.

Puspa D., Kathmandu, Nepal

ONE IN A BILLION

MARCH 1988

Having had a few drinks before an academic cocktail party, I greeted the Dean with the only Chinese words I knew. A few weeks later, at a similar celebration, I agreed to leave in six months for a year-long teaching assignment in the heart of the People's Republic of China. I'd started the worst part of my drinking several years before when I'd spent the year teaching in Poland; and I knew that I would die drunk and disgraced in China. But I had given my word that I would go.

The psychologist I soon latched onto didn't think it was a good idea. My wife and kids weren't very certain either. Of course, I drank with abandon as I despaired about my future. The next few months turned out to be my dizzying drop to the bottom.

Two months before departure, I went for the required physical examination. I'm not sure why, but I blurted out that I thought I was an alcoholic. After looking at my responses to the famous twenty questions, the doctor agreed with my diagnosis and asked what I wanted to do about my alcoholism. I said I was willing to do anything — except go to AA. Fortunately, in this case I followed my old pattern of doing exactly what I said I'd never do. On short notice, I contacted a sober colleague and AA member whom I'd been watching from the corner of my eye to see if his life could be as good without drinking as he made it seem. He took me to a meeting, assigned me two sponsors, saw that I had copies of the books, and a meeting schedule for each day of the week.

Sponsor Dick had me talk with him each day about how Step One worked in my daily affairs until he thought I was ready for Step Two. Sponsor Jerry laughed at my worry about the three-letter word in the Third Step and asked me what Step I was on — Step One, of course. At one meeting, I realized that I had hope! When a chronic sense of sadness just lifted and went away, I learned that alcohol truly is a depressant. In all my confusion, I knew I'd found something I wanted, and I wasn't drinking.

What might have sounded like an adventure to some people, made me heartsick when I sobered up. I mentioned in meetings that I was going to China. At one of them, a large red-headed man with a booming voice took me aside, put his arm around my shoulders, and told me I'd be all right, that my Higher Power was transportable and that the Steps worked just as well in China as at home. He also told me about the Loners service. All I needed to do was leave my name with the General Service Office, and they would help me make contacts with other AA members who were in places where it was difficult or impossible to get to meetings. I phoned them and gave them my name and Chinese address.

On a hot August day, two and a half months sober, I made my farewells to family and my new AA friends, and got onto the plane, Big Book in hand. I got off the plane in the middle of China, almost exactly halfway around the globe from my Michigan home. I was greeted by a delegation of my Chinese hosts, whisked off to my living quarters at the university, and told to rest before there would be a banquet in my honor. My head was spinning. I kept smiling and going over the Serenity Prayer.

In my room waiting for me was mail from the States. I opened the large envelope and took out a letter from the General Service Office which began, "Dear Jim, my name is Lois and I'm an alcoholic." I read the rest through tears of gratitude and relief. What she had sent me was a large packet of AA materials. Alcoholic that I was, I wanted to sit down and read everything at once. I did manage to read a little and to see that the packet contained a directory of names and addresses of others like myself around the world who could be contacted. Just then there was a man at the door telling me it was time to go to the banquet.

Ushered to the seat of honor, I glanced at the table before me and saw that at my place was a row of drinks: a bottle of beer, a glass of wine, and a glass of *maotai*, the Chinese vodka. There was no water or tea. Before I could sort out my thoughts and feelings, everyone rose for a toast to my arrival and to Chinese-American friendship. Maybe it was because I had just glanced at the AA pamphlets, or maybe it was because of the letter from GSO, or maybe it was because of what my sponsors had worked on with me, or maybe it was the sum total of the two months of meetings, but surely it was my Higher Power that gave me the choice of not picking up a glass. I explained that I was allergic to alcohol and that if I drank even a drop, I'd fall down unconscious. I wasn't lying — although the actual effect might be a little slower. My hosts sent someone for a bottle of orange pop, the first of dozens during the next twelve months. Chinese-American friendship continued.

Soon I had a routine that revolved around AA. Upon awakening in the morning and before I went for instruction in Chinese

Tai Chi exercises at daybreak, I read from the Big Book and from Hazelden's *Twenty-four Hours a Day*, prayed and meditated, and asked for guidance. After teaching in the morning, there was a long, traditional Chinese rest break during which I wrote to my wife and children and to someone in AA, either at home or around the world. Before sleep, I read from the pamphlets or the meeting by mail provided by the *Loners-Internationalists Meeting* (*LIM*), read some more from the Big Book, and expressed my gratitude for the day's sobriety.

Everything was not always well. I missed my wife and my sons. I missed my sponsors and AA friends even though I'd known them only briefly. I wanted to talk to another alcoholic. Then it began to rain and didn't stop for more than forty days and forty nights. The living and working conditions were difficult. I would occasionally and melodramatically remind myself that I was the only certified alcoholic in the People's Republic of China — one in a billion!

One night after a couple of months, at bedtime, I was feeling particularly lonely and isolated. I picked up where I had left off in my reading, the beginning of the "Women Suffer Too" story in the Big Book, when someone knocked on my door. It was a man with a letter sent from another Chinese city a few hundred miles away. I opened it immediately. It began, "Dear Jim, my name is Trish and I am an alcoholic." By return mail she had a letter from me, and then I had another one from her, and so it went.

She returned to the States at Christmas time. By then, though, letters had started coming to me because of the *LIM* bulletin — Peter from Wales, Luciano from London, Ken from Australia, and other people from exotic places such as Hollywood, California, Grand Forks, North Dakota, and the good ship USS Stamp. Dozens of letters came, and I had no trouble finding someone to write to each day. A number of people wrote regularly, and Peter M. from Wales became my sponsor-by-mail. Bless them all. What wondrous things greeted me each day — the experience, strength, and hope that not only lifted the compulsion to drink but brought me back to the human community.

Just before Christmas, I got a letter that began in that marvelous way, "Dear Jim, my name is — and I am an alcoholic." This time it was from an Anne who was coming to China for a short period of work and would be in my city, Xi'an, for three days. Could we meet? Could we! The day finally came and I walked into a hotel lobby filled with tourists and had no trouble spotting Anne. Hers was the lively and smiling face beaming right at me. The parts of those three days that we could be together were just like an extended AA meeting. We talked about the Steps, about staying sober a day at a time, about letting go and letting God. That sounds so ordinary, but it was a highlight of my life.

On New Year's Day, my wife and two teenage sons arrived to spend the rest of the year with me in China. I had missed them but had been grateful to have time to work my AA program alone. They had seen me sober for two months before I left, of course, but they had had years of drunkenness before that. Some old habits came back in a flash. For instance, after months of practicing getting help with my own daily affairs and letting others take care of theirs, I, the Old China Hand, started making arrangements and giving advice about how they should do things. It didn't take long to have fear and anger more present than faith and serenity. Fortunately, the daily willingness to practice the Steps *and* my wife's enthusiasm for her Al-Anon program let us muddle through. I remember realizing, after I'd done something particularly unpleasant, that it was a Tenth Step situation. It was a little matter, but it was so difficult for me to admit I was wrong to her and the boys. I asked for help to do it, did it, and waited for the fallout. The only fallout was my astonishment that nothing particular happened. We went on with our lives. We lived in very close quarters and had, mostly, just ourselves for companionship. We got along — and with more laughing than I ever remember in our household. Without realizing it, I had entered into an important part of my Ninth Step work.

As we pedaled our bicycles through the city streets or into the countryside, socialized with Chinese friends, or traveled together around China, I marveled at my good fortune in having had the opportunity to live and work in China. And I'd been so sure a year before that I would go there to die alone. But there was no mystery about why this difference between the expectation and the reality. The AA Fellowship had shown me principles to guide me in a new way of living. Not drinking a day at a time and doing my best to put the Steps into the center of all my affairs not only worked to end the drinking but to change my thinking, feeling, and behaving.

In June, my first AA birthday arrived and also another knock on my door. This time it was Nancy, an alcoholic from the States who was on vacation and who had been writing to me through the *LIM* network. She had with her a one-year token. Imagine that! I am always struck by the generosity of the spirit that we show to suffering and recovering alcoholics.

A year to the day that I left for China, I arrived back home. My first desire was to get to a meeting of my home group, the Dignitaries Sympathy Group (neither dignified nor sympathetic, some say) and listen to their stories. It was a joyful reunion. Some newcomer asked me how I could stay sober in China. I remember telling him that it's no different there than here, that the God of our understanding and the AA program are wherever we will go.

I added that my worst day sober in China was better than my best day drunk at home.

I never think of the phrase, "Dear Jim, my name is — and I'm an alcoholic" without a surge of emotion. I'm so grateful for the *Loners-Internationalists Meeting,* which makes it possible for some lonely alcoholic somewhere in the world to open a letter today and read these life-giving words: "Dear friend, my name is — and I'm an alcoholic."

J. M., East Lansing, Michigan

A LONG WAY FROM AKRON

JUNE 1995

It's the sun and wind in that place I will always remember. I was standing on the porch of the old tin-roofed building that served the area variously as general store, town hall, butcher shop, brothel, and beer hall, looking at the dilapidated bus in which I'd been traveling across Zimbabwe for six hours. The wind swirled clouds of dust across the yard. A scrawny, half-starved African dog trotted by. In the scant shelter provided by a little group of thorn trees, a few old women were trying to sell avocados and bananas to travelers. I was at a bus stop somewhere between Filabusi and Mbalabala on the Bulawayo Road. As far as I knew, the place had no name.

I wondered if I'd find an AA meeting at my journey's end. For the past month, I'd been visiting the rural school where my fiancee worked as a Peace Corps Volunteer. Since sobering up in April 1991, I'd never gone more than two days without a meeting, so despite regular prayer, meditation, and reading from AA's *Daily*

Reflections and the Big Book, the strain of living immersed in a foreign culture was beginning to tell. A week before, as I stood in the doorway of my hut watching the children laugh and yell as they ran to get to school on time, a feeling of dread and depression had crept upon me. Although the Zimbabweans were friendly and welcoming, I'd begun to feel like an isolated stranger in a strange land. I noted this incipient erosion of my sobriety with a shiver. Instead of the warm African late winter sun, I felt a chilly darkness encroaching. My alcoholism had followed me all the way to Africa. I knew the symptoms, I knew their consequences, and fortunately (because of AA) I knew the cure. So that weekend, when my fiancee and I went to the little town of Masvingo for a couple of days of rest at our favorite backpacker's lodge, I told her that I wanted to try to find another alcoholic to talk to. This is the most basic tenet of our program, but in Zimbabwe it was not always easy to follow.

Of course I said nothing to the owners of the lodge, a kindly older couple named Bruce and Iris. When I'd proposed marriage to Noel on an earlier visit to their place, they had happily told us that we were the very first people to get engaged there and had given us a bottle of wine with which to toast one another. Noel drank a glass or two, but I'd confined my toasting to a cold "mineral," the Zimbabwean term for a soft drink. We simply thanked them for the gift. Most Zimbabweans have never heard of AA, so there would have been no point in telling them that I was a member.

The International AA Directory listed a Loner in the Masvingo area, a man who lived at a fairly remote Catholic mission. But when I'd tried to contact him two weeks before, I was told the man had died recently — sober. In the capital city of Harare, there were two AA groups listed, but Harare was forbiddingly distant — a long and difficult bus trip that ended with arrival in town after dark. I was willing to take my chances with Harare's numerous thieves and muggers, but perhaps that wouldn't be necessary. A meeting was also listed for Bulawayo, Zimbabwe's second largest city. An early start from Masvingo would ensure an arrival in late afternoon (barring breakdowns, flat tires, and interminable waits while the bus driver or conductor negotiated for safe passage with the police). Still, I hardly knew what to expect. The group might not even be there, it might have moved, the information in the directory might be out of date or, worst of all, the phones might not work. (Problems with the phones — where phones exist at all — are practically a daily occurrence in Zimbabwe.) It wasn't unusual for the government to change a phone number without telling anyone, including the person whose number had been changed. I decided, however, that all this projection of difficulties and obstacles was yet another good reason to find a meeting. I had that familiar feeling that my disease was talking to me.

The driver began revving his engine and honking his horn (the signal that he'd had enough beer and was ready to start), so I boarded the bus and jammed myself and my backpack into a narrow, rickety seat. The ancient engine roared and spewed black diesel fumes. The conductor banged loudly on the side of the bus and then let out a burst of whistles and bird calls — his announcement of departure. We swayed onto the empty highway. In the distance the smooth, rocky domes of the rounded mountains near Mbalabala loomed above the dry, brushy veldt. Jivey African beer-hall music blared from the scratchy speaker wired above the driver's head. An old woman in a ragged red sweater sat across from me, grinning and holding in her arms a live chicken. I thought wistfully of AA in America, of the warm spring evening more than a year before, when Noel and I had stood on the neat brick sidewalk outside Dr. Bob's house in Ohio, looking at the friendly light pouring from the open doorway. I smiled back at the old woman and said "Maswere sei, ambuya?" ("How are you, grandmother?") I was a long way from home.

Two hours later, in Bulawayo, I stepped off the bus across from the old Selborne Hotel. I was immediately surrounded by the usual clamor of street urchins begging, men hawking everything from cheap watches to homemade drill bits, and women selling potatoes, mangoes, and bananas. I pushed my way through the crowd and then went across the street to the hotel. Soon I was settled in a single room, its fixtures typical of the 1940s. A large electric fan turned slowly overhead. There was a bath, but no shower. A note on my pillow informed me that mosquito nets were available on request. But best of all was the nearly antique black phone on the nightstand.

I began by trying to place a local call to the first phone number listed in the AA directory under Bulawayo. My progress was impeded by language difficulties; English is the official language of Zimbabwe, but it's not indigenous. At first, the hotel operator and I couldn't understand each other at all, though we were both speaking English. My first effort met with total failure: I was connected to a tire service somewhere in town. The man on the other end began a spate of rapid-fire Ndebele. When I could understand him at all, he seemed to be quoting tire prices. I thought wryly of Bill W., standing in the lobby of the Mayflower Hotel fifty years before and making phone calls. I summoned all the patience I could and proceeded slowly. In the course of an hour, I was able to have the operator place calls to each of the numbers in turn. The last number was the lucky charm. It was the home number of a man named Tony, and although he wasn't there, his housekeeper gave me his number at work. I made the call and Tony answered. I breathed a great sigh of relief and told Tony I'd been out in the bush and hadn't been to a meeting in five weeks, and that I thought it was about time to find one. "Well then," he answered with typical British reserve, "I should think that's quite right." When I asked where the meeting was, so that I could take a taxi there, he said I'd never be able to find it and offered to send someone around for me. I agreed happily.

I took a bath and ordered tea from room service, and about an hour later my phone rang. The caller was a man named John, who said he was in the lobby waiting for me. He spoke with a clipped British accent. "You'll know me when you see me," he said. "I'm a short arse." I was really happy to sit down to dinner with him in the hotel restaurant. Over dinner, John told me a bit about himself. "I went to Botswana to go drinking and didn't get back for two years," he said. Sober now and with his own place to live, John was really grateful — grateful enough to come over to the Selborne and spend his evening with a stranger who had asked for help.

After dinner, John and I were picked up by Cliff, a local farmer who drove the most beat-up Mercedes I've ever seen. It seemed that the unofficial tradition of AAs driving tired old cars extended even to Zimbabwe. In Africa, it's unusual to own a car at all, and I found out later that those AAs who did, usually made the rounds and picked up several other members en route.

All AA meetings are good, but I enjoyed the one we attended that night more than any I've been to before or since. It wasn't that the meeting was different from those I go to in the United States; on the contrary, my gratitude was for the similarities. The familiar signs proclaiming the Slogans hung on the walls, the Preamble was read, the Serenity Prayer recited. About the only difference was that we drank tea instead of coffee. The Bulawayo meeting was small but very much alive. I had the same experience there that I've had in Michigan, Wisconsin, New Jersey, Maryland, and South Africa: alone in a strange place, I suddenly had a half dozen instant friends. I didn't know it then, but I'd be fortunate enough to return three more times to this meeting, to help the group with a Twelfth Step call, and to be invited to their homes and offices. Local information — from the best places to stay to where to rent a car — was easily available.

After the meeting, we sat around the room and talked a bit about what AA was like in the United States. The primary difference, of course, is that near my home in Connecticut I can hop in my car and go to two meetings a day if I wish. In Africa, I had to hike out of the bush to the tar road and then wait hopefully for a bus. Since the buses don't run on any discernable schedule, this meant I had to wait however long it took for the correct bus to happen by. If I was lucky, going to a meeting was a two-day proposition. I was expressing my frustration about this when May S., who had chaired the meeting that evening, spoke up. "Didn't you say you've spent some time in Masvingo?" she asked. She looked thoughtful.

I answered that I did, and asked whether there were a meeting there that wasn't listed in the directory. "There used to be a meeting in Masvingo a long time back," she said. "But I think it disbanded. We do have one woman there still, a Loner named Iris."

Iris? It couldn't be! "Does she run a lodge for backpackers?" I said.

"Why yes," said May. "Don't tell me you know her?"

"I've been staying at her house for the last three days," I said, beginning to marvel at my Higher Power's latest practical joke.

"Well," said May, smiling, "that's a good one. How long did you say it took you to get here to find this out?"

Next morning I boarded the early bus for Masvingo. It seemed I was back there in no time. I hitchhiked to Iris and Bruce's place, wondering what Iris would say when I told her the story. When I arrived, I found that May had managed to get through to her by phone. Iris stood in her kitchen smiling at me. "Oh dear," she said in her reserved, kindly way, "I guess giving you a bottle of wine for an engagement gift wasn't such a grand gesture after all." Iris was to have a beneficial influence on my recovery for the rest of the three months I spent in Africa. She showed me it was possible to have real and happy sobriety even when living in an area remote from meetings.

What was it that led me to stay at Iris's lodge, when she was the only AA member left in the entire town? Perhaps it's an example of the kind of communication Bill W. was wondering at when he wrote, "Why, for instance, at this particular point in history has God chosen to communicate his healing grace to so many of us? Who can say what this communication actually is — so mysterious and yet so practical?"

Jeff C., Ashford, Connecticut

A HEALTHY APPETITE FOR BEER
OCTOBER 1996

As a twenty-four-year-old Scottish emigrant arriving in South Africa in 1969, I was struck by many of the differences between the country of my birth and what was to become my adopted homeland. Although my drinking was yet to become a problem for me (or others), the most significant beauty of South Africa in my eyes was that booze was cheap. This was a drinker's paradise. The letters I wrote to my fiance, who was to follow me to South Africa some months later, informed her not so much of the physical, social, or practical aspects of South Africa but told her, "You can get drunk for a Rand" (about eighty-five cents in U.S. money). In retrospect, this was strange behavior because getting drunk, while not an unknown experience for me, was not yet a priority.

For quite a number of years to come, being in South Africa as a young husband was great. The lifestyle was one of the outdoors, discovery, *braaivleis* (barbecues), innumerable friendships, fun, and prosperity. During this time I left the printing industry where I was a graphic arts photographer and took up a sales career in office equipment. I don't believe that one occupation should be blamed for creating more alcoholics than another but some careers certainly produce more opportunity. Professional selling is one of them. Not only do you get paid for doing it, you can drink on expenses and on company time with drinking buddies.

Slowly but surely I began to make the most of my new drinking opportunities both at work and socially. Without my realizing what was happening, drink was slowly but surely taking control of my life. I didn't see myself as a drunk, just as "one of the boys" who had a healthy appetite for beer. In 1975, having gained some considerable experience in a tough and competitive sales environment, I decided that as the father of a baby boy I should settle down and find employment with a secure income rather than the uncertainty of sales commissions. I joined the marketing department of an international plastic and chemicals company. This only expanded my opportunities for drinking. Now I could drink without it directly affecting my income. I still honestly believed that I was just a regular guy who enjoyed social drinking to the fullest. Ours is a progressive disease and my dose of the illness was no exception. The next symptom to manifest itself was the "geographic change."

I accepted a position in Cape Town where I was to set up and run a plastic bag factory on behalf of a Johannesburg company. I wasn't the first, nor will I be the last to say, "It will be different when I move." Cape Town is one of the world's most beautiful cities, and I thought this was going to be the beginning of a new and better life. (No prizes for guessing that this was not to be.)

I drove alone to Cape Town while my family followed by air. I'm now able to see that the 1,000 mile drive to Cape Town was my first easily identifiable alcoholic experience. It took me two days to get there as I completed the longest pub crawl I'd ever managed. At the new job, I felt inadequate and ill-prepared for my responsibilities, and this soon showed in my performance. Simple tasks took on the proportions of major undertakings. Problems were neglected or concealed with predictably calamitous consequences. I felt lonely, misunderstood, persecuted, and thoroughly miserable. My skills were not in question; my behavior and ability to apply myself was. It was inevitable, after two years of squandered opportunity in Cape Town, that I embarked on another geographical change; this time back to square one.

I joined a large national chemical company and was once again selling plastic raw materials to manufacturing companies. The next six years saw the continuing advancement of the disease of alcoholism and the erosion of my faculties. I was fortunate in that I didn't have the same exciting experiences of many of my contemporaries in alcoholism. I've never spent a night in jail, never lost a job, house, spouse or family, nor did I have a motor accident. That doesn't mean that I didn't suffer any less trauma than those who did experience more tangible damage. In fact I might have found sobriety sooner if I had. However, that was obviously not part of the plan my Higher Power had for me.

Shortly after arriving back in Johannesburg I joined a well-known service club and was soon elected to the position of clubhouse convener. What a windfall. This post included the management of the bar, the answer to a drunkard's prayer — round the clock access to booze. The club met once every fourteen days yet I found it appropriate to take stock of the bar a couple of times a week. Newspapers and magazines which contained any reference to alcohol abuse were destroyed or hidden. If I drink only beer, I thought, how can I be alcoholic? A drinking buddy and I once sat in a pub debating this very point. After six hours or so, clutching our bar stools to retain possession, we concluded that one couldn't become alcoholic unless drinking spirits or wine. Anyway, we could give up beers if we really wanted to. Such is the wisdom of the alcoholic.

I became an expert in avoiding situations where my daily and uncontrollable shakes would be a problem. When offered coffee in a customer's office, I always said, "I just had one, thanks." When meeting people for a business lunch I made sure that I had sipped a hand-steadying couple of drinks beforehand. Signing checks required imaginative strategies, as did handling documents and opening locks with keys. Not that I wanted a drink. Alcohol simply was necessary to function. I did most of my drinking at a quite pleasant pub near my home. It is hardly surprising that as a very regular guest, I had a lot of drinking friends there who would welcome me with a brimming full beer tankard as I walked in the door. While this was most gratifying, it had disadvantages. Slurping one's beer like a dog from a bowl tends to invite caustic comment from even the closest pub friend, even if he'd been in a state similar to yours ten minutes before. To avoid these harrowing experiences and to ensure a steady hand, I would first visit a low-down cocktail bar where I knew no one and endured my one or two "regmakers" in private and darkness. (In South Africa, the pick-me-up drink, usually taken in the morning, is called a regmaker, loosely translated from the Afrikaans as "right maker" and pronounced *rech*, as in Scottish loch, and *maaker*. Our local AA magazine has been named Regmaker in memory of the life-saving drink.) This disease of ours told me that this behavior was normal for a conscientious and dedicated drinker like me.

The life of an alky isn't an easy one. The freedom of sobriety was for me still a long way off. Only a fellow alcoholic can appreciate the depths of despair one can sink to. I so often wished that someone would put me on a desert island where there was no drink and I could get sober. Contacting AA never even crossed my mind. Stepping off the curb to cross the street became an ordeal, as did virtually all of the things I now take for granted. I like to recall these days while I celebrate doing with ease the things that once terrified me.

Even bad things come to an end. I reached my personal rock bottom when I attended a two-day training session at work. I was determined to put on a good show and prove to everyone, and to myself, that I could handle the situation. While I hadn't yet been reprimanded, I'd earned quite a reputation for screwing-up and smelling of beer. I decided I'd only have two drinks the night before (why is it always two drinks and never one or three?) and be in fine fettle for the day ahead. Predictably, that morning I was in as bad a state as I'd ever been in. My colleagues from around the country were standing looking down from the open French doors at the top of a small flight of stairs. I approached the bottom of the stairs with my body trembling and my mind in turmoil. Reaching the first step, my legs shook like jelly as the assembled people watched. Somehow I made it to the top in a series of rigid lurches. I can still see their faces. Some people gaped in amazement, others shook their heads in sympathy. I shuffled up to my manager, told him I was not well, was going home, and would call him later. I made it back to my car, sat soaked in sweat, and said to myself, "Well, this is it. I've got to do something about my drinking, right now." Instantly I felt better. The feeling of misery and weariness lifted from my shoulders and was replaced by one of hope and anticipation. I almost shouted with joy. I had just had my first spiritual experience.

I went home and told my wife that I was going to see our doctor to do something about my drinking. I told the doctor that I had a drinking problem and wanted to stop. "You see, doctor, the real problem is my shakes. I only drink to control my shakes, so if you can give me something to stop the shakes, I won't need to drink anymore. Simple, huh?" I was already climbing onto the pink cloud of newfound sobriety and was completely taken aback when he told me he certainly could stop the shakes, but, he said, "There is nothing I can do for this." He tapped the side of his head. "You get yourself to AA and get properly fixed up. If you don't, I'll send you to a rehab clinic." I elucidated that I wasn't bad enough for AA, most certainly not for a clinic. But I would think about it. Still feeling on top of the world next day, I reported for work. Before very long, my manager came to my office and said with genuine concern, "Dave, we are a bit worried about your drinking." I told him that I was too and had done something about it. This began a wonderful trusting relationship of support which endures to this day, more than eight years later.

I can't remember too much about what was said at my first AA meeting but I vividly recall being astounded to hear that I wasn't the only one to have shakes, fears, and suffering. I left that meeting filled with hope and wonder.

Today I have freedom from the sovereignty and power of alcohol. No more need to lie and believe those lies myself. I can cross the road without stumbling and hold my head up high and shoulders back. I can plan my daily routine without scheming where to fit in a regmaker. I can visit customers in the afternoon, and not just those who want to drink. I can live without fear of window envelopes, the telephone bell, my manager asking to see me. (Many's the time I took the blame for things because I didn't know if I was at fault or not, having been in a blackout.) I don't have to ask what I did yesterday because I can remember. I am in control of my life and can look anyone in the eye.

One of the beautiful highlights of my sobriety is the loving relationship I share with my young adult children. My son Scott and I probably do more things together than most fathers and sons get to do. Daughter Claire will ask me to go to the cinema, coffee shop, or mall, and we have a lovely time together. Scott and Claire attend a local health and racquet club gymnasium and they asked me to enroll and join them for sessions. What a transformation. What a liberation.

While I wouldn't recommend that anyone become an alcoholic, I believe that sober alcoholics living the AA way of life have been blessed with a gift. It's a gift that can't be bought, that can't be won in a lottery, that can't be stolen, forged, or rented.

Dave G., Edenvale, Gauteng, South Africa

GRUPA UNA

JULY 1990

My wife and I lived in Romania during 1984-1985, and during all that time — quietly, to avoid the attention of a distrustful government — the two of us met together as AA Group Number One, or Grupa Una, in our apartment in Timisoara, Romania. The popular national drink, *tuica*, a kind of plum brandy, was offered to us everywhere, and we had to learn to say no thanks tactfully, without offending our hosts. At Christmas, we left Romania, traveling on the Orient Express from Transylvania through Hungary to Vienna. How exciting it was to be in a free country with bright lights and pastries and shops stuffed with goods of every imaginable sort — a severe contrast to bleak Romania, with its empty shelves and universal suffering. It was an incredible joy to find a wonderful AA meeting in the Vienna woods — our first meeting in many months with more in attendance than the two of us!

My wife and children had to fly home to Washington State from Vienna, and I climbed back on the venerable Orient Express to make the long journey back to Romania and the town of Timisoara. And what I couldn't say then, because of possible government reprisals, I can finally say now.

The shabby local train finally deposited me — alone and lonely — back in frigid Timisoara, and I went about my business of teaching literature at the university there. I certainly saw many candidates for Grupa Una, but I was quite hesitant to say anything to anyone in a country where suspicion and fear were a daily fact of life. If a Romanian associated or socialized with an American outside the university classroom, he or she had to file a report with the secret police (the Securitate) explaining the circumstances. I had reason to believe my apartment was bugged, and we had to be very careful what was said in letters or by phone. In addition, the government was very hostile toward any new or different club or organization, fearing that such structures might be a cover for "subversive" political activities. So far as I could tell, no Romanian had ever heard of Alcoholics Anonymous, and so I kept quiet, keeping my personal contact with the Fellowship through reading AA literature and softly playing tapes in my back bedroom.

All this changed when Juliet (as I shall call her) came to my apartment one dark night. Juliet was an attractive young Romanian woman, well educated and fluent in English. She traveled by train each day to a nearby village where she taught school until late afternoon, and returned again by train to Timisoara. And there she was, standing in my apartment, nervous and apprehensive. She motioned to me that she wanted to write something down, so I gave her an old IBM card from my desk. On it she wrote, "Please don't say a word about what you see here. I need a long, secret talk with you. Come downstairs — I'll be waiting in the street." She slipped out the door; I waited a minute or two, put my coat on, and walked down the dark stairs and out into the night. I followed her into a nearby apartment building and upstairs to a rear flat. Inside, in a dimly lit dining room, Mama sat drinking tea. Juliet introduced me to her mother, made two ersatz coffees, and we all settled down around the dining room table. Juliet said, "I need so much to hear the message you bring from America. I heard you lecture at the university, and there was something about what you said I need to know." I was mystified as to what to say — certainly alcoholism and

AA were at the moment far from my mind — so I began talking of my life at the university in America. Somehow, in the next few sentences, I made some kind of reference to alcohol or drinking. Suddenly Juliet's eyes brightened and she said, "You know, I won a car as a prize and I got drunk and crashed it to bits." Now I was startled — and because I felt once again that strange almost mystical flash of Twelfth Step identification — I took a deep breath and began talking about my drinking and finding AA and what AA was all about. Juliet sat perfectly still, her eyes getting wider and wider. And then she began to gush forth telling me about *her* drinking. Neither of us could talk fast enough to get it all out — and we both experienced that moment of joy known to all those in our Fellowship when we share our experience, strength, and hope. In that amazing instant, Juliet realized why she wanted that "secret" talk with me; she had felt the presence of the AA program in me, even though I had never mentioned AA by name.

Her happiness, her relief, were tangible. At one point, I said "Wait!" and ran out, down the steps, up the street to my flat where I gathered up an armload of AA literature. I ran back to Juliet's apartment and dumped it all on the dining room table. "Here," I said, "all this is for you to read — soon!"

And read and study she did! Grupa Una had its first Romanian member, and she proved to be the answer to a twelfth-stepper's dream. We had a meeting almost every day, but we had to be very careful of the Securitate. My apartment was out, as was hers. Juliet had wanted to twelfth-step a friend, whom I will call Victoria, and so we often had a meeting in her "safe" apartment, usually in a back bedroom. Sometimes we would meet at the open air market, and walk through the streets of Timisoara, holding fast to the Romanian tradition of becoming silent when other people walked nearby. Other times we would have a meeting casually sitting on park benches. Always we were worried about the Securitate, but Juliet would say, "I don't care, the AA is more important to me than the fear of the Securitate!"

Juliet took to AA like a Romanian duck to the Black Sea! She asked me more questions than I could answer. Assuming at first that I was the resident "expert" of AA, she felt I should indeed know everything. With Mama, and with the mamas of other Romanians newly introduced to the program, there was another problem: they assumed I was the "higher power" sent from America to help their children! It took some talking with the alcoholics *and* family members to convince them that I was just another drunk from America who had found a way, through Alcoholics Anonymous, to stay sober a day at a time, that I was neither special nor unique.

But their faith in AA regularly moved me to tears. The first weekend Juliet had the literature, for example, she stayed at home. On Monday, I noticed she seemed quite tired. When asked why, she said she had been sitting up copying the Big Book by hand. Shocked, I told her that I was giving her my copy to keep forever, that she didn't need to copy a single word.

Grupa Una proved to be a traveling group — meeting from place to place as circumstance dictated. At times peripatetic, the group would grow in numbers, and then diminish. Juliet was always on the lookout for prospective members. I remember one Twelfth Step call with a Romanian woman in a crowded, noisy bar, with Juliet translating for me as I tried to explain the Steps and Traditions of AA. The air was thick with the blue smoke of Turkish cigarettes, and the din made conversation almost impossible. Yet even in this exotic environment, the AA message somehow got through.

Grupa Una stayed a functioning group during the remaining five months I was in Romania, and Juliet took her Fifth Step with me. We thought we were keeping clear of the Securitate, but the day before I was to leave, I was kept at the university on a pretext. When I returned home to my flat, someone had been there. My personal tapes and AA tapes had been electronically erased. I felt I had to tell Juliet and the others, and they put a brave face on for my sake, telling me not to worry. Leaving Timisoara was something akin to a death, considering the circumstances, but loving goodbyes were said, the train began to move, and tearful waves continued until we were out of sight of each other.

I was shaken by what had happened and, to confirm my fears, the train came to a sudden halt at the border and the border guards, in association with the Securitate, came directly for me, took me off the train and to a small room for interrogation. They asked many questions about students, colleagues, and friends, but I told them nothing. They warned me "not to write ill of Romania," and thoroughly searched through my luggage, apparently looking for manuscripts. This continued for about an hour, but finding nothing incriminating, the guards finally shouted, "Get back on the train," and I did. The train jolted forward, and in a few minutes we were in Yugoslavia.

Back in America, I wrote and exchanged letters with Juliet as often as I felt I could, and we talked from time to time by telephone. We had agreed on a simple code in letters which served us well, and we were quite circumspect on the phone. I was never able to tell her of my experience at the border, and we were both afraid to speak openly of AA. It was too risky to send her AA literature; instead, I tried to tell her indirectly how much support she and the others had over here because everywhere I went in

America, AA members wanted to know how Grupa Una was doing. And so time passed — four long years. And then, to our thrilled amazement, the Romanian revolution took place, and suddenly AA could be brought into the open.

Juliet's letter arrived three weeks after the revolution. But when I read it, I realized that we had *not* been successful in avoiding the Securitate, that their eyes had been on our little group, probably from the beginning. Juliet wrote these lines which tumbled my heart:

"They [the Securitate] visited me six months after you left Romania. In deep despair and scared to death by their presence, I decided I could not lose AA for the Romanian alcoholics need it badly and I could not cooperate with the Securitate either — what remained was the compromise, the lie. I thought that was God's will; I'll never know if I was correct. By no means was I permitted to correspond without reporting the topic of every letter and of every one of your phone calls.

"I didn't tell them more than what I thought they had already found out and they pretended to be satisfied. But their presence in the air almost killed me through fear, self-pity, and depression. The words *fellowship, cooperation, group,* and *God* had to be avoided at any price, as illegal. Courage and martyrdom are notions I'm learning extremely slowly and I didn't want to end in jail.

"In a word, all these years I have been scared to death and I haven't told you the truth. I used to be the only AA here and they would have said AA was political if I had acted as a revolutionary. So, I had to watch, and suffer with my people.

"It's the greatest of miracles that I have not touched a drink all this horrible time. What has kept me sober if not a loving God? He wanted me to survive up to now and he did his work. He never failed me."

In the face of this demonstrated courage, the hardships, the handicaps, the repressive conditions seemed only to toughen the resolve to keep AA vital and central to day-to-day living. And so Grupa Una *is* indeed alive and well. The AA program did its work, as it always has. Darkness may have been crowding in but the light of AA never went out, and that light can now flourish and grow ever brighter, not only in Romania, but throughout the world.

F. P., Spokane, Washington

The Home Group

IN THE GRIP OF THE GROUP

JANUARY 1993

When I finally decided to stop drinking and call AA, I thought about it for weeks. I was afraid of many things — afraid of being ridiculed by my fellow drinkers, by my friends, and even by my own family for not being able to control myself. They would be embarrassed if I admitted I was an alcoholic.

I was also afraid I might not qualify to join AA. Alcoholics drank "real" alcohol. I might be rejected if they found out I had drunk only beer.

I was also afraid they might think I was some kind of do-gooder who went around town joining various social clubs and organizations, just to have a cause to work for.

I was afraid I might not be able to quit. I might fail and let someone down — again. I often told the same tired joke: "It's easy to quit drinking. I've done it many times." I was good at telling that one. But I prayed very hard, and agonized much, and I finally made the call.

At my first meeting, I apologized to the group. I honestly admitted I was only a beer drinker. It was difficult to say, but it felt good to clear the air. I half expected to be kicked out of the meeting, but I was gently assured that there were beer drinkers in AA. In fact, there were some at that very meeting! I felt better, but I wanted to clear up a few more things. So I bravely said, "I am not a joiner. This is the first club I've joined since 4-H." This brought the house down. I knew right then that I was home.

I remember seeing a movie about some early members of AA. These courageous people devoted many hours of their own time to Twelfth Step work. When an AA had a slip, someone went right to his side and picked him up from the bars. From that scene I got the impression that this is what AA folks did. I envisioned we would go bar-hopping, snatching up perfectly happy drunks, dragging them to AA meetings.

This is not how AA works. I soon learned about our Twelve Step program. I was told that the Steps were designed by the pioneers of AA to help us remain sober. I was eager to start, and expected to get some kind of a home study course, with questions later. But I was told I had already started. I was amazed to learn I'd already taken parts of the first two Steps. I had admitted I was powerless over alcohol and that my life was unmanageable.

I was also reminded of what I'd said to the group at my first meeting. I had somehow admitted to strangers that I'd prayed for guidance before calling AA. They had me and they knew it. "You have already sought out a power greater than yourself," they informed me. I was bewildered. I couldn't make my case. They remembered every word I had uttered at that first meeting. I had never had so much attention. No one had cared before, or knew how to show me the way out of my dilemma. I didn't know it at the time but I was discovering a power greater than myself — the love of the AA group.

In my meetings I learned more about the First Step, and why it was necessary that the alcoholic "hit bottom," before making that call. The AA literature says it very clearly:

". . . few people will sincerely try to practice the AA program unless they have hit bottom. For practicing AA's remaining eleven Steps means the adoption of attitudes and actions that almost no alcoholic who is still drinking can dream of taking. Who wishes to be rigorously honest and tolerant? Who wants to confess his faults to another and make restitution for harm done? Who cares anything about a Higher Power, let alone meditation and prayer? Who wants to sacrifice time and energy in trying to carry AA's message to the next sufferer? No, the average alcoholic, self-centered in the extreme, doesn't care for this prospect — unless he has to do these things in order to stay alive himself.

"Under the lash of alcoholism, we are driven to AA, and there we discover the fatal nature of our situation. Then, and only then, do we become as open-minded to conviction and as willing to listen as the dying can be."

John G., Salinas, California

⤳

A NUDE AWAKENING

MARCH 1990

Ever dream you were in a restaurant and had no clothes on? Or that you were in an AA meeting naked as a jaybird? Well, for us fortunate recovering alcoholics at a nudist camp ensconced amid the magnificent Douglas firs of the Oregon forest, it's not a dream, it's a reality.

Welcome to the Nude Beginnings meeting of Alcoholics Anonymous. My name is David, and I'm an alcoholic. I am also, among other things, a nudist and a chef.

When it came time for me to semi-retire, it was only natural that I should semi-retire from the world of textiles (clothes, to you) and live permanently and year-round in a nudist park. I found one near Tucson, Arizona, where I could spend the long winter months, and one near Eugene, Oregon, where I could enjoy the summers. The camp in Oregon also needed someone to operate its small restaurant on weekends. What could be better for a semi-retired chef?

Before I even opened the front door of the cafe (now known as David's Bistro-in-the-Buff), I hung two beautifully done plaques near the cash register, where everyone could see them. One said "Live and Let Live," and the other said "Happy, Joyous, and Free." Near the exit door, appropriately enough, I placed a third message which proclaimed, "Keep Coming Back." The signs mean something to nonalcoholics, too, of course, but the real joy comes when an AA member spots them, surmises just who might have put them up, and discreetly asks me, "Are you a friend of Bill W.?"

However, the greatest thing these proverbs did was to bring enough of us AA folk together so that we could have our very own AA meeting right here in camp.

On Saturday evening the restaurant closes at six o'clock. The crew puts things away, finishes the clean-up work, makes fresh coffee, and at seven-thirty we open the doors again for the meeting.

It's an open meeting closely patterned after the seven A.M. Attitude Adjustment Hour in Palm Desert, California — the meeting that got me sober and saved my life. We try to maintain an upbeat, positive exchange right smack in the middle of now.

There were four of us at our first gathering: Betty with thirty-one years, Roy with twenty, Robin with five, and me with nine. So great was our joy at what we were doing that faces beamed, eyes sparkled, and laughter abounded. It was a pretty giddy affair. Then as Sue and Patsy and Keith heard about our meetings and came in, the excitement started all over. Sue celebrated her first birthday with us, Patsy her sixth, and Betty's daughter Michelle, who had also joined us, celebrated her fifth. Two nonalcoholic visitors attend regularly, as does a member of Al-Anon. And because we are primarily a summer resort with many visitors, we get AA people who are here for only a weekend or so.

We're not sure what will happen come October or November, because the chilly rains of the Oregon winter aren't too conducive to running around outside in the all-together. Camp business declines drastically, the restaurant goes into hibernation, and some of us leave for sunnier, if not greener, pastures. Nevertheless, you can rest assured the AA slogans will remain in the boarded-up Bistro-in-the-Buff, and come springtime, we will return and some trusted servant will again be saying those magical words,

"Welcome to the Nude Beginnings meeting of Alcoholics Anonymous. My name is — and I'm an alcoholic."

The real idea of all this is to show you that AA is indeed everywhere. Next year we plan on having a midnight meeting in the hot tub — as soon as we can find a waterproof Big Book!

So come visit us.

Come celebrate your birthday.

And wear your birthday suit.

David W., Marana, Arizona

WHO'S SITTING NEXT TO YOU?

MARCH 1991

I know who you are. You are "X" who attends the ABC Meeting at the XYZ Club where AAs meet in Anywhere, U.S.A.

I saw you there the other night at the eight o'clock meeting. I don't know how long you've been sober, but I know you've been coming around for a while because you spoke to a lot of people who knew you.

I wasn't one of them.

You don't know who I am. I wandered into your meeting place alone the other night, a stranger in a strange town. I got a cup of coffee, paid for it, and sat down by myself.

You didn't speak to me.

Oh, you saw me. You glanced my way, but you didn't recognize me, so you quickly averted your eyes and sought out a familiar face.

I sat there through the meeting.

It was okay, a slightly different format but basically the same kind of meeting as the one I go to at home.

The topic was gratitude. You and your friends spoke about how much AA means to you. You talked about the camaraderie in your meeting place. You said how much the people there had helped you when you first came through the door — how they extended the hand of friendship to make you feel welcome, and asked you to come back.

And I wondered where they had gone, those nice people who made your entrance so welcoming and so comfortable.

You talked about how the newcomer is the life blood of AA. I agree, but I didn't say so. In fact, I didn't share in your meeting. I signed my name in the book that was passed around, but the chairperson didn't refer to it. He only called on those people in the room whom he knew.

So who am I? You don't know, because you didn't bother to find out. Although yours was a closed meeting, you didn't even ask if I belonged there.

It might have been my first meeting. I could have been full of fear and distrust, knowing AA wouldn't work any better than anything else I'd tried, and I would have left convinced that I was right.

I might have been suicidal, grasping at one last straw, hoping someone would reach out and pull me from the pit of loathing and self-pity from which, by myself, I could find no escape.

I might have been a student with a tape recorder in my pocket, assigned to write a paper on how AA works — someone who shouldn't have been permitted to sit there at all but could have been directed to an open meeting to learn what I needed to know.

Or I could have been sent by the courts, wanting to know more, but afraid to ask.

It happens that I was none of the above.

I was just an ordinary drunk with a few years of sober living in AA who was traveling and was in need of a meeting.

My only problem that night was that I'd been alone with my own mind too long. I just needed to touch base with my AA family.

I know from past experience that I could have walked into your meeting place smiling, stuck out my hand to the first person I saw and said, "Hi. My name is — . I'm an alcoholic from — ."

If I'd felt like doing that, I probably would have been warmly welcomed. You would have asked me if I knew Old So-and-so from my state, or you might have shared a part of your drunka-log that occurred in my part of the country.

Why didn't I? I was hungry, lonely, and tired. The only thing missing was angry, but three out of four isn't a good place for me to be.

So I sat silently through your meeting, and when it was over I watched enviously as all of you gathered in small groups, talking to one another the same way we do in my home town.

You and some of your friends were planning a meeting after the meeting at a nearby coffee shop. By this time I had been silent too long to reach out to you. I stopped by the bulletin board to read the notices there, kind of hanging around without being too obvious, hoping you might ask if I wanted to join you, but you didn't.

As I walked slowly across the parking lot to my car with the out-of-state license plates you looked my way again. Our eyes met briefly and I mustered a smile. Again, you looked away.

I buckled my seat belt, started the car, and drove to the motel where I was staying.

As I lay in my bed waiting for sleep to come, I made a gratitude list. You were on it, along with your friends at the meeting place. I knew that you were there for me, and that I needed you far more than you needed me. I knew that if I had needed help, and had asked for it, you would have gladly given it. But I wondered . . . what if I hadn't been able to ask?

I know who you are.

Do you remember *me*?

Fran D., New Orleans, Louisiana

SERENIDAD IN CENTRAL SQUARE
JUNE 1989

My name is Barbara and I'm an alcoholic. I'm an alcoholic, that must always be remembered. But I'm many things besides. It's always been several things at once with me: homework and the radio blaring. Working two jobs at the same time. When I first started going to meetings, I couldn't sit still unless I brought my knitting.

That's the spirit in which I started going to Spanish-speaking AA meetings — to improve a language I love and will always speak imperfectly, *and* to get in one of the four meetings a week I require of myself.

What little Spanish I know I picked up at a leisurely pace by living in South America for nearly thirteen years. I am married to a Colombian, and now I teach English as a Second Language to Hispanics here in Cambridge. And I am curious: will the vocabulary of alcoholism and recovery be any different? Will it really be the same program I have come to know and trust?

El Grupo Serenidad, which meets in a room of its own behind the storage room of the Cambridge Food Coop on Massachusetts Avenue, is the oldest Hispanic group in the area. I've noticed it there as I've passed through Central Square on my way to work. Last week, I noted down their meeting times, and today, Friday, I've resolved to stop in on my way home from work.

Central Square is the center of a very hip world: vegetarians, esoteric boutiques, practitioners of yoga and African dance, drunks, Harvard and MIT students on bicycles — all these worlds collide in the space of a few city blocks. I push my way through the usual throng, down the stairs to the Food Coop and into the meeting room. I am the only woman in the room, a middle-aged Anglo-American female. They all look at me dubiously.

The meeting starts with all of us standing as the chairperson, Victor recites the St. Francis Prayer in Spanish at lightning speed. (All the names used in this article have been changed.) We sit; Victor reads the Steps and Traditions. Jorge, whom I shall come to love, is walking around with a piece of paper on which he's noting the names of speakers for the evening. He comes to me. Can I do it? I nod.

Elias speaks. A Central American. The slang is different. Rich obscenities. He apologizes to me. *Goma,* I guess, means hangover. Members of the audience feel free to speak out, banter, but when it gets too loud Victor tinkles a little silver dinner bell and frowns. Then laughs. Victor is *picaro* — mischievous. Both Victor and Elias wear their names sewn on their blue work shirts: they work for an auto shop. Elias has four years and is so grateful to be sober. "Bee Weeson says." I wonder, Who is this Bee Weeson? I don't understand. But there he is looking down at us from a photograph over the podium. Bill Wilson.

Jorge speaks: "I didn't drink today." Gratitude. Jorge's life as a drunk was very amusing. Now it's very serious. He's the one who worries about service, about others keeping their sobriety. There's one in every group. There has to be. He scolds that not enough people come to the *sesiones de trabajo* (workshops). I'm handed a cup of coffee. Victor tinkles the bell. I'm next. What will I say? I've decided not to plan it.

My father met Bill W. once, I tell them, placing my cup of super-sweet coffee on the podium in front of me. I want to tell them about those early AA meetings that took place in my house forty years ago when I was a child. It feels like a link. I never thought I'd be an alcoholic like my father; but it happened. Denial . . . the words come to me. Blackouts. How do you say that, I ask them. *Lagunas mentales,* Jorge says. Mental lakes. What wild poetry. It's why I reached bottom, surrendered. I couldn't see beyond the mental lakes. And yet, because of the mental lakes, now I have this wonderful, joyous life. They're nodding: yes, they know, they know.

Next week, when I go back, Jorge includes me in his greeting. They call me *la compañerita* ("the little companion"), their voices filled with affection. It's in a happy, relaxed state that I claim my seat this night.

Mario relates his drinking to womanizing in a way that's shockingly honest. Others take up the theme. I've never heard this link made before. They seem to see it as a Latin problem. Machismo. They speak as if giving up drinking is a painful sort of castration in their culture. I can't articulate how deeply I admire this honesty, how they seem to me like real men in the fullest sense, sober as they are, and learning to be faithful and gentle to their families. Healed men. I feel my own alienation from the male sex healing.

On one of the nights I stand at the podium distractedly telling my story, I get into an area of my alcoholism that has been previously unexplored: my pre-drink period, the period when I lived in Colombia. I didn't drink there, I hear myself saying, but I took pills.

For years, I watched my father-in-law take pills for anxiety and sleeplessness. And when I began feeling these same symptoms, I simply walked into pharmacies and asked for these drugs — no prescription needed. It was years later I learned that I'd been taking Thorazine daily.

I was a pharmacy freak, I tell them. I loved all the literature that came in the pill bottles, read every word of it. I recall the panic I felt, returning to this country. What would I do? I manipulated doctors and for years I feigned symptoms of schizophrenia. They are laughing with me as I probe this dark area. I told them how I began to hate myself for all this deception. It was too complicated. So I turned to something I could buy on my own. Something minor: alcohol.

I send one of our Waltham drunks to check out this meeting. I will meet him there, I tell him, but he doesn't show up. When I go upstairs, later, to get the bus, he's there. "I couldn't find it." I start to explain how it's right down the stairs when I note his condition. All the way back to Waltham on the bus I have to endure his drunken ragtime.

They don't find us, but they find the bars, Victor says; he doesn't have my benign feelings toward Central Square. He drank there.

Another week we have a hilarious fight. The meeting isn't clearly listed as Spanish-speaking in the meeting book, so a lot of *gringos despistados* show up, looking for a convenient early meeting. They are informed of another meeting at Youville Hospital but many simply stay; they're confused, discouraged. This is a meeting, after all, and you can get something from the aura at most meetings. An effort is made, on these occasions, to speak English. I'm trotted out to make a long talk, and the others do their best; but it's uncomfortable, and resentment is building, especially as some of these people are court-ordered and merely there to get a signature confirming their attendance.

But some of these people are appreciative, and have a genuine need for an early meeting like this one.

Such is the case with the pretty young actress who comes this week. She is in a play at the Alley Theater at eight o'clock. Do we mind if she stays for the meeting?

Victor, who is chairing, and not supposed to speak, addresses her at length, showing off his English which is very good. The girl is very pretty and appreciative, but there is a growing noise of dissension in the outer room. The silver bell is tinkled to no avail. I speak. No one is listening. Luis, very uncomfortable, tries in English. He can only tell his story in baby terms.

"Not supposed to be an English lesson . . ."

"Should have stayed home tonight . . ."

I hear these murmurings from the growing buzz outside. The girl is oblivious. Finally she has to go, after Victor makes her another pretty speech.

Those outside come back in. Someone makes a long speech about Victor's abuses: speaking from the chair, getting away from Traditions. Victor faces him down. This was a drunk, he says. All drunks deserve attention, even English-speaking ones. The bell is tinkled. All this should be discussed in business meetings, not from the podium.

Finally Jorge speaks: "I didn't drink today."

He adds, as always, "And I don't *think* I'm going to!"

Laughter. Wonderful healing laughter. They can look at me again. They haven't been able to through all of what went before. We didn't mean you, someone says.

Oh, I know, I say. I know. This isn't an English lesson. Or a Spanish lesson either.

Laughter and pain — the pain of Central America underlying all. Like a machete kept under the bed and flashed out of sleep.

It's not what made them drink. Nothing but alcoholism makes you drink, we know. So it isn't mentioned much, except incidentally in telling their stories: Mario, from the Jamaica Plain Group, describing how he had to sleep under the dining-room table of a friend's apartment, sneaked drinks from his hostess's decanter to numb the friction of fifteen people crowded together in one small apartment. The pain of wife and children left behind in a Guatemalan village. Carmelo, from the Somerville Group, served in the army and carries a piece of metal gunshot in his head which, if dislodged, could paralyze or kill him.

He prays it won't. He's prayed away the symptoms it was causing him. It's in Carmelo that I feel the deep Central American mysticism brought to bear on "Bee Weeson's" St. Paul-like experience. It could have all gone into fanaticism, as Carmelo himself admits: he recalls standing on soapboxes and ranting. Now he's focused at this podium in Central Square, buttressed by our Traditions of poverty and service, as they are intimately understood by this group.

So I've found the answer to my question: it's the same program. And it isn't Spanish lessons.

"You know what they call blackouts in Spanish?" I idly

comment to a young college student, John, who's in my Step Group in Waltham. "Mental lakes."

"Perfect!" he shouts. "It's perfect!"

Barbara de la C., Waltham, Massachusetts

A NEAR FATALITY ON THE INFORMATION SUPERHIGHWAY

MARCH 1996

A year ago I was sober but an emotional wreck. I was going through a phase in my sobriety in which I found myself depressed and unwilling to reach out to my fellows in Alcoholics Anonymous. This emotional state eventually led to my relapsing. The first beer that I drank almost led to my death.

For some time now, I've been meeting with other recovering alcoholics on the Information Superhighway. Recovering alcoholics from all over the world share experience, strength, and hope with each other in an e-mail group. Many of us have become good friends without ever having actually met. I had been sharing about my depression and feeling of hopelessness with others on the Internet prior to my relapse, and I also attended this e-mail group while on what I hope to be my last drunk.

One day during this drunk, I was at my computer pouring down a deadly mixture of vodka and pills. I "posted" a note to the group which many members interpreted as a suicide note. I was coming up on an overdose and eventually passed out on the floor. A group member named Chris, who lives 3,000 miles away on the East Coast, read of my suicidal despondency and called the police and fire department while I lay on my floor passed out. The paramedics arrived at my door and rushed me to the intensive care unit at a local hospital. I was told by the hospital staff that I would have died had not Chris tracked down my address and taken action.

I was held at the local jail after my release from the hospital and then transferred to the state mental hospital on a suicide hold. At the time, I resented the person who had dared to save my life. I really didn't care if I lived or died. I had no hope left. Much of the usual trouble that I incurred while drinking had happened all over again — jails, hospitals, institutions.

Today, I am sober once more and gratefully attending meetings. I traveled to San Diego for our International Convention where the first meeting I attended was the AA and Computer Networking meeting. My sponsor and I walked into the meeting room and there they all were — all of my cyber AAs in the same room and in person. As I found out later, Chris had already shared with the group about his experience with me. I got to meet and talk to and hug Chris, a man I'd never met face to face, but a man who made it possible for me to return to Alcoholics Anonymous and start anew.

This experience set the tone for my stay in San Diego. I felt part of the other 60,000 walking, talking, laughing, grateful miracles who met in San Diego to celebrate sobriety.

Larry T., Pasadena, California

KIDS R US

APRIL 1994

When I first came into Alcoholics Anonymous, I often had to bring my two-year-old daughter with me to meetings. Not once did anyone complain when she used to crawl around under the tables and untie everyone's shoes. Instead she and I were met with smiling faces and loving embraces. There were plenty of times when my daughter would speak out loud during a meeting (two-year-olds don't understand the concept of whispering). There were plenty of times when she got tired of trying to keep still, got frustrated, and started to cry, and when that happened, someone in the group would just get up, take my child out into another room, and entertain her. And when I'd walk into a meeting all stressed out (and didn't even know it), someone would see my anguish and pick up my child so I could sit still in the meeting. People would take shifts with her so I could get a good grip on the AA program. I never had to worry that they weren't treating her well. I just accepted their gift to me. Thank God for those people for their compelling love toward me and my daughter.

Since then, a lot has changed in my life. I've accepted this beautiful program and my life has flourished. I'm now married and have two more children, and I still bring them to meetings. My oldest child is seven, and she still attends meetings along with my three-year-old.

People no longer get up and take my children out of the

meeting when they start to fuss, and I don't expect them to. I can handle my kids myself now. But I often find myself at my home group taking care of a newcomer's children, giving back what was so freely given to me. And, yes, I've gotten frustrated with unruly kids at meetings, but I know if I keep giving as much as I received, I will truly learn what brotherly love is all about.

We now have baby-sitting at my home group so that parents can feel at home and accepted. Whenever I hear someone use the excuse that they can't go to a meeting because they have children, I say, "Yes, you can — I do it all the time." I offer to go with them and watch their kids in another room if the kids can't sit through the meeting. I do it because it was done for me.

It makes me feel sad when people say they are made to feel uncomfortable in a meeting because they've brought their children. Some are even asked to leave because their children are being too loud. Isn't our primary purpose to stay sober and help others to achieve sobriety? Instead of demanding quiet from children, can't we ourselves take the children into another room so that their parents can get a grip on this wonderful way of life? Anytime I do something nice for someone else I feel so good inside. I could never do that when I was drinking.

Alcoholics Anonymous has given me my life back. It's given my family a loving and caring sober mother and wife. I can't begin to tell you how grateful I am that my children don't have to suffer the hell of growing up in an alcoholic home. When my oldest daughter was three I found her playing with her dolls, pretending they were all in an AA meeting. It made me smile. Because of their exposure to this program, my children automatically run up to their friends and hug them — it's fellowship in action. I know so many people today that have come to love and care for my children as if they were their own. All my sober family is also my children's family.

By the way, most of the people who helped me get sober and watched my child didn't have children. They just had lots of love.

Jackie C., Kissimmee, Florida

TOGETHER WE CAN

JANUARY 1990

Two months after I picked up my four-year chip, I decided I was tired of meetings and resentful that I had a disease that required meetings. I rationalized that I could stay sober without Alcoholics Anonymous; after all, weren't there many alcoholics who were sober without AA?

I attempted to examine my reasons for wanting to quit meetings. I still liked AA, although I had lost some of my original thrill for it. My basic reason related to the resentment I had against religion. I felt that as a child, I'd been sold a bill of goods based on fear; I was told if I didn't come to church every Sunday morning, I wouldn't be a good person and something bad would happen to me. And so, similarly, I didn't like the warnings of fellow alcoholics that I would get drunk if I didn't come to meetings. As an alcoholic I was full of the rebellious nature that Bill W. frequently talks about.

I heard the comment several times in meetings, "I come to meetings because I'm afraid if I don't, I'll get drunk." When I heard that comment, my automatic reaction was rebellion. I didn't want to come to meetings out of fear of getting drunk; I wanted to come not to avoid a painful consequence but to gain something positive, such as release from fear and rebellion and a better way to live.

One thing I'd learned in my four years of meetings was that talking about what bothers me helps it lose its power over me. I chaired the discussion meeting of my home group and confessed that I had been debating in my mind whether I could stay sober without Alcoholics Anonymous. I believe that God speaks through people, and by the time the meeting was over, I had tears in my eyes, goosebumps on my arms, and the feeling of a Higher Power at work in the group. It took some courage for me to speak up in a group that I knew was going to let me have it with both barrels, but I try hard today not to hide my thoughts and feelings.

The discussion started on my right with Joan. My feelings on the subject were nothing new to her as she had already thought what I thought and tried it. She'd had five years' sobriety, quit going to meetings, and relapsed. It took inpatient treatment for her to get sober again and, she assured me, she doesn't want to test statistics again.

Next was one of my favorite alcoholics, Edward. With eighteen years' sobriety, he doesn't mince words. I'd really looked up to him when I came in with nothing much but a big mouth and chip on my shoulder. He was a big dose of hope for me when I had two weeks dry because I thought, "If this man still comes to meetings after all these years, then maybe it will work for me." He believes in keeping it simple. He looked at me and said, "I can't believe you would think of something so stupid!"

Next, a chronic slipper, who'd never been able to stay sober more than three months. I bet he could stack his start-over chips to the ceiling. He explained to me that someone might come through the doors of AA who needs me to be there. Now this might not mean much to someone else, but to me, it touches my heart. Because when I came through the doors of AA, I didn't think I had anything anyone else could use or needed. What a miracle the Fellowship has wrought! I, who felt like a worthless, useless soul until I found AA, now have something that someone else may want. By the grace of God, I'm one of those people talked about in the Big Book who are "uniquely useful to their fellow man."

And the last person, the one who brought the tears to my eyes, was the newcomer at his first meeting. He trembled and shook, this big giant fellow. His voice quivered as he told about running from himself and his alcoholic demons so hard and so fast for so long. He had come to a standstill only two nights before and couldn't face life anymore. With tears in his eyes, he said he couldn't go on anymore. He'd tried everything he knew to stay sober, even church, and he was looking for someone he could talk to who would understand that he was "just a drunk." He said he felt something in this room, he didn't know what it was, but he knew that we were there for him and that somehow we understood.

With goosebumps on my arms, I thanked my Higher Power for my answers once again and for the privilege of being a part of the Fellowship of Alcoholics Anonymous. I realized that sitting there in that meeting had nothing to do with fear, but was about love and the sharing of experience, strength, and hope with one another.

S. R., Martinsville, Virginia

Overcoming Adversity

HOW TO MAKE A WHEELCHAIR FLY

AUGUST 1987

I am in a wheelchair for the rest of my life as a direct result of my alcoholism. Alcoholism kills and it also paralyzes. I am living proof of that.

I drank for over twenty years and was involved in many car accidents while intoxicated, yet I always seemed to walk away unharmed. On the night of December 23, 1976, however, I was in another accident. Once again I was in a blackout, but I didn't walk away from this one. I severed my spinal cord.

Two months after the accident I was drinking again. I never once admitted to myself I was in that wheelchair because of booze. I drank for eight years after the accident — in and out of hospitals, surgery, psychiatric wards, suicide attempts. Institutions were my home, though I never admitted it.

By the grace of God, in September 1984 I was admitted to a detox and rehab at the Bronx VA hospital. I was the first wheelchair patient to go through rehab. I was still unique.

I chose my sponsor while in rehab, and he's still my sponsor today. I have a special relationship with him and I love him. I can say that today about another man and not feel like a sissy.

My first experience with AA outside of an institution was at a meeting which was totally accessible to my wheelchair. But the next outside meeting was held in the bottom floor of a brownstone in Manhattan. I had to be carried down the steps and it was very frightening. I had to admit total powerlessness over the situation and turn it over to God. One day at a time, I made meetings all around the city, some accessible, some not so accessible.

I have a home group now, and I'm very proud of it. I get carried up and down a whole flight of stairs every Monday. There are times when fear rears its ugly head, but I've come to realize that if I fall I'm supposed to fall. I go after my sobriety with everything I have inside me — the same way I went after a drink. That's the only way it works for me. I'm grateful to be alive and I'm grateful to be sober.

Service is an important part of my recovery. I chair two institutions meetings and answer phones one day a week at intergroup. I know I have to give this precious gift away in order to keep it. Alcoholics Anonymous has given me the life I was always searching for in a bottle or a pill. It has given me a God of love. I'm never alone anymore.

I'd like to say to anyone in a wheelchair or with some other physical challenge, this program works. There are still times when the disease tells me I'm not an alcoholic, but meetings are my medicine. I strongly suggest you take the positive action and get to one today. Asking for help doesn't come easily to an alcoholic, but when I reached out people responded.

If you're thinking about drinking, please remember that it could put you in a wheelchair for the rest of your life. You don't have to do it. I did it for you.

B. N., New York, New York

NO LONGER ALONE

MARCH 1995

In a dimly lit and crowded basement room in New York City, I raised my hand and said for the first time, "My name is Julie and I'm an alcoholic." A great sense of relief came over me as I felt joined together with the recovering alcoholics who sat around me.

During my active drinking years, I'd suffered from a few major depressions that had required hospitalizations and shock treatments. In 1979, a psychiatrist diagnosed me as having bi-polar affective disorder, more commonly known as manic-depressive illness. I had been prescribed Lithium at that time, but I would discard it and drink instead.

At age twenty-five, I was a devastated alcoholic. Over a period of twelve years I'd become a daily drunk. My life was in a shambles when I arrived at AA and surrendered myself to God and the First Step. "Don't drink and go to meetings," I was told by my fellow AAs. I quickly found two solid sponsors who are with me to this day. I shared. I cried. I laughed and I complained, but through the grace of God and AA, I found sobriety. I thought to myself, I'm not crazy, I'm an alcoholic, and I just want to get well.

In the second month of my sobriety I was referred to an internist who worked with many alcoholics. He told me that I had alcoholic hepatitis and that my liver was enlarged due to my abusive drinking. He said, "You're a very sick young woman, but you can recover if you don't drink."

As the early days of my sobriety passed, I found myself sleepless at night, full of creative thoughts, ideas, and plans. I collected phone numbers at meetings, and called people at odd hours of the night. I began eating less, talking more, and becoming over-elated, euphoric, and erratic in my behavior. After about sixty days of fragile sobriety and regular attendance at AA, I got the notion that I should travel to Spain and trace my ancestral roots. I was financially bankrupt but talked incessantly about flying to Spain. On a follow-up visit to my doctor, he noticed an elevated and excitable mood, coupled with irrational thinking. He insisted that I go to a rehabilitation center for alcoholics which was located in Pennsylvania. I was resistant at first until he said that he would no longer treat me if I didn't go. I trusted and respected this man's judgment, so I took his advice and traveled by train to the rehab. I was at the facility for only two days when the staff noticed my rapid mood changes and irreverent outspokenness. I was then isolated from the others in an intensive care room, where I was notified that I was being transferred the next morning to a psychiatric institute nearby.

The psychiatric institute was set in a lovely wooded area with Victorian-styled houses for the patients. I stayed there for six weeks, celebrating my ninety days of sobriety by calling friends in AA in New York. After discharge, it was necessary for me to live with my parents as I was unemployable for over a year due to my health. With two dollars and two tokens for the subway given to me by my mother, I traveled from the suburb of Queens into midtown Manhattan to attend my home group. Eventually I met people in AA near my house and settled into local groups. (I still make it a point to take in a meeting at my first home group at least once a year.)

Due to my psychiatric disorder, it was necessary for me to be under the care of a psychiatrist. I needed to take prescribed medication to control my mood swings and still do. Each day I take prescribed medication for my illness just as I make a daily AA meeting for my alcoholism.

I'd like very much to say that all has been well since I got sober and entered treatment, but that's not the case. I have experienced setbacks from time to time — severe manic episodes and crashing depressions. More times than I care to remember I've wanted to drink due to these setbacks. But because of my continued involvement in AA, I've been able to stay sober.

I discovered that I can apply the Twelve Steps suggested in AA to my recovery from manic depression. In the rooms of AA I've found the comfort, love, and support I need to pick up the pieces and try again after my setbacks. And I'm not alone in my journey. Over the years I've met and shared with many other recovering alcoholics who also have to grapple with a psychiatric disorder.

With the grace of God and the help of AA, as I write this I am approaching my eighth sober anniversary. While disabled for a few years by my manic depressive illness, I managed to return and finish college with honors. Both of my sponsors, along with my family, will be attending my graduation commencement in June. I decided to write this article to say to the many recovering alcoholics with a psychiatric illness: you can recover a day at a time and live a happy and useful life. I know because I've done it.

Juliana, Flushing, New York

⊂

ANOTHER HAND TO HELP ME ALONG
FEBRUARY 1997

December 15, 1993: the Christmas season was in full swing, my wife and I were busy with jobs, kids, and all the extra preparations that kids and holidays sometimes require. I'd been in Alcoholics Anonymous for two and a half years. Fortunately I had a good sponsor who'd helped me through the Steps when I was willing to take them (and sometimes when I was unwilling). When I came to AA I was out of work; by this time I had a full-time job.

My mother had been in the middle stages of Alzheimer's disease, staying in a full-service retirement home some miles from us. My wife and I gave her all the time we could spare, at least one day a week, but I'd grown resentful over the time she took from the rest of our activities. Mom had been in and out of the hospital several times for major and minor problems, so I wasn't too concerned when her doctor called us on December 12 to tell us she was putting Mildred in the hospital for a few days for a "mild case of pneumonia." I was able to make it in to see her three days later, already feeling guilty at waiting so long. On the way I stopped and bought a beautiful red poinsettia for her room. As I approached the desk in her section I could see the nurses behind the counter in frantic activity on the phones. I put the plant on the desk and asked which room Mildred was in. The activity stopped and they looked at each other and then at me. I said I was her son and had come to visit. One of the nurses said she was sorry to tell me that Mildred had died an hour earlier.

All the self-absorbed business of the day came to a sudden, quiet halt. I looked down at the bright red flowers. My first feeling was embarrassment at having brought a plant for a dead person. I asked if someone would like it in their room. I started to sweat. I felt a huge black hole opening up inside of me. I mumbled some inanities, then started moving toward the door. I wanted to run far away. I think I started to cry.

One of the nurses, a middle-aged woman who had the look of long experience with life and death, came around the counter and took my arm in both hands, holding me firmly. She looked up at me and said that Mildred was right down the hall, had not been disturbed, and it would be good if I went in and said goodbye to her. That was the last thing I wanted to do — it was asking for more courage than I had in me. But she held my arm firmly and kept telling me it would be good to go talk to Mom for a while, to tell her goodbye, tell her I loved her. Suddenly we were at the door and the nurse pointed at the drawn curtain. "She's right in there, and there's a chair by the bedside. Spend as long as you want. I'll make sure you're not disturbed."

I'd made amends to my mom some months back, but felt they weren't complete because she was unable to comprehend fully what I was telling her. Now I sat down, took her hand, and made amends. I told her I loved her and was sorry she had suffered. Finally I was quiet and just sat with her awhile longer. Somehow, we were at peace with each other.

I left the hospital in a fog. I couldn't tell how I felt. I remember a fleeting thought: "What a great excuse to drink!" I went home and called an AA friend. It turned out he had nothing going on, and he said, "Why don't you come over and hang out?" I went, and later on a couple more AAs dropped by. We spent the afternoon doing nothing in particular (I was numb). I had dinner at home, then the same guys picked me up to go to a new meeting thirty miles away, basically a speaker's meeting. It was perfect since the last thing I wanted to do was talk. After the meeting, coffee. Then home. And sleep.

In earlier days, my mother's death would have made the major tragedy list, good for untold days of drunkenness and self-pity. But at every step there was another hand to help me along. I know God works through people, if we place ourselves in his care. My sponsor tells me that death is just another part of life, and that it isn't up to us to call the shots, just to do God's will the best we can on a daily basis.

And there is always grace for the days I'm helpless, as I was that day.

Bill R., Allyn, Washington

BREAKER, BREAKER

MAY 1993

Somewhere in Indiana, I pulled my eighteen-wheel tractor trailer off the interstate and into the truckstop. It was seven o'clock on a Monday night. My home group in Toms River, New Jersey, would be starting its meeting in an hour, and this was anniversary night. I'd been promised by my boss that I'd be back in time so I could celebrate my second anniversary. (I'd been on the road for my first one as well.) Now I had all four of the HALT symptoms: I was hungry, angry, lonely, and very tired.

I climbed out of my rig and walked into the truckstop to refill my coffee thermos and to call home.

Molly answered the phone on the first ring. Her slight Irish brogue picked my spirits up right away. She told me that she was real proud of me, that my sponsor and several other people had called to congratulate me, and that my name was on the cake. She told me to drive safe and hurry home. I thanked my Higher Power for all the people in my life who hadn't given up on me when I had.

It took me eighteen years of being "around" AA to obtain those two years of sobriety, and all I did was go to meetings and say my prayers. A good friend told me that I had finally received the gift of surrender.

As I pulled back out onto the interstate, I noticed police and emergency vehicles everywhere. According to the voice on my CB radio, a young man, apparently drunk, had staggered onto the roadway and been hit by a truck. Another voice on the radio said, "I thought God took care of drunks and fools." I added my comments by saying he had taken care of me for the past two years.

Another voice came over the radio. He asked for the guy who hadn't had a drink for two years. "Go ahead," I replied. "You must be a friend of Bill W.," the voice said. "My handle is 'Just for Today,' " he said. I told him mine was "Camel Jockey."

"Hey, Camel Jockey, how about getting a cup of coffee? I sure could use a mini meeting." "No problem," I said. "There's a truck stop as soon as we cross into Ohio."

After we met up at the truck stop, I explained to Just for Today — whose real name was Bob — that it was my anniversary, and I'd been looking forward to getting home to celebrate with my home group. We talked about AA for a while. I found out that Bob, like myself, was finding it difficult to make meetings, what with tight schedules and dispatchers wanting their loads delivered by yesterday.

It just so happened that my company was looking for team drivers to run coast to coast. I suggested to Bob that we team up and this way we would be able to help each other. He said he'd think it over, discuss it with his sponsor, and get back to me within the week.

The following Saturday he called to tell me that he was interested and was going to my company for an interview.

That was over a month ago and Bob and I are now trucking coast to coast. We have meetings and listen to each other's tapes and read our books. I don't have that lonely feeling anymore.

I'm writing this article because we felt there may be other truckers out there in the same position we were in — missing the Fellowship when they're on the road.

So if you're out there jamming gears and you feel like you're a prisoner of the white lines, give old "Just for Today" or "Camel Jockey" a yell on the CB radio. We'll either be on channel 19 or channel 12. Or just ask for "Friends of Bill W."

George B., Beachwood, New Jersey

WHEN OUTSIDE ISSUES CREEP IN
MAY 1992

I stood in my living room and screamed that I was quitting AA. My Al-Anon wife was stunned. She couldn't believe what she was hearing, and all she could do was cry.

I'd been sober for seventeen years and in that period I'd devoted myself to AA. For me, Alcoholics Anonymous was not an avocation but a vocation. I averaged four meetings a week and spent many, many hours in service. My house was often like Grand Central Station — a stopping-off place for drunks. I had no interests outside of AA and work. I had a small business and never lost the opportunity to help the out-of-work newcomer by giving him a job. Most of the time, these newcomers took much and gave little. My business suffered, but since money was not my sole objective, I persisted in this practice against sound advice.

Living in a small community, I could really see how AA had an impact. I enjoyed being part of AA's growth, while I watched with a certain amount of sadness as the traditional Twelfth Step call was being made obsolete by treatment facilities. I also watched with some skepticism as the God of our fathers was replaced by the therapist. But I tried very hard to avoid controversy on outside issues and encouraged members to keep their eye on the ball — the ball being, of course, the suffering alcoholic. I encouraged cooperation with outside agencies.

I was totally enamored with the Fellowship, though I accepted that as an organization we had our sins. I was most concerned about ego and power-driving within myself and made every effort not to abuse the Fellowship by trying to have everything done my way. I was delighted to support any AA venture that could strengthen our Fellowship. My enthusiasm was unlimited in AA. However, all this was about to change.

I come originally from a country where the racial majority is, in the United States, a minority. I refused to discuss with AA members why this group of people wasn't entering into the Fellowship in the same numbers as the majority. My refusal was based on our

Preamble. Our job, I often said, was to carry the message, period
— not get involved with social issues or make social statements,
though surely we should provide opportunity for everyone.

I looked at prejudice as just another of our many character
defects. It was up to the individual to deal with it the best way he
or she knew how. Our program deals with it forthrightly and honestly in our Preamble by stating simply that we are totally inclu-
sive.

I was accused of being naive, of not accepting the political realities of the world we live in. I was told some members felt they
were being discriminated against. But I continued to refuse to be
drawn into the argument.

Meanwhile, a few members, not as naive as I was, and
well-versed in the political realities, had their way and a general
group conscience meeting was called to clear the air. In the spirit
of AA, and attempting to face the realities and sincerely believing
that AAs would do the "right thing," I went to the meeting. Prior
to the big meeting, my own group held its own group-conscience
debate on the subject. After much discussion we came to the conclusion that we were doing the best we could and that no one was
being denied access to our group.

However, the general group conscience meeting — as I had
feared — turned nasty, with members accusing other members of
prejudice. There was much pain and hurt. Our members were
divided. A few power drivers, believing in the rightness of their
position, lashed out and took everyone's inventory according to
their own bias.

I couldn't believe what was happening. Charges and counter-
charges were being laid. Everyone was suspected as a bigot.
Newcomers were being told to avoid certain meetings because the

members were prejudiced. Martin Luther King and Malcolm X were quoted. We had become embroiled in outside issues. It was hard to believe that the older members involved couldn't see how destructive this was to the Fellowship.

I was stunned. Then came the resentment, a resentment so deep that it dogged my heels for three years. I could not let go of it. I became angry for allowing the resentment to persist. But it was as if a light had gone out of my soul. My perceptions of AA changed. I found myself at meetings counting the number of people in racial groupings.

Gone was the enthusiasm. Where once I was truly color-blind, I now saw AA in terms of black and white. In their eagerness to prove lack of bias, groups started pushing into service those with a minimum amount of sobriety. It no longer seemed to matter whether people were reasonably qualified. The color of their skin became more important.

I became sicker and sicker. My group recovered, as it always does, but I remained scarred. Consumed with anger, self-pity, and resentment I slowly deteriorated. I became rigid in the Fellowship. At every meeting I harped on the Preamble. But the joy had gone. No longer was AA the same for me.

I tried to become a defender of the AA faith. I argued against outside literature permeating AA. I constantly reminded members that AA was not about the "inner child" or being shame-based.

And I became sicker and sicker. I judged members as I became harsher and harsher. I lost my business because I was so consumed with anger and self-pity. I couldn't sleep. Gone was my childlike delight in the Fellowship. I had finally entered the grown-up world of "political reality." And I didn't like it for one minute.

So there I stood in my living room, screaming, "I have had

enough of AA!" I let loose with a tirade of all the anger that had been building up for years. There were distortions, of course, but hidden behind every accusation there was a grain of truth and perhaps more than just a grain.

At that point I had truly bottomed out emotionally. I had every intention of quitting AA. I didn't, but it was close.

Of course I was wrong. But in this diatribe is a warning, not simply that we must learn to live and let live, and that self-pity and resentment will drive us back to drink. Not simply that I was not "working my program" and that "I was not walking the spiritual walk." All this is very true.

But how many have experienced similar things? How many of us have made AA their whole life and then watched as this life was torn apart because we didn't accept the "political realities." How many of us have left AA? If there are others out there who are no longer going to meetings because of similar goings-on I would like you to know that I understand.

I am speaking to those who gave the Fellowship their best shot, who once believed that AA should stick to its primary purpose of helping others to achieve sobriety.

I made a big mistake in trying to protect our Fellowship. But I'll tell you straight out that AA needs a few champions right now. We mourn the loss of our extinct species in the world – AA may one day be among them. I would urge any of the old-timers to return and hold steady. Keep your eye on the newcomer.

Anonymous

~

YOU MEAN YOU'RE *STILL* MARRIED?
AUGUST 1989

Staying married and staying sober. Sometimes it seems impossible to do both at the same time. In the AA circles I travel in, there are a lot of people, men and women, who are no longer married to the spouses they were with when they finally hit bottom. I understand why. In my early sobriety, Ella and I fought more than when I was drinking. Or perhaps I just remembered every word without my booze to ease the misery. It seemed to me that living with Ella when I was drinking had been hell, but trying to live with her and trying to learn to stay sober was double hell — with no pain killer.

I was trying to follow the AA program and live one day at a time. But every time I did one little thing wrong, she would drag out the past and hit me with it. She was going to some Al-Anon meetings but didn't seem to be getting the program — in my opinion. All she appeared to be learning was how to tell me how to work my program. I was sure if she would only listen to me, I could straighten out *her* program.

Then I got a sponsor who also had a wife. Tim had only a year of sobriety and he and his wife were still capable of getting into a good one. Maybe that's why I was attracted to him as a sponsor. If he could work a program with his wife, maybe there was hope for me. Meeting him at his home, I found that his wife wasn't as bad as I'd expected. But then I knew how Ella and I saved most of our bad stuff for when we were alone. Over coffee, Tim's wife, Barbara, asked me to bring Ella the next time I came over. This sounded like a good idea. Barbara knew a bit about the program. Maybe she could teach Ella something.

As I got to know Tim and his wife better, I noticed that seeing Barbara did Ella a lot of good. Ella was also asking Tim about things. At first this burned me, since I figured I could have given her the same or even better advice! But I came to realize a difference. Ella was likely to listen to Tim's and Barbara's views whereas she often ignored mine. I also discovered that if Tim wasn't available, Barbara could give me something to think about until I could see him. Since many of my problems were with Ella, I found Barbara's suggestions useful. I realized maybe Al-Anon did know a few things.

Ella and I began to attend more meetings — AA and Al-Anon meetings held at the same time in different rooms or open meetings where spouses could attend together — and we began to know more couples in recovery. We were all having the same problems. Both AAs and Al-Anons were finding it difficult to get along with their unreasonable spouses. The resentments from the past continued to disrupt our todays. Ella and I could agree on the problems another couple was having — usually contributed to by both partners, as we saw it. But we were surprised at how difficult it was for us to look objectively at ourselves as a couple. In spite of the difficulties we were having (or maybe *because of* our problems), some married people began to ask how we were working our individual programs. This was embarrassing because I realized that my understanding of what the program suggested I do was better than I was actually doing. But I tried to be honest in admitting this to fellow AAs. As a result, talking over other people's problems taught me more about what I had to do. Sometimes I had to go home and make a newly discovered amends to Ella.

As I read the Big Book more closely, I found that there was plenty of information on family recovery. Initially, I'd been unable to think beyond my own sobriety to the need for family recovery. This included my need to practice patience, tolerance, and forgiveness for my wife. From the beginning of sobriety, I expected her to demonstrate these attitudes toward me. I didn't realize how long it was going to take both of us to learn to practice these attitudes. In reading about AA and our co-founders, I found that recovering as a couple was what Bill and Lois W., and Dr. Bob and Anne S. had learned to do. Dr. Bob and Bill had talked with their spouses as well as the alcoholics they were working with. Lois and Anne also talked with alcoholics as well as with spouses.

Family recovery is part of the AA program for those of us who are still married when we come into AA. But recovering together is as hazardous as recovering alone, or perhaps even more so. If I'm recovering alone, I only have to deal with my own dry drunks or slips, but if I'm recovering with a wife I have to allow her the same opportunity for mistakes. Together, we have twice as many opportunities for slips and dry drunks as we have separately. But if I can work my AA program and allow my wife to work her Al-Anon program, together we have the potential for experiencing the recovery as a couple that Bill and Lois, Bob and Anne, demonstrated.

Our individual recovery has to be a priority for each of us. We each have our own sponsors in AA and Al-Anon. But we also needed to know, observe, and talk with recovering couples, and be available to new couples. We benefit by realizing how much remains to be done in our own recovery: "We are not saints." Perhaps what we have most to offer is a recognition that our recovery as a couple continues to be difficult. To "practice these principles in all our affairs" seems hardest in those relationships which are most important to us.

After nine years of agonizingly slow recovery, we are more in love with each other, and have a deeper love for our child, than in the days before alcohol. This is a love that we have had to relearn from each of you, married and single. Thank you for giving us the opportunity to follow the winners.

J. P., Mississippi

⌒

SOLEDAD'S SEARCH
NOVEMBER 1995

My father was born in Mexico. My mother was born in Laredo, Texas. My parents were married in June 1963, and I was born in San Antonio three months later. My mother gave birth almost annually, to six children in all.

When I was a toddler, my dad took me with him to the bar in town. He gave me a drink from his mug. He explained that I had to be very still so that I wouldn't fall off the barstool, then he went to the restroom. While he was gone, I picked up his beer mug and drank from it. After that first drink, I couldn't get enough to satisfy the incredible compulsion for more that set in once I started to drink.

Neither one of my parents had even gone close to the sixth grade. My father worked as a laborer. My mother ironed clothes to help make ends meet. My father hunted javelin, deer, and rabbit. Occasionally, he also came home with an armadillo or a rattlesnake. That, too, was good eating. When I was about five years old, he taught me to skin rabbits and help him skin the deer. We also had chickens. My mother usually slaughtered one to fix dinner.

On one occasion my dad was cutting up some deer meat and the ax landed on his hand. I didn't realize then that it was probably due to his drunkenness. I saw the blood gushing out; it scared me and I ran to tell my mother.

Another terrifying incident was when my mother was cleaning up some hens she had just killed. She ordered me into the house to get a bowl. I refused and she got very upset and as she motioned with her arm for me to go on and do as she said, the knife slipped out of her hand and stuck me in my breast. I screamed, cried, and ran to tell my dad what Mother had done. I didn't care if Dad beat her because of what had happened.

My father often cursed and yelled at us. His form of discipline was to whip us very hard with his belt until we were in so much pain we could hardly move. Most of the time my mother knew better than to say anything. She knew she could get hurt herself when he was drunk or mad enough.

When I was seven years old, my parents decided we had to move. They'd been talking about it for a while, then one night some Mexican illegal aliens in search of something to eat wound up at our house. They said they had jobs waiting for them in Garrison. My parents called and spoke to the prospective employer who said he'd be glad to give my father a job too. Our whole family was welcomed, so we moved.

I started school, but I had to walk a long path to the main highway. I was afraid of the cows. My dad's boss must have been a big shot in the town because he arranged it so that the school bus would pick me up at the front door of the little cottage we stayed in. Neither one of my parents had mastered the English language, but most of the time they made themselves understood; however, I didn't know one word of English. Due to the language barrier, I found it truly difficult to learn. When I was eight years old, our family moved to Houston and I was placed in an ESL (English as a Second Language) class. Many kids ridiculed me. They called me "wetback" and constantly picked on me. My self-esteem was low enough before that, thanks to my father.

When I got to junior high, I met a friend who taught me how to dress "cool." I began to get suspended from school for fighting and truancy. I also started drinking beer, smoking cigarettes, and using inhalants.

At the age of twelve, I read a "Dear Abby" letter from another twelve-year-old who said that her father was coming into her bedroom in the middle of the night and fondling her. I could hardly believe it because the exact same thing was going on in our house. Abby suggested that the girl tell a school counselor, her mother, or the police. I felt that I couldn't tell my mother so I went to the school counselor with the column. I told her the girl and I had the same dilemma. She called in the authorities. I was asked to identify my father and he was taken into custody. Since he'd never been in trouble before this, he received only five years' probation. He was also ordered to move out of the household immediately. My mother kept asking me if it were true, while my father insisted that he hadn't done anything wrong. I couldn't understand how she could possibly doubt that I was telling the truth. Naturally, the word of what had happened was all over school and in the general area where we lived. Engulfed with guilt, shame, and confusion, I drank more and more. I wanted to forget that it had ever happened. Boys, supposedly friends before this, tried to make advances. My mother didn't help. When she became so overwhelmed with having to do everything for us herself, she would say, "If you hadn't opened your big mouth, your father would still be here helping me!" These words, from my own mother, haunted me for the longest time.

I began to run away from home, the first time with my twenty-three-year-old boyfriend. We lived in Galveston with his sister, and drank and drugged together. We got into terrible fights. He beat the living hell out of me.

After about eight months, I went back home and returned to school. Two years later, I worked as an exotic dancer. My mother found out and urged me to return home and go back to school. I did, but my alcoholism and experimenting with drugs continued to be a problem. I became pregnant out of wedlock when I was eighteen.

By this time, either I would pass out somewhere or get locked up for being under the influence. I felt that my luck would soon run out and I'd get locked up for a lot longer time than a few days. I didn't want to go to prison.

Like my first sexual relationship, all the significant ones that followed were basically the same. I had a knack for picking real losers just like my dad. They were all convicted felons, alcoholics, drug addicts, and abusers. Needless to say, I thought very little of myself.

After the birth of my three other children, I found sobriety through Alcoholics Anonymous. I have struggled through plenty of hard times in sobriety, with my children and with all the responsibilities that go with trying to live life on life's terms. My oldest daughter still lives with my mother, but she's very proud of me. My life today is truly very good compared to the way it was. My landlord is not threatening to evict me. When I go into a pawn shop, I am there to shop, not to pawn my stuff to get drunk. Recently, when I was pulled over by a cop, he actually gave me a traffic ticket and allowed me to get back into my own car. What a big, big difference! Just the fact that I have a car amazes me. In my drinking days, I sold my car, because drinking was much more important. Thank God I found AA.

Soledad P., Houston, Texas

⌐

THE CARE AND FEEDING OF RESENTMENTS
AUGUST 1991

I want to say a few words about the care and feeding of resentments. Why do I work so ceaselessly to convince myself (and others) that a resentment is justified? It has the same corrosive effect on my enjoyment of life whether justified or not.

I do it because nothing reaffirms my sense of nobility quite as strongly as a good, justified resentment. Whether it is the flaming variety or merely smoldering, it spreads warmth and sometimes even exhilaration.

You see, I am right and the other guy is wrong. That knowledge nourishes my self-esteem. So whenever the fires of my resentment simmer down, I toss another log on the coals to be sure I keep it alive. I review and make notes from time to time of the specifics of the resentee's injurious behavior.

Occasionally anger craves action. But there seem to be only two courses open to me: practice the "honesty" part of the program by telling the resentee just what's wrong with him, or keep it to myself and keep the fires burning.

The former course would probably lead to an angry confrontation that I shrink from handling. The latter course would result in the fires spreading eventually to other aspects of my consciousness and behavior — even to unrelated areas. I can't seem to find any way to build a firebreak that will permanently confine the flames of a resentment to its specific object.

Eventually, I become so uncomfortable that I have to do something about it.

But what to do?

First of all, I must face the fact that the resentment process is not only fruitless, it is self-defeating. Justified or not, the resentment, and my efforts to bolster its justification, will eat away at my peace of mind and my enjoyment of life.

Meanwhile, the person I resent couldn't care less. Here I am burning myself to a crisp over something he or she may not even be totally aware of, something I can't change. At the root of my resentment is a compulsion to change things I cannot change — to wit, another person. So maybe what I need to do is take a look at changing myself.

When we first come around AA, we're urged to do just what we are told. We might not like it, we might not even agree with it: just do it. When the action gets the predicted result, we're astonished and sometimes a little annoyed. But almost against our will, we come to understand and believe. We've never been able to achieve these ends by just thinking, but our action and its results can open the door to understanding and belief.

So maybe the thing to do about my resentment is to act.

But act how?

I was told to act "as if."

That seems to call for selling myself on two points:

1) In the long run I will feel better if I can get rid of the resentment. But what about the fact that I'm right? That brings me to point two.

2) Over time I can feed my ego and feel even more righteous by shedding the resentment than by concentrating on how right I am. Now I can ponder on how noble I am to have gotten rid of the resentment and to be treating the resentee on a "Do-unto-others basis." In brownie points, generosity ranks above rightness any day in the week.

So, there's the carrot. I will feel better if I can give myself credit for being generous.

But how do I go about being that way?

Here are several actions I am trying to take. To some extent, they seem to be working.

1) In many cases the resentments are traveling under aliases with passports bearing such names as "hurt feelings," "ungratefulness," and "honest desire" to set the record straight. Now is the time for unmasking the aliases. Is the real identity of the resentment perhaps "wounded ego," "self-pity," or "territorial imperative"? By any chance, is it caused by the fact that I did something that I felt was kind, thoughtful, or unselfish for the resentee, and he is not reacting with adequate appreciation? If so, I must ask God to help me remember that anything I do with the label "kind," "thoughtful," or "unselfish" I do because it makes me feel better to do it than not to do it. How can I demand gratitude for something I did to make myself feel better?

2) I try to understand how the resentee feels. What makes him do the things I resent? Are they intended to hurt me or are they in response to some inner compulsion of his own? Rarely do I find that the injurious action was designed to hurt me. Rather it is usually in answer to the pressure within the resentee. This concept helps me to take some of the edge off the resentment.

3) I must initiate some friendly contact with the resentee —

whatever would have been a normal contact if there were no resentment. I try to act as if the resentment didn't exist.

4) Regardless of the reaction I get, I must pause and enjoy the fact that I made an effort to overcome the resentment.

When my wife, who has been in AA for years, read to this point in the manuscript, she suggested a fifth idea. She said, "Instead of *asking* God for help to erase the resentment, *thank* him for helping. Thank him in advance and thank him afterward. That sort of puts your commitment on the line." Good advice.

So has any of this worked for me? Not always and not totally. But I am enjoying life a lot more than when I first set out on this course. Because of my actions and attitude, the resentee is giving me less and less cause for my resentment. Far more important, I have no need to justify my feelings by tending and refueling the resentment. With no fuel, the resentment slowly burns out and I begin to be free.

I hate to admit it, but AA is right again.

And now, gentle reader, one final word. You probably assume that I wrote this in the spirit of sharing. Not so. I wrote it in the ardent hope that from time to time I will read this piece myself.

B. F. P., Vero Beach, Florida

FLIGHT PATTERN

MAY 1993

Next fall when you see geese heading south for the winter, flying along in a V formation, you might like to consider what science has discovered about why geese fly this way.

It has been learned that as each bird flaps its wings, it creates an uplift for the bird immediately following. By flying in a V formation, the whole flock adds at least seventy-one percent greater flying range than if each bird flew on its own.

People who share a common direction and sense of community can get where they are going quicker and easier, because they are traveling on the uplift of one another.

When a goose falls out of formation, it immediately feels the drag and resistance of trying to go it alone, and quickly gets back into formation to take advantage of the lifting power of the bird immediately in front.

If we have as much sense as a goose, we will stay in formation with those who are headed the same way we are going.

When the lead goose gets tired, it rotates back in the formation and another goose flies point.

It pays to take turns doing hard jobs.

Geese honk from behind to encourage those up front to keep up their speed.

We too say something when we "honk from behind."

Finally (now I want you to get this), when a goose gets sick or is wounded by gunshots and falls out, two geese fall out of formation and follow it down to help and protect it. They stay with the ailing goose until it is either able to fly or until it dies; then they launch out on their own or with another formation to catch up with the group.

If we have the simple sense of a goose, we will stand by each other like that.

Anonymous, Surrey, British Columbia

Interviews

SPELLBOUND BY AA: AN INTERVIEW
WITH NELL WING

JUNE 1994

*N*ine years after the Fellowship of Alcoholics Anonymous began in Akron, Ohio, the Grapevine magazine published its first issue in June 1944. Three years after that, Nell Wing arrived in New York. A young woman in her late twenties, Nell had decided to go to Mexico to pursue a career in sculpture. In the meantime, she wanted a temporary job to earn a little more money for the journey. The agency where she applied for a temporary job told her about an opening at the headquarters office of Alcoholics Anonymous. Nell knew about AA, having read Morris Markey's article "Alcoholics and God" in the September 1939 Liberty magazine, and through other magazine articles in the early forties, as well.*

In 1947, she started working in the office of the Alcoholic Foundation (now the General Service Office), and in 1950 became Bill W.'s secretary. Within a few years, she became close friends with Bill and his wife, Lois, and on weekends she regularly went up to Stepping Stones, their home in Bedford Hills, New York, to help Bill with correspondence or research, or just to keep him and Lois company.

After Bill died in 1971, Nell continued her close association with the General Service Office and with Lois. She organized the AA Archives, and in 1993 published a memoir called Grateful to Have Been There. *Nell never got to Mexico, but she worked for AA for thirty-six years. She still travels frequently around the country, speaking to groups about AA history. Two Grapevine staff members interviewed Nell Wing at the Grapevine office in New York.*

GRAPEVINE: You've described the Grapevine as having an "improbable history." What did you mean?

NELL WING: It's miraculous that the Grapevine is still in existence fifty years later. The Grapevine doesn't have what a lot of magazines have, like ads or a sales force. It has to stick to its primary purpose and basically that's to ask members to write articles and to share their stories. But the Grapevine has kept going because there are many, many people who understand and appreciate it. There are always enough members who find it useful and helpful in maintaining sobriety and keep it going. Some even read it long before becoming members of AA.

GRAPEVINE: What was it about the Grapevine that Bill W. found so appealing?

NELL WING: He quickly saw it as a means of carrying the message.

And since he couldn't connect personally with all groups and areas in AA on a regular basis, he used it as a primary source of sharing and explaining the important issues that he wanted accepted by the Fellowship. It took several years, as we know, before there was a steady and enthusiastic growth of Grapevine readers. But Bill thought that sharing his ideas in print this way was important. It was there — you could read it, you could think about it, you could refer to it later.

GRAPEVINE: That was one of the reasons for writing the Big Book — so the program wouldn't get "garbled" in transmission.

NELL WING: Exactly. If it's in print, it's a matter of record. And the fact is, Bill was perhaps his own worst enemy in trying to get his ideas across. He could pound you into a corner, so to speak, because of his frustration when his ideas were not understood and accepted by the trustees and the membership at large. So the Grapevine was an effective way for him to reach people — without the pounding!

GRAPEVINE: The Grapevine is now fifty years old, and we're considering what our role for the future will be. Do you have any thoughts about where the Grapevine fits in?

NELL WING: Preserving the experience — to my mind that's what you do in the Grapevine. The Grapevine's purpose is similar to the purpose of archives in general: to preserve the past, understand the present, and discuss the future. So many young people are coming in today and they need to know about the history of AA.

GRAPEVINE: What was your first acquaintance with alcoholics or AA?

NELL WING: My dad was a teacher and a justice of the peace in our small town. I knew about alcoholics very early on because the state police would often drag guys over at three in the morning, rapping on our door. And many of these drunks were professional people in our town or nearby towns, and perhaps good friends of my dad's. Occasionally he'd pay their fines for them — when you've been out drinking until three A.M., who has any money left to pay fines with?

I read about AA in the September *Liberty* magazine — sitting in my college dorm — in 1939. So when I first came to work at AA, I knew about it, and I also knew that a drunk was not always a Bowery bum.

GRAPEVINE: You worked with Bill W. for twenty years. Tell us more about him.

NELL WING: As I said, he could be adamant about what he knew had to be accomplished. He had the vision to see what was needed in order to preserve the Fellowship. But everybody liked to argue with Bill, and he liked to argue, too!

Listening to Bill was some experience. When Bill would be talking, say at a banquet, many in the audience would be very moved and even weeping at what and how he shared. He could touch you in ways that were really remarkable.

Generally, he could learn from experience. Like for example when he was advised to set the tone and tense for the text of the Big Book: don't say, you must do it this way. Just say, Look, this is what we do. He was a teacher but not a preacher!

GRAPEVINE: What's amazing is that he listened.

NELL WING: I always think how Bill was so much like the

philosopher and writer William James. Both Bill and James were spiritual, though not necessarily deeply religious; they were also both pragmatic New Englanders. Bill had a way of talking about a deep faith inside himself the way James did. Bill liked to read about different interpretations of what God was like. He was very philosophical, and James's *The Varieties of Religious Experience* was very meaningful to him, as it was to many AAs both in those early years and since.

GRAPEVINE: How were Bill and Dr. Bob different from each other? Was Bill the greater risk-taker?

NELL WING: I think so. Dr. Bob, as a doctor, believed in being cautious and advising people how to evaluate ideas and solutions, to weigh them carefully — have everyone in agreement before taking action. Bill believed in putting the goal forward and aiming for it. No matter who liked it or who didn't like it: aim for that goal. Bill always thought way ahead. Dr. Bob was the monitor, evaluator, the ground level, the supporter of Bill's ideas, even perhaps not always agreeing with the timing of an idea. Another miracle! A perfect match! A wonderful partnership, indeed. Yes, Dr. Bob was the right person to balance Bill. His view was, Keep it simple. Bill had vision; that was one of his gifts — he could see the road ahead.

GRAPEVINE: Where do you think he got this?

NELL WING: I don't know. He simply was of that character. He had a need to think ahead to the next step, a sense of direction, an ability to judge what the needs were, and a great ability to bring different streams of thought together. But he took time to think things through. People said that up at Stepping Stones, Lois was the one who did the yardwork, the plumbing, and the daily things that husbands usually do. It was true. Bill would be walking a lot, contemplating, just thinking ahead.

GRAPEVINE: Did Bill have a sense of humor?

NELL WING: Yes, he'd knock us off our chairs sometimes. He'd tell Lois and me something funny that happened to somebody he'd heard about, and the way he told it, we would just absolutely go into hysterics. He could tell a naughty story, too. It wasn't that he was always pristine about everything. In the office, Bill and I used to share a big room; I was at one end and he was at the other end. So I saw the "passing parade," as it were — people coming in to see him. Occasionally somebody would say, "Hey, Bill, I just heard this," and then tell a joke currently making the rounds. And Bill would look at him as if the guy was crazy. If he didn't relate to a story or it didn't have a spark, he'd just kind of look at you. The poor guy would be standing there, so disappointed that he was telling Bill a joke and Bill wasn't laughing.

GRAPEVINE: Lois and Bill never had children. Do you think they wanted them?

NELL WING: Lois did, certainly. She always wanted children but she had three ectopic pregnancies back in the twenties. She and Bill tried to adopt but the adoption facility said they needed a friend who could recommend them, and the friend they asked — an old friend of Lois's — said that quite frankly she didn't think it was the right thing to do, because of Bill's drinking. So they never got the go-ahead to adopt.

But Lois loved children. Up at Stepping Stones, young kids would come running over to visit with her. She didn't treat them like silly children but would talk to them as if they were adults.

And even years later, the grown-up children would come back and see her. At Halloween time especially there were always lots of neighborhood kids — I never think of Halloween without remembering Bill and Lois. Lois always had the table full of pumpkins and treats. When the children knocked at the door she'd be there to give them a little something. Then the kids would pull straws to see who got the biggest pumpkin.

GRAPEVINE:: You mentioned before about Bill reading. Did he like to read?

NELL WING: He read a lot in earlier years. One of Bill's great attributes was that he could listen and learn. And a lot of very well-informed people came to visit Stepping Stones over the years. A lot of ideas were expressed there and talked about.

GRAPEVINE: Did Bill imagine that AA was going to be as big as it is today?

NELL WING: I remember in the late 1940s I said, "Bill, this Fellowship is going to go all over the world." He laughed and said, "Nell, *you* can say that — I can't." But the growth was phenomenal. After the war, many servicemen in AA were stationed overseas and were responsible for getting AA started in Japan in the late forties and in Frankfurt, Germany. Actually, in Japan, the program started out with thirteen steps, not Twelve. And do you know what the wives were called in Japan? The Chrysanthemums. Wives were invited to open meetings — well, not invited, but tolerated, and they definitely did participate!

GRAPEVINE: Any thought on what made AA so successful?

NELL WING: You know, one reason is that Bill wanted to avoid the mistakes of the past. He paid great attention to what made the Washingtonians and other similar movements fail back in the nineteenth century.

GRAPEVINE: That's true, especially in a Grapevine article in 1948 — "Modesty One Plank for Good Public Relations." [In this article, Bill discusses how the Washingtonians veered from their initial singleness of purpose — which was helping alcoholics — and how they didn't have a national public relations policy — a Tradition, as AA does.]

NELL WING: Yes, that was a marvelous article. But there were also plenty of things going on in the present that helped shape AA policy and Traditions, too.

GRAPEVINE: Such as?

NELL WING: Well, for one thing, when Marty M. was soliciting for the new National Committee for Education on Alcoholism (later the National Council on Alcoholism), she made a big error in 1946. She said that whoever contributed to the NCEA would also be contributing to AA, or that AA would benefit from it. Well, that created some explosion! Bill was traveling and speaking out West and AAs were bombarding him with questions: "What's going on? What is this woman saying?" The trustees of the Alcoholic Foundation had their first press conference because of this, explaining that what Marty said was not endorsed by AA, and that the trustees had nothing to do with the solicitation announcement. Bill and Dr. Bob had earlier let their names be put on the NCEA letterhead because Bill was very supportive of what Marty was doing in the field of alcoholism. Bill never believed that AA had all the answers for every alcoholic. He always said that whatever worked for the individual was what was needed. Anyway, the Marty M. controversy lasted four years — it was a fast and furious business at the time. But it helped galvanize acceptance of the short form of the Traditions, which were later accepted in 1950 at the Cleveland Conference.

GRAPEVINE: While Bill was clearly one of the Fellowship's old-timers, it seems he was often at loggerheads with other members about a variety of things.

NELL WING: Well, when he wrote the Twelve Concepts in 1959, most of the Fellowship wasn't interested at all. And in the early fifties he proposed a change in the ratio of alcoholics to nonalcoholics on the Board of Trustees. And nobody wanted to hear about that proposal, either. Nevertheless, both the Concepts and the ratio proposal were eventually accepted by both the Board of Trustees and the Fellowship as a whole.

GRAPEVINE: These are more examples of how Bill looked ahead.

NELL WING: Absolutely. That's why he was so concerned about establishing the General Service Conference in 1951. By the late 1940s, it was no secret that Dr. Bob probably didn't have long to live. [Dr. Bob died in 1950.] And Bill was wondering how much time he himself might have. He wanted and expected the Fellowship to be able to go on without him and Dr. Bob. But nobody wanted to face the fact that he was going to die some day.

GRAPEVINE: Weren't there a number of projects Bill wanted to get to in the years following Dr. Bob's death?

NELL WING: In 1954, Bill had the idea of creating a writing and research team to help him with, among other things, a major history of AA. Bill's depression was still with him and he knew that if he could give a lot of time to doing something specific and keep at it, that would help the depression. He wanted to do a good, thorough history and also put together a new edition of the Big Book. The scope of the history project proved to be too much, though, and had to be scaled back. Nevertheless, the result was *AA Comes of Age*. The new edition of the Big Book finally did get completed, and Bill was also eager to do a summing up of what he had learned, the wisdom that had come up through the Fellowship. He had a very precise idea of the kind of book he wanted to write, but he wasn't able to do it. In the end, what took its place was *As Bill Sees It* — not a bad substitute!

GRAPEVINE: What were Bill's depressions like ?

NELL WING: Most times you didn't know he was going through it. His depressions came and went. Sometimes, not often, but occasionally, when he was dictating to me in the office, he would just put his head in his hands and weep for a bit. The worst of these depressive bouts were between 1945 and 1955.

What he accomplished, AA-wise, despite his depressions, is a miracle. So many people wanted Bill's advice — not just AA and Al-Anon friends, but nearby neighbors at Bedford Hills. They'd ask if they could come over to Stepping Stones, and Bill always said yes to everyone.

To get away from the phone ringing and all the people, Bill and Lois would often go away in the middle of the week — to their "hideaway," they called it, a small rented cottage ten or fifteen miles away. Lois would write and work on Al-Anon matters and Bill would catch up on correspondence and memos regarding current AA projects.

Then, once a year they often took an overseas trip, usually in the fall, and in the spring they would take a trip around the United States and Canada, visiting AA friends and discussing AA matters. Harriet, the housekeeper, would pick up their mail, and I'd go through it to see what needed to be answered right away and what could wait for their return.

GRAPEVINE: Bill seems to have taken every opportunity possible to communicate — through memos, letters, Grapevine articles, the Big Book, the "Twelve and Twelve," traveling around, talking to groups.

NELL WING: Yes, he was a terrific communicator! And he felt intensely the need to share his plans for AA's future and to receive endorsement of them — despite the often feisty opposition from some.

Right here, I would like to mention the Grapevine book, *The Language of the Heart,* for I think it's a most valuable book. If you want to know what Bill W. was all about, read that book!

GRAPEVINE: Tell us about working in the Archives of the General Service Office.

NELL WING: I wanted the Archives started, as did Bill. My father, who valued history, had a huge library at home, and after college I took a course in library science and liked it. I always thought that it was very important to preserve AA history, preserve how it started and how it grew — to remember the mistakes in order to avoid future ones. It certainly was important to Bill, but it was hard to get others to understand the need for setting up an Archives. In Europe, in the fifties, archives were thought to be very important, but were not generally so considered here in the United States.

We're a "now" people; we don't always think about the future in terms of preserving the past.

In 1954, a fellow named Ed B. was hired to help Bill with his writing projects. Ed was a wonderful guy — a writer, a criminologist, and just newly sober — but he didn't think it was important to preserve all the material we had collected and researched. Our desks were opposite each other and I'd watch him going through pamphlets and letters, throwing many of them in the wastebasket. I'd say, "Hey, Ed, we can't throw all this away." I knew from experience that each of Bill's letters contained at least five different ideas! Ed had had a laryngectomy — so he'd write out a note, "No, that's not important any more." I didn't argue, but after he left work at four o'clock, I'd take everything out of the wastebasket and put it all safely away in storage boxes until I could sort it out.

I'm especially grateful that Bill so strongly believed in preserving AA's experience. He knew the importance of getting things done, and had a special gift for timing. I often think, suppose he hadn't possessed certain leadership abilities — where would AA be now? Maybe some little sect, who knows? I think it was destined. I think the Higher Power set this up, I really do. The fantastic success of AA is like a big puzzle and there are pieces that you know fit in, but you just don't know where until you look back into the past.

GRAPEVINE: How has being so close to the Fellowship affected you?

NELL WING: Well, I always like to say I'm on the outside looking in. About a week after I first came to the office, I attended an open AA meeting at a meeting hall on Forty-First Street. I remember a gentleman sharing his story and I found myself weeping — while everyone else was laughing! Right from the start, I was spellbound by AA. One person helping another who had a similar problem — that is still a stunning idea to me.

Over the years, I've gained some spiritual gifts myself. Most nonalcoholics who are familiar with AA feel the same sense of growth.

GRAPEVINE: Hanging around with a bunch of drunks for this long — it can only go up from here!

NELL WING: I'll tell you something, I don't know people who have lived and learned and reacted to life like AA members. I've been taught — and I'm grateful. Every morning when I wake up, I express gratitude for what's happened to me.

AN INTERVIEW WITH THE AUTHOR OF "DOCTOR, ALCOHOLIC, ADDICT"
JULY 1995

D*r. Paul's story "Doctor, Alcoholic, Addict" was published in the Third Edition of the Big Book; his remarks on acceptance, which appear on pages 449 and 450, have been helpful to many AA members over the years. This interview was conducted by telephone to Dr. Paul's home in California.*

GRAPEVINE: How did you come to write the story that's in the Big Book?

DR. PAUL: The editor of the Grapevine — a woman named Paula C. — was also the chairperson of the committee to review the stories. She wrote to tell me that the magazine was going to use an article I'd written on why doctors shouldn't prescribe pills for alcoholics. So she knew my writing a little bit and she asked me if I had a dual problem and would I be willing to write an article about it for consideration in the Big Book. My reaction to that was the same as my reaction when it was suggested I come to AA — I thought it was one of the dumbest ideas I'd ever heard and I ignored her letter. Later on she called and asked for the article, and I lied and said I hadn't had time to write it. She extended the deadline and called me a second time. I had a gal working in the office with me who was in the program, and she thought it would be nice to have typed a story that might end up in the Big Book, so she said to me, "You write it, I'll type it, and we'll send it in." So that's what we did. But by that time they had done another printing of the Second Edition, and I thought, Fine, that means they won't use it. But Paula said she liked it and the Grapevine published it with the title "Bronzed Mocassins" and an illustration of a pair of bronze mocassins. Eventually it was put in the Big Book, but the title was changed, and my guess is that they wanted to show that an alcoholic could be a professional and be an addict, but that wouldn't make him not an alcoholic. It worked well but maybe it overshot the mark, and now one of the most uncomfortable things for me is when people run up to me at a meeting and tell me how glad they are the story is in the book. They say they've been fighting with their home group because their home group won't let them talk about drugs. So they show their group the story and they say, "By God, now you'll have to let me talk about drugs." And I really hate to see the story as a divisive thing. I don't think we came to AA to fight each other.

GRAPEVINE: Is there anything you regret having written in your story?

DR. PAUL: Well, I must say I'm really surprised at the number of people who come up to me and ask me confidentially if what they've heard on the very best authority — usually from their sponsor — is true: that there are things in my story I want to change, or that I regret having written it, or that I want to take it out because it says so much about drugs, or that I've completely changed my mind that AA is the answer, or even that acceptance is the answer. I've also heard — on the best authority! — that I've died or gotten drunk or taken pills. The latest one was that my wife Max died and that I got so depressed I got drunk. So, is there anything I'd like to change? No. I believe what I said more now than when I wrote it.

GRAPEVINE: Do you think that your story might help those who are dually addicted?

DR. PAUL: I think the story makes clear the truth that an alcoholic can also be an addict, and indeed that an alcoholic has a constitutional right to have as many problems as he wants! But I also think that if you're not an alcoholic, being an addict doesn't make you one. The way I see it, an alcoholic is a person who can't drink and who can't use drugs, and an addict is a person who can't use drugs and can't drink. But that doesn't mean that every AA meeting has to be open to a discussion of drugs if it doesn't want to. Every meeting has the right to say it doesn't want drugs discussed. People who want to discuss drugs have other places where they can go to talk about that. And AA is very open to giving the Steps and Traditions to other groups who want to use them. I know this from my own experience, because I wrote to the General Service Office and got permission to start Pills Anonymous and Chemical Dependency Anonymous. I did that when I was working in the field of chemical dependency. We started groups but I didn't go to them because I get everything I need from AA. I don't have any trouble staying away from talking about drugs, and I never introduce myself as an alcoholic/addict.

I'm annoyed — or maybe irritated is a better word — by the people who keep insisting that AA should broaden to include drugs and addictions other than alcohol. In fact I hear it said that AA should change its name to Addicts Anonymous. I find that a very narrow-minded view based on people's personal opinions and not on good sense. History tells us that the Washingtonians spread themselves so thin they evaporated. Jim B. says the greatest thing that ever happened in AA was the publication of the Big Book, because it put in writing what the program was and made it available all over the world. So wherever you go it's the same program. I don't see how you could change the program unless you changed the book and I can't see that happening.

GRAPEVINE: It's a question of singleness of purpose?

DR. PAUL: That singleness of purpose thing is so significant. It seems to be working; why would we change it? I can't think of any change that would be an improvement.

GRAPEVINE: Nowadays drunks often come to meetings already dried out, but that wasn't always the case.

DR. PAUL: No, it wasn't. You don't get Twelfth Step calls as dramatic as they used to be. Now I find that if you're called upon to make a Twelfth Step call, it'll be on somebody who is in the hospital. You find out when they're available and not in some other kind of meeting, and make an appointment. But this might change as the number of treatment programs begins to fade out.

I used to make "cold turkey" calls, where the alcoholic hadn't asked for help. One time I went to see this guy who was described to me as a big husky fellow. He was holed up in a motel. I found out from the manager of the motel that he was on the second floor, and as I was walking up the outside stairs to get to his place, I thought to myself, if this guy comes charging out the door, he could easily throw me over the stair railing and I'd end up on the concrete. So I thought, well, the good news is I'd probably be one of AA's first martyrs. Then I thought, yeah, but I'd be an anonymous martyr. I made the call anyhow, and he got sober for a while.

GRAPEVINE: In your Big Book story, you say that acceptance is the key to everything. I wonder if you've ever had a problem accepting what life hands you.

DR. PAUL: I think today that my job really is to enjoy life whether I like it or not. I don't like everything I have to accept. In fact, if everything was to my specifications and desires there would be no problem with acceptance. It's accepting things I don't like that is difficult. It's accepting when I'm not getting my own way. Yes, I find it very difficult at times.

GRAPEVINE: Anything specific?

DR. PAUL: Nothing major, though it sometimes seems major that I have to accept living with my wife Max and her ways of doing things! She is an entirely different person than I am. She likes clutter, I like things orderly. She thinks randomly and I like structured thinking. We're very, very different. We never should have gotten married! Last December we were married fifty-five years.

GRAPEVINE: I guess she knows your thoughts on this matter.

DR. PAUL: Ad nauseum.

GRAPEVINE: You're still going to meetings?

DR. PAUL: I'd say five or six a week.

GRAPEVINE: Do you and Max go to meetings together?

DR. PAUL: Max isn't in AA, she's in Al-Anon and she's still very active in it. But I go to Al-Anon too, and that helps a great deal, and Max comes to open AA meetings with me and that helps too. It's kind of like Elsa C. used to say: when two people have their individual programs, it's like railroad tracks, two separate and parallel rails, but with all those meetings holding them together.

GRAPEVINE: Do you think you'd still be married if you hadn't gone to meetings all these years?

DR. PAUL: I'm sure we wouldn't. I initially thought that the Serenity Prayer said I'd have to change the things I couldn't accept. So I thought, well, we can't get along so it's time to change the marriage. I used to go around looking for old-timers who would agree with me and say that's what the Serenity Prayer meant. But Max and I finally made a commitment to the marriage and stopped talking about divorce and started working our programs. In fact we tend to sponsor each other, which is a dangerous thing to do, but we help each other see when we need more meetings, or need to work a certain Step or something like that.

GRAPEVINE: Do you have, or did you have, a sponsor?

DR. PAUL: Early on I was talking to a friend of mine, Jack N., who was sober a couple of months longer than I was. Jack and his wife and Max and I used to go to AA speaker meetings together. I was telling him how my home group was nagging at me because I didn't have a sponsor, and on the spur of the moment I said, "Why don't you be my sponsor?" and on the spur of the moment he said to me, "I'll be your sponsor if you'll be my sponsor." And I said, "I don't know if they'll allow that." But we decided to try it and it worked out. He calls me because I'm his sponsor and I call him because he's my sponsor so I guess we call each other twice as often. We're still sponsoring each other. That's been going on for twenty-seven years. He moved to L.A. but we stay in touch, mostly by phone.

GRAPEVINE: Is there a tool or a slogan or a Step that is particularly useful to you right now?

DR. PAUL: Pretty much every morning, before I get out of bed, I say the Serenity Prayer, the Third Step Prayer, and the Seventh Step Prayer. Then Max and I repeat those prayers along with other prayers and meditations at breakfast. And I say those three prayers repeatedly throughout the day.

I grew up thinking that I had to perfect my personality, then I got into AA, and AA said, no, that isn't the way we do it: only God can remove our defects. I was amazed to find that I couldn't be a better person simply by trying harder!

What I've done with a number of problems — like fear and depression and insomnia — is to treat them as defects of character, because they certainly affect my personality adversely. With depression, I've never taken any antidepressants. Instead, with any defect I want to get rid of, I become willing to have it removed, then I ask God to remove it, then I act like he has. Now, I know God has a loophole that says he'll remove it unless it's useful to you or to my fellows. So I tell him I'd like my defect removed completely, but he can sleep on it, and in the morning he can give me the amount he wants me to have, and I'll accept it as a gift from him. I'll take whatever he gives me. I've never done that when he hasn't removed a great deal of my defect, but I've never done it when he has permanently and totally removed any defect. But the result is that I no longer fight myself for having it.

GRAPEVINE: That's a helpful way of seeing things. It makes defects into a gift.

DR. PAUL: That's right. And it's the Rule Sixty-two business [see *Twelve Steps and Twelve Traditions*, p. 149]. It's like Father Terry always says, "Be friendly with your defects." In fact some poet said, "Hug your demon, otherwise it'll bite you in the ass." Poets can talk like that.

GRAPEVINE: Has your sponsoring changed over the years?

DR. PAUL: I do a lot more stuff by telephone. When I'm speaking at a meeting, if I think of it, I give out my home phone number. So I get a lot of phone calls from all over the country. People ask me if I'm willing to help them as a sponsor and I tell them, well, you call me every day for thirty days, or maybe sixty or ninety or whatever, and then they call me every day, and we get to know each other, and during that time we find out what it's like to be relating to each other. It's kind of a probationary period. Then if they still want me to be their sponsor, we'll go ahead and if they don't, we move on and there's no loss. And this gets them accustomed to calling, so when they have a problem, they don't have to analyze it at great depth and decide if it's bad enough that they should bother me with a phone call. I haven't personally been doing each Step individually with people as much, but I've redone all the Steps myself on an average of every five years. And every time I've done that, my sobriety has stepped up to a new plateau, just like the first time I did them.

Sometimes people call me because they're feeling in a funk, their sponsor has moved away or died, or they've moved away from their sponsor, or the meetings don't mean much anymore. They aren't getting anything out of AA. And because of my relationship with pills, I've had a lot of people come to me and say they've got — what do you call it? — a "chemical imbalance." They're seeing a counselor who says, "Yeah, you're depressed," and the counselor wants to start them on an antidepressant. My suggestion is, if you want to do something like that and you haven't done the Steps in a number of years, do the Steps first. And repeatedly people will do that and decide they don't need the pills.

GRAPEVINE: When you speak at out-of-state AA meetings, does Max go with you?

DR. PAUL: I don't go unless she goes.

GRAPEVINE: Why not?

DR. PAUL: Because I decided I didn't come to AA to become a traveling salesman and be away from home. So we go where it's a big enough event that they can take us both. And what's really more fun is if it's a mixed event where Max can speak, especially if she gets to speak first. She likes that. She likes to say that I say that she tells a perverted version of my drinking story. Then she points out that I was the one who was drinking and she was the one who was sober.

GRAPEVINE: There are many more young people in the Fellowship now. Do you think young people have special problems because they're getting sober at such an early age?

DR. PAUL: People always say they're so glad to see the young people come in, and I agree, but I'm glad to see the old people come in too. I like to see anybody get sober. It's hard to say whether your pain is greater than my pain or mine's greater than yours. I'm sure that young people have problems, but we all have problems — gays have problems, people who are addicted to other drugs have problems, single people have problems. I can't think of anything more of a problem than being a woman alcoholic trying to get sober, married to a practicing alcoholic male, and with a handful of kids. That must be about as big a problem as you can get. Everybody has special problems.

I've said it often and I haven't had any reason to change my mind: the way I see it, I've never had a problem and nobody will ever come to me with a problem such that there won't be an answer in the Steps. That gives me a great deal of confidence. I think the program — the Steps — covers everything conceivable.

I'm getting way off from what you asked me. I can't give short answers. I often tell people that the more I know about something, the shorter the answer, but when I don't know, I just make up stuff.

GRAPEVINE: Did you find it helpful at some point to become familiar with the Traditions?

DR. PAUL: I find the Steps easier to understand than the Traditions and the Traditions easier to understand than the Concepts. In fact, I find the long form of the Traditions considerably easier to understand than the short form, and I find that the long form is much more specific on the idea that AA is for alcoholics and not for just anybody who wants to come in. A lot of people like that phrase "The only requirement for membership is a desire to stop drinking," and people interpret that to mean that if you're willing to not drink, you can call yourself an alcoholic and a member of AA.

That's not at all what it says. I think it means that if you're an alcoholic with a desire to stop drinking, that's the only requirement for membership.

GRAPEVINE: How many years have you been sober now?

DR. PAUL: Twenty-seven.

GRAPEVINE: Twenty-seven years of meetings. Have you seen any changes in the way the meetings are conducted?

DR. PAUL: All I see is that there are more meetings and bigger meetings and more variety of meetings. I just love to see AA grow. I enjoy meetings. I've been to meetings in Singapore and Hong Kong and Japan, but I think the most interesting was when Chuck C. and Al D. and I were vacationing in the Cayman Islands and we couldn't find any meetings. We were twelfth-stepping alcoholics there and we decided we all needed a meeting, so we went to the local newspaper and got some publicity. We had a public information meeting, and we got a regular meeting started. As far as I know, that meeting is still going.

GRAPEVINE: So you haven't gotten bored by Alcoholics Anonymous.

DR. PAUL: Well, I thought about that some years back. Why is it that so many people aren't around any more? Where do they go? It seems to me that most of the people who leave AA leave because of boredom. I made up my mind I wasn't going to get bored, and one of the things I do when I get bored, if I can't think of anything else to do, is to start a new meeting. I've probably started fifteen or twenty. The most recent one was last November. I got a couple of friends together and we started a "joy of sobriety" meeting — it's a one-hour topic discussion meeting and it has to be a topic out of the Big Book and it has to be on the program and how you enjoy living the program. It's fast-moving and we just have a lot of fun. It's a great antidote for depression.

GRAPEVINE: What's the most important thing you've gotten from AA?

DR. PAUL: This whole thing is so much more than just sobriety. To be sober and continue the life I had before — that would have driven me back to drink. One of the things I really like about AA is that we all have a sense of direction, plus a roadmap telling us precisely how to get there. I like that. All I want out of AA is more and more and more until I'm gone.

AN INTERVIEW WITH THE AUTHOR OF "PHYSICIAN, HEAL THYSELF!"
OCTOBER 1995

D*r. Earle's story "Physician, Heal Thyself!" appeared in the Second and Third Editions of the Big Book. Dr. Earle was interviewed by telephone at his home in California by a Grapevine staff member.*

GRAPEVINE: What is the background of your Big Book story?

DR. EARLE: I'd met Bill, and he and I had become very friendly because we had the same kind of a hot-flash story — Bill sobered up with a big hot flash and so did I. Physical sobriety came to both of us on a golden platter. He got hold of a tape of a talk I'd made at Folsom Prison, and he said he wanted to put my story in the Big

Book, and I said, "Sure." So that's the way it happened. It was typed from the tape recording. I think I helped with some of the editing of it.

GRAPEVINE: What do you think of the story now?

DR. EARLE: I would say again what I said there: that I lost nothing materially, that I was on the "skid row of success." As a matter of fact, I made more money the last year of my drinking than I'd made in my whole life. (More than I've made since, too!) But the skid row of success is just as uncomfortable as the actual skid row in a down-and-out area of a city.

When I came to AA, we had a lot of low-bottom snobs who would look at everybody else and say, "What do you know about drinking? I've spilled more on my tie than you've ever seen." Then pretty soon we got some high-bottom snobs who said, "At least I didn't have to go as far down as you did before I came to AA." I think these comparisons between high and low bottoms make no sense because alcoholism is like pregnancy — either you are or you aren't. A woman can be in early pregnancy and not show, but she's still pregnant. With alcoholism, there may be degrees but it's all the same disease.

GRAPEVINE: And unmanageability can manifest in a variety of ways.

DR. EARLE: Yes. I don't know how many dozens of times I tried to stop drinking, and I could do it — but I couldn't stay stopped. I remember one time, a Sunday, that I was looking in the bathroom mirror, and I looked terrible. I said to myself as I'd said many times before, "I'm going to stop drinking for good. I'm going to go on the wagon forever" — a very dangerous statement. And I was pretty good on Monday, Tuesday, Wednesday, and Thursday, but on Friday I came home and went to the kitchen and poured a big glass of vodka and drank it down. And as I drank it, I said, "Earle, you said you weren't ever going to drink again." Somehow, I just could not stay stopped. But the last day of my drinking I had a tremendous flash of awareness about what addiction was and what had happened to me and then the craving to take a drink disappeared and has never resumed.

GRAPEVINE: What happened?

DR. EARLE: I talk about it some in my Big Book story. The only thing I knew about AA was what I'd read in Jack Alexander's article [*Saturday Evening Post,* March 1941]. It said that one of the founders, Dr. Bob, was a doctor, and I'm a doctor — I'm a gynecologist and I'm also a psychiatrist — so I identified with that. On the last day of my drinking, I talked to a friend of mine about AA. My friend gave me a piece of paper and there were twenty-four or twenty-five statements on it directed toward the drinker who's planning on stopping. Now that wasn't me. I didn't plan on stopping. In fact, I thought I had the problem licked — once again. I had gotten a concoction that I thought wouldn't get me drunk — vodka over ice. Plus, I hadn't ever considered myself alcoholic. I hadn't used that word. A drunk — yes. I couldn't stop drinking and stay stopped — yes. But in those days we used the word alcoholic to mean somebody on skid row, and I wasn't on skid row.

I don't recall leaving my friend's house (I wasn't totally blacked-out that day — I was kind of browned-out), but I do recall being on my deck in Mill Valley trying to make out what this piece of paper said. I was just so drunk I couldn't read it. So I asked my wife to read it to me and she did. And she read one thing that said, "Don't stop drinking for anybody else except yourself." That made a very deep impression on me; to this day I've no idea why. And the next thing she read was, "Don't consider yourself a martyr because you stopped drinking." I've forgotten what the other statements were, but those two just hit me across the face like a baseball bat. I broke down and cried. Of course crying was par for the course in those days. Bing Crosby was popular then and I'd listen to his songs and I'd cry, or I'd be driving along and I'd look up at the sky and I'd see a lovely cloud and I'd cry. I'd look at my wife and daughter and cry, and I suspect they looked at me and cried too.

Well, that evening my wife patted me on the back and went into the house, and I sat there and I'd never felt so depressed in my life. Now, I'm a reasonably happy guy. I have my downs, like everybody does, but in general I kind of radiate above the line. But this was the deepest I'd ever felt. I was feeling just terrible. I don't know how long I sat there — for a long time. Finally I looked at my watch and I realized it was time to ascend my stairs — we lived on the side of a mountain — and go up to the barbeque area and make the fire for dinner. I remember going up those stairs and being so drunk I was afraid I'd fall. There were no handrails on those stairs. I got to the top stair and I looked at my drink and I had just a little bit left in the bottom of the glass, and I thought, "This small amount won't do any good, I'd better go down to the kitchen and make a big drink and bring it back up." So I turned around, just feeling terrible, down and depressed, and all of a sudden a very remarkable thing happened to me. It was as though an explosion occurred inside of me. I felt pain in every segment of my body. I have no idea why this happened. At that instant I heard the words, "This is your last drink." Well, I certainly hadn't planned on this. *This is your last drink!*

I looked at my glass and poured out what was there. I'd already had my last drink. I never felt so relieved in my life. God, I felt good. I felt just tremendous. It suddenly occurred to me: "Earle, your trouble is that you call yourself a drunk; you're not, you're an alcoholic." At that instant the craving to take another drink evaporated from me and believe it or not, it has never once returned.

I saw my friend the next day and I went to AA and I got turned on by AA and I've been turned on ever since.

GRAPEVINE: When was that?

DR. EARLE: I came into the Fellowship on the fifteenth of June, 1953. So by the time this article is published [October 1995], it'll be forty-two years and I'll be eighty-four years old. I still go to AA meetings several times a week. I think it's the greatest. I have a lot of fun there.

GRAPEVINE: In the Big Book, you talk about operating on a woman with a tumor and how that brought you a sense of the Higher Power. Can you tell us any more about that experience?

DR. EARLE: When I came into AA I knew all about psychological things but I had never thought of a power greater than myself — that really hadn't crossed my consciousness. So in AA they said you needed to find a power greater than you were. Jimmy B. and Hank P. were the guys responsible for the phrase "as you understand Him" and I talked to Jimmy and Hank, I talked to Bill, I talked to Chuck C. — I kept asking, "What's all this Higher Power stuff?"

When I was about nine or ten months sober, I operated on a woman and took out a large uterine tumor. I took out the sutures on the sixth day, and the wound was tightly healed together. How come? As I was pondering this, the woman's husband called me.

He said, "I want to thank you for curing my wife. We are deeply appreciative." And she got on the phone and said the same thing. I said, "Well, I'm glad to be of service," but when we hung up, I asked myself, "Did you cure her?" And I thought about the wound and how it had healed, and while I didn't underestimate my diagnostic ability or my surgical ability, I wondered if I really could say I'd cured her. Well, I couldn't account for it. I thought, maybe the nurses at the hospital cured her, because after all they had spent more time with her than I did. I spent many hours in surgery with her, but after that I just spent a few minutes twice a day making rounds. But I realized that as valuable as the nurses were and as lovely as they were, even they could not bring about a cure. And then it finally became perfectly clear to me that inside of every human being there is a healing power. I had cut my finger and it had gotten well; I'd broken a bone and it had gotten well; I'd operated on this woman and she had gotten well. How come? That to me, in its simplest form, is a concept of a power greater than I am.

GRAPEVINE: What was your impression of Bill W.?

DR. EARLE: I thought he was a hell of a great guy. I went back to New York and I met Nell Wing [Bill's nonalcoholic secretary], and some others, and they took me in and introduced me to Bill. He was a great big tall, long, lanky guy. And he and I took to each other just like a duck takes to water. We sat and talked for an hour or two, I think, and we just talked back and forth — what had happened to him, what had happened to me — and we became fast friends almost instantly. He was a guy who felt very deeply about things, and he'd had a remarkable experience that had brought him to the conclusion that he might sober up the world. And to begin with, he went off to do just that — to sober up the world. But pretty soon he quieted down and just sobered up those around him. I went back to New York many, many times and spent time with him. He had a room in a hotel under the name William Griffith. He didn't use his last name because people could find him. He and I would spend all day long talking about things, talking about one thing or another — we shared all kinds of stuff.

Let me tell you about one of my trips back to New York. I looked at Bill and he just looked terrible. And I said, "Bill, how do you feel?" And he said, "I don't feel well at all." I found out that whenever guests came to AA headquarters, Bill would take them down to a little ice cream shop around the corner and he'd buy them ice cream and cake and coffee. He was doing nothing day after day but drinking coffee and eating ice cream and cake. And I said, "Bill, you know, this isn't the best diet." He said, "I guess it's not. What shall I do?" So I put him on a high protein diet and he went on that diet and got to feeling just great. And people said, "Bill, you look so good — what happened?" And Bill said, "My gynecologist put me on a high protein diet."

GRAPEVINE: Have you had periods in sobriety that were emotionally difficult?

DR. EARLE: Oh my, yes. So did Bill — you know Bill had a long depression. Let me tell you how I got at some emotional rest. Years ago, a medical college in the South asked me to go to Saigon as a visiting professor to help the Vietnamese set up a new department in gynecology and obstetrics. Before I left, I went back to see Bill and Lois and Marty M. and some others, and I spent about eight or nine days back in New York before I went to Asia. Bill took me to the airport and on the way there he said, "You know, Earle, I've been sober longer than anyone else in our organization. After all I was sober six months when I met Bob. But," he said, "I don't have too much peace of mind." He said, "I feel down in the dumps a hell of a lot." So I said, "So do I, Bill. I don't have much serenity either." I was sober by this time maybe sixteen, seventeen years. He said, "Do me a favor. When you get over to Asia, see if you can investigate, firsthand, the various religions in Asia. That means Hinduism, Buddhism, and Taoism, and Confucianism and ancestral worship and the whole shebang." And I said, "All right, I'll do it." And he said, "Stay in contact with me and maybe we can find something in those religions. After all, we've taken from William James, we've taken from all the Christian religions. Let's see what these others have."

So I hugged Bill and got on the plane and went to Asia. I had three or four rest and relaxation periods a year but I didn't rest and relax. I was determined to find something that would bring peace and serenity to me. I spent a lot of time in Nepal and in Indonesia. I spent time in India. I went into these places looking, looking, looking for serenity. I spent two or three years just driving to find out something. I tried meditation, I read the Bhagavad Gita, the Vedas — everything. I went to an ashram on the southeast coast of India, run by a very famous guru and saint. There were about a hundred and fifty East Indians there. I was the only Westerner and they welcomed me. I wore a dhoti — that's a white skirt that men wear — and I wore one like the rest of them did. We all ate on the ground on great big banana leaves over a yard long. There would be food on the banana leaves and you'd make it into a ball with your right hand and throw it into your mouth. There were no knives or forks at all, so I did what they did. I didn't like the taste very much but I did it.

I happened to be there at the time of the Feast of Dewali. Dewali is like our time of Easter; it's the time of renewal. We were awakened on the early morning of Dewali around two o'clock. This ashram was located at the base of a mountain known as Arunachal. Now Arunachal in Hindi means sun, and the myth goes that one of the gods, Rama, lives inside of this mountain. We were told we had to walk around the base of this mountain — which was a ten mile walk — and as we walked, we were yelling to Rama. If you do it in a very firm and believing way, it's said that Rama will come up and wave at you and bless you. I was there, and I did it. We walked around and we were yelling "Rama, Rama, Rama" hoping that Rama would come up and bless us all. They all walked in their bare feet. I didn't, I wore my shoes. Gosh, I was tired. But I walked all night long, the whole distance.

After that event, I came back to my little apartment in Saigon, ready to return to my medical work. I was so beaten because I'd been driving and searching and clenching my fists for almost three years (and I kept writing to Bill about all this, you know). And I came into my apartment and I suddenly collapsed on the floor. I lay there breathing kind of heavily and I said to myself, "Oh, to hell with serenity, I don't care if it ever comes." And I meant it. And do you know what happened? All of a sudden the craving to find serenity utterly evaporated — and in its place there was serenity. The trouble was the search . . . looking out *there* for what was right *here*.

You know, we only have this given second. There's always now. Once I realized that, serenity became mine. Now — I'm speaking about emotions — I haven't sought one single thing since that day because it's all right here. I often say to people at meetings, "You're trying to find peace of mind out there. I don't blame you, but it isn't out there. It's here. Right here."

Now, do I think there is a supreme being, a God? Sure I do. Of course. But do I have any religious beliefs? No. Religion demands that you do certain things and my life in AA isn't like that. AA is a very loose-jointed organization. People say there is only one way to work the program. That's crazy. We talk about the "suggested" Steps, which are guides to recovery, not absolutes. Chapter five of the Big Book says that "no one among us has been able to maintain anything like perfect adherence to these principles." If we had all the members of AA standing here, everyone would have a different idea what AA is all about. Bill's idea was different from Dr. Bob's, yours will be different from mine. And yet they're all based on one thing and that is: don't drink, and use the Twelve Steps in your own way.

GRAPEVINE: Do you sponsor people differently now than you did years ago?

DR. EARLE: I don't think I do. Maybe these days sponsees tend to talk about not only their drinking but a little more about the relationship problems, and so we get into conversations about their wives or sweethearts and some emotional problems.

GRAPEVINE: So whatever changes you find in AA, you're not uncomfortable with them?

DR. EARLE: Well, some AA groups have turned into kind of psychological forums and that isn't AA to me. Maybe it is, I don't know. Here's the way I feel about it, correct or incorrect: AA is my family, and every family has a mix of people in it. Every family has people who are braggarts who think they know everything — every family does. Every family has people who whine all the time — every family. And every family has people who go out and do very well and succeed at the art of living. So when I hear the whiners — well, they're kind of a bore, but on the other hand, a family always has boring whiners in it.

GRAPEVINE: Did your marriage change after you got sober?

DR. EARLE: Oh my God, yes — I've been married four times. I was sober about fifteen years before I got divorced the first time. I'd been married thirty years. It was a marriage that was not very successful. My wife and I went on different paths, but we were victims of the idea that good boys and girls don't get divorced. Finally I said to Mary, "You know, I think we ought to get divorced," and she said, "I think so too. We don't have much in common." So we had a very sensible, quiet, straightforward divorce. But you can't hang from the rope for thirty years and not miss it when it's cut down. So, after that I got married twice for very short times to two very fine women, good friends of mine today. Then I had a long time when I wasn't married and then I met my current wife and we've been married fifteen years. She's sitting right here next to me, by the way, working on the computer.

GRAPEVINE: Is there any Step that is a particular help to you?

DR. EARLE: I like that Tenth Step pretty well. When you make a mistake — stomp on somebody's toes — you can straighten it out right away. I think that's a pretty valuable Step.

GRAPEVINE: What is your view of the Eleventh Step?

DR. EARLE: Let me say something which might be heretical to many people. I think that God's will and my will are identical. I think that it was God's will that I become addicted to alcohol and amphetamines so that I could find AA and get sober. And so I feel that the greatest thing that ever happened to me were the alcohol and drugs that I took, because that brought me to where I am, and I need to be here. If the casting director who runs this whole universe were to come to me and say, "Earle, you're going to live your life over again," I would say, "All right, but I want to live it exactly the same way — all the misery, all the drinks, all the amphetamines." All the stuff I took, I'd do it exactly the same way. Why? If I didn't do it exactly the same way, you and I wouldn't be having this conversation, and I live on such things. So, the Eleventh Step is great but I don't need to pray for God's guidance. It's here all the time.

GRAPEVINE: So God's will for you is to be sober.

DR. EARLE: That's right, but he had to get me drunk first.

GRAPEVINE: Is there anything you'd like to say in conclusion?

DR. EARLE: I think AA is the greatest thing alive. And I think that we do need to check on what's happening in AA, and I think we need to look at AA as a family. AA cannot be the same way it was when Dr. Bob and Bill were here. I think that we need to go along with changes in AA but let's not forget the Twelve Steps. Let's not forget those suggested Steps that we can use to make ourselves more aware of what's going on. Because to me the greatest thing in life is to be aware of what's happening all the time.

I'm not a church-goer — I'm in church all the time. To me, prayer is utter awareness. I don't know if that makes sense to you but it does to me. It's being aware of things, of what's going on around me all the time, in a given second. That to me is a form of prayer, that to me is a form of righteousness, if you want to use that religious word.

GRAPEVINE: A Buddhist might call that awareness "mindfulness."

DR. EARLE: Christians call it a state of grace. We in AA have a bit of a state of grace.

~

AN INTERVIEW WITH THE AUTHOR OF "THE INDEPENDENT BLONDE"
MARCH 1996

Nancy F. *is the author of "The Independent Blonde," which appeared in the Second Edition of the Big Book. She was interviewed in the Grapevine's offices by two Grapevine staff members.*

GRAPEVINE: How did your story get in the Big Book?

NANCY F.: We had several writers around and they wrote my story. I didn't write the story — someone wrote it for me. I don't even remember being interviewed. I never thought much about my story, to tell you the truth. I don't even think I knew it was in the Big Book.

GRAPEVINE: Your story was picked because someone knew you?

NANCY F.: We all knew each other in those days. Because we were all in one clubhouse.

GRAPEVINE: It was a small world, wasn't it?

NANCY F.: Absolutely, and we were all together. In those days, nobody was anybody. Not like today. Nobody had any money, everybody was poor. Everybody was coming back from the war, so nobody had anything really. I don't mean we were hungry, I don't mean that. I had an apartment and so forth. But we were all sort of starting from scratch. We used to go down to Greenwich Village and eat for fifty cents by candlelight.

There was great camaraderie in the clubhouse. It was on Ninth Avenue and Forty-First Street. Nobody was on Ninth Avenue and Forty- First Street in those days, so the first time I went to a meeting, I thought there would be a bunch of bums. Then I thought, you're one too, so you better get over there. I decided not to get dressed up because I didn't want to look better than everybody else, and when I got there, Park Avenue was there and everybody was there. So I learned my lesson — never think you're better than anybody else, just go. It was quite an education to see how everybody was suffering the same disease. I met people like Felicia. I never knew a princess before. I never knew a countess before! I can tell you, I never could have gotten anything like that anywhere else. And there was a humanity in all of us for each other. I was so welcome. It was the first time I felt welcome.

GRAPEVINE: You did a lot of Twelfth Step calls in those days.

NANCY F.: Oh yes, we went everywhere. We'd go on buses all over to speak. People's houses, or rented rooms. So many lived in such lonely rooms, all by themselves, no bathroom. When I came into AA I was about thirty-nine years old. That was in 1945. There was another woman who was as young as I was, and they picked us to go to hospitals and drying-out places because we were younger and presentable. In those days, if you were a drunk from a rich family, they put you away. You were hidden in hospitals and all kinds of places. So she and I bought little hats with flowers on them and we had little black dresses and pearls, and that's how we'd go. I was very naive; I said, "Gee, there's bars on the windows and no door-knobs." I saw so many young, young rich women, incarcerated by their families.

Once we went to the apartment of Miss X [a celebrated actress] and she told us such wonderful stories, we forgot why we were there. We didn't have the nerve to tell her that she was a drunk. Later she did get sober.

GRAPEVINE: Did you take literature on Twelfth Step calls?

NANCY F.: There wasn't much literature. We'd just go and talk and be friendly and say how long we were in AA and where to go to meetings. But our intensity when we were talking to drunks was very effective, because they knew how we felt. They knew that we cared about them. And nobody had cared about them in so long. So that's how it worked for us. We didn't have any spiel of any kind. We'd say, "You'll be okay, and you'll go to meetings with us and we'll come and get you, and if you have any trouble, call us right away." It was very simple but very effective.

I didn't like the families in the beginning. I was mad at the families. I wouldn't talk to anybody but the alcoholic. A friend of mine said to me, "Nancy, I think that it's time that you begin to accept families." And I said, "Do I have to?" She said, "I think that it would be a good idea." I respected her but I thought, I'll think it over but I'm not ready yet.

I had never felt like I was anything in my whole life, that I had anything to give and then here I was told that I had something to give someone — well, I could hardly wait to go on those Twelfth Step calls. I didn't care if somebody lived in Philadelphia or Hoboken or Timbuktu, I would go. I was so eager to give what I had. I went right from the First Step to the last Step. For me it was just wonderful. I got in with people and I cared for somebody. You see, I had never cared for anybody, not even myself. When you care for somebody, you begin to heal yourself. You don't even know it.

I left home when I was fourteen. My mother died when I was three, my father remarried when I was fourteen, and my stepmother threw me out. When you're thrown out, you don't feel like you're anything. You know something's got to be wrong with you or they wouldn't have thrown you out. And they tell me that, psychologically, I felt abandoned by my mother. So here I was in AA and there were people who told me I had something and that they had the same thing that I had — you can't imagine how important that was.

One woman at the clubhouse was a scrublady and I think I learned more from her than anybody. She lived in a tenement house, happy as a lark. Her name was Annie and she came in when she was sixty-seven and she died when she was about seventy-four. I was in a beginners meeting when she came in. And she laughed at me and said, "You're jealous of me because I've had a few drinks and you can't have any." I said, "You're so right." The rich ladies used to come down from Connecticut on Friday night and they'd look at Annie, and she was poor, she was uneducated, she had nothing, but she was sober, and she was having a ball. She was having the best time she'd ever had in her life. And there was no way, looking at Annie, that you could complain. These women couldn't say their alimony was cut off or they were getting divorced because Annie was sitting there with not a word of complaint. She had a quality that was so easy, so simple. She used to curse a lot when she spoke and a priest would be in the audience and she'd say, "Excuse me, Father, but I'm trying to be careful."

GRAPEVINE: Was this Annie the cop-fighter, whose story was also in the Big Book?

NANCY F.: That's right. She lived on First Avenue across from a church. She got sober and then she got drunk again and she went up to High Watch Farm, and when she came back, I said to her, "Now you have to make an amends list, but don't tell me your story because you'll hate me if you do. You've got to find somebody you can tell your story to. You can have a priest or Dr. Silkworth or whoever you want." She said, "I'll take a priest." So we found a good old fellow of a priest, and I said, "Now remember, he's no better than you are so don't be afraid of him. This isn't confession, you're just going to tell your story." They met at my apartment and I made coffee and then I told Annie, "You come over afterward to the meeting." We had a Friday night meeting a couple of blocks from there on Fifty-Eighth Street. So she came over afterward and she was so relieved. The first time she did go to confession, she said, "Father, I'll tell you everything, but don't ask me how many times."

I was in the hairdressing business and Annie used to come to the beauty shop I had and I used to charge her a dollar because I never wanted her to think I just gave her anything because she was very proud. So I'd charge her a dollar. One time she got a job up in the country and they charged her six dollars and she said, "Hell, I can get it done for a buck up on Park Avenue." I gave more permanent waves to people who had never seen a beauty shop. Every time somebody wanted a job, I'd grab them and give them a permanent wave, set them up to get the most.

GRAPEVINE: You mentioned Dr. Silkworth. Did people regularly talk to him or see him?

NANCY F.: Oh yes. If we were in trouble, we'd go to Dr. Silkworth. If we were in a situation and we didn't know how to get out of it or were afraid we might get drunk, we could talk it over with him. He was a very simple, wonderful man. He said to me once, "The day that you can sit down and just be honest with yourself in this situation, you will know what to do." That was the kind of a man he was.

GRAPEVINE: You knew Bill W. Did you ever go to Bill to talk?

NANCY F.: No, no!

GRAPEVINE: Why not?

NANCY F.: I was in awe of Bill. It would be like going to God! Also I didn't think that was his job. But he was around all the time.

GRAPEVINE: Did he speak at meetings a lot?

NANCY F.: Yes he did, and he was a lousy speaker. He said so himself — he laughed at himself. He always thought it was kind of funny.

GRAPEVINE: Why wasn't he a good speaker?

NANCY F.: I don't think he was interested really. It just wasn't his main thing. He knew he wasn't any good and he didn't care and it wasn't really important to him. He always used to say, "If they want me to get sober on, they'll never get sober." He meant if you wanted Bill W. to get you sober, that's the first thing that would get you drunk.

GRAPEVINE: What about meetings? How often did you go?

NANCY F.: I went to the clubhouse every day from eleven o'clock in the morning when they opened up until they closed at night. It was the only place I felt safe. It was a church and they held the meetings in the church part and then in the basement they had a card game, which I never knew. But I heard later there were very hot card games down there. You could eat at the clubhouse too — upstairs we had a restaurant. You could have coffee any time of the day and night. Eventually we went broke. I remember we had two refrigerators and we used to say that only drunks would buy two refrigerators since we only needed one. Excessive behavior cost us. We were $5,000 in debt and the landlord didn't trust us and wanted us to get out. Norman B. was a great member and he gave everybody money; he was a rich man when he came in and he gave all his money away. We had a meeting of a hundred people, and Norman got up and said, "You bunch of drunks, you've spent all the money at bars — threw it away. Now go home, search your conscience, write a check, and send it in. Let's move out of here with honor." And that's what we did.

GRAPEVINE: Do you see a big difference in meetings today?

NANCY F.: There's not as much giving and Twelfth Step work. People are busy and working harder, I guess, than we did. We seemed to have more time. But I don't know. I know we didn't get eased off alcohol as people do now in treatment centers. We went through it and I think it was a different experience in humility and suffering. You'd be getting off a drunk for days. And never be so miserable, never. I didn't know anything about pills. I never knew what a sleeping pill was. If you were not in that "set" you didn't know about drugs. I never heard of cocaine, people didn't have it in those days. So it was different. It was only alcohol. Now it's quite different. People will say, "I'm a druggie," and make some of the alcoholics mad. I think if you're suffering, you're suffering, but I don't have a strong opinion about it.

GRAPEVINE: Tell us more about your early days.

NANCY F.: I was in a women's group for many years. Marty M. had asked a woman named Elizabeth to have a women's meeting in her home, because she lived on Fifty-Eighth Street in midtown Manhattan. Elizabeth's husband was the alcoholic; she was not. For fifteen years I went there every Friday night until she gave it up.

Once I had to hospitalize my landlady; this woman was a drunk and I put her into Knickerbocker Hospital. And that night Elizabeth said, "Nancy did the most wonderful thing today." And I thought, what did I do? I had never been praised before and I felt so warm inside and I thought, This is wonderful. And then I thought, Maybe there is something about me that she sees. If a woman like that sees something in me, maybe there is something. Elizabeth started me off, she encouraged me. Whatever she told me to do, I did. She took me in sort of as a member of her family. For the first five years, I did nothing but go to AA. I couldn't do anything else — didn't know anything else to do.

GRAPEVINE: Then you started your hairdressing career?

NANCY F.: I was in business for twenty-six years on my own. I always said to Elizabeth, "I'm afraid of everything." And she said, "But that never stops you from doing things." She just nurtured me. I told her I should take lessons in English, and she said, "No, you should take lessons in speech." So she sent me to George Dixon who coached Rex Harrison in *My Fair Lady*. George had a sign up over his door which said, "Create yourself; everything else has been done." I went there for a year. I went everywhere: churches, psychology, therapy. Whatever Elizabeth suggested, I would do. She was the one who taught me that there was something inside of me — that I could do things. You know, Marty M. [a founder of what is now the National Council on Alcoholism] was going to hire me as a speaker. She sent me to Yale to take alcoholic studies and I was thrilled. Oh my God, I thought, I won't have to work hard, I'll go there and I'll go around speaking. Oh it will be marvelous. Because I had to go out to hair-dressing shows and I was scared to death to do that; I had to improve my skills and work hard and go into business and learn about labor laws and all that. See, I didn't want to do that. Then Elizabeth said to me, "Do you think you should earn your living over what's wrong with you?" "Oh," I said, "is that what I'd be doing? No, no that's not what I want to do." So I came back and told Marty that I wasn't going to work for her. I want to tell you, I never did such a difficult thing. But I had to do it. I wouldn't have liked myself if I didn't.

GRAPEVINE: You were married?

NANCY F.: I met my husband when I worked on a ship. He was an officer on a ship; he was a big tough man, very handsome. He was in the Navy during the war. He could drink and never get drunk. Well, he got drunk but he was never like I was. I was sloppy. Sometimes I'd go to sleep and sometimes I'd fight. I'd say things that I didn't have the courage to say when I was sober. One day he beat me right down to a pulp and I took care of myself from that day on. When I left him, I just took my coffeepot, no furniture. I looked at that furniture and I said to myself, "The next time you belittle yourself for sticks of wood, let me know." And I never asked anybody for anything again. I found the answers in myself, which was the greatest thing that ever happened to me.

GRAPEVINE: You went back to school in sobriety?

NANCY F.: I went to high school in my fifties and went to college when I was seventy. I called up a therapist I'd gone to and I said, "How can I prevent myself from being frightened of old age? I'm watching a friend of mine who's scared to death about getting old — and she's got a companion and children and everything. How can I prevent it?" And he said, "Go to school." So I did.

GRAPEVINE: What did you study?

NANCY F.: Behavioral science. A lot of psychology and sociology.

GRAPEVINE: Did you have a career goal in mind with that major or did you just like the subject?

NANCY F.: I just knew I wanted to spend my time in some way and I loved to learn and I liked to write. I went to college for nine and a half years.

Saturday night I'd go out. I always went out on Saturday night. And at six-thirty on Sunday morning, I'd get up and write my papers. I got people to help me. The day I passed algebra, I was coming down Fifth Avenue and I was crying and laughing. I thought, "I know what makes me happy — accomplishment, doing something that I never thought I'd be able to do." I was exhilarated.

A friend told me, "Work hard and try to get an A." He was working for me to get cum laude and I didn't know what he was doing and I said to myself, "I'm lucky if I stay in school, let alone get an A." But he nurtured me, you know. Everybody nurtured me. I graduated cum laude. I really enjoyed it. When I graduated, the graduates had to walk several blocks — I was on my cane by then — and all my friends were in the car driving along behind me. They thought I was going to faint and they said, "Get in the car." And I said, "Get in the car? My God, I worked nine and half years for this. If you think I'm not going to walk in this parade, you're crazy!" It was a wonderful experience.

GRAPEVINE: Do you miss going to school?

NANCY F.: No, today I live in a Quaker community where there's a lot of things being done. I'm teaching English to migrant workers.

GRAPEVINE: Are you a Quaker?

NANCY F.: I've been a Quaker for two years. They do things. I like that. It impressed me that a lot of women had lived wonderful lives, men too. So I said to them, "How do you get to be a Quaker?" And they said, "You just write a letter." So I said okay, and I wrote a letter.

GRAPEVINE: How did you feel about a Higher Power when you came into AA?

NANCY F.: I didn't believe in God, and I didn't want to hear anything about it. But I said maybe there's a power without him. I was mad at my father and I was mad at men and I didn't want any authority figures. I had a human being in my mind as God. I didn't know if I was more scared of God or my father. But after I got sober I went to a man who taught that if you think right, you'll be all right. I went searching around. I believe that there's a universal something in the world. And I don't question it too much, but I know it's there. If I behave right, I'm tuned in on it. I believe in a force because I experienced relief from myself and my emotional problems when I first got sober. You know, in the beginning everything comes up, one right after the other. It makes you dizzy.

GRAPEVINE: So whatever defensiveness or feistiness you had about the Eleventh Step, you managed to resolve it.

NANCY F.: Yes, but I didn't go deeply into a lot of things. For example, making amends — there was nobody left to make amends to. I was by myself. But I went back to my job, because I had quit my job, and I made amends like that. But I didn't do very much other than work with people. I'm much better that way than I am on trying to solve the mysteries of life. Working with people, that's where I get my satisfaction.

AA has given me so much. AA was the greatest education I ever got. Where else could I have gotten that kind of education? For nothing? For a dollar a week?

Is AA Changing?

SURRENDER — NOT SELF-IMPROVEMENT

FEBRUARY 1990

Being a frightened perfectionist, my reaction to change is to "view with alarm for the good of the organization," as Bill W. says. In this article, however, I want to do two things: share a little of how I cope with my craving to control AA, and mention one change that I really do fear.

"Is AA changing?" Sure it is; it's alive. It changes because those of us who are in it change, once we surrender to the process of recovery and to our Higher Power. And we change in good ways we couldn't have asked for or imagined. I can't predict the course of AA any more than I can predict my own. I trust that our Higher Power is steering the Fellowship as long as we keep to our primary purpose — to carry the message to the alcoholic who still suffers.

AA changes because the world changes. Not to change is not to adapt; not to adapt is to become extinct. I don't want that to happen to AA. All of us have lives outside AA that put us in contact with new ideas and new pressures. We bring the stuff of our daily lives into meetings to share with the group, not only the bad stuff, but also the good, our triumphs and breakthroughs. Some of those good things are new insights, new ways to apply the principles of recovery, new techniques or new concepts that enhance the AA program. Some I welcome, some I feel hesitant about. But my recovery depends on the survival of the group. I want the group to work for you so that, when I need it, it will be there for me. I want it to be receptive and supportive of you so that, when I need it, it will be receptive and supportive of me.

One of the changes that stirs the pot is the presence of addicts in AA meetings. I myself am an antique, that rare and fabulous beast, a "pure" alcoholic. These days, that's a setup for terminal uniqueness. In my first year I announced to my sponsor that I didn't think I was a real alcoholic because I'd never used cocaine. He stared at me in stupefaction, then laughed, thank God, and asked some well-aimed questions: what was the First Step? The Third Tradition? Had I ever heard "identify, don't compare" as a guide to listening in meetings? In other words, the point he made was that I can use my alcoholism to isolate, to avoid hearing what my fellows in recovery have to say, and to excuse myself from the footwork of the program.

I used to think that my recovery was second-class, because my story didn't include the medicine cabinet and syringes. I used to compensate for my innocence of drugs by sharing not experience, strength, and hope, but theories, wishful thinking, and doubts as to what my story could offer hard-core folk. It helped neither them nor me. It took me a while to realize that, as the Big Book says, "no matter how far down the scale we have gone, we will see how our experience can benefit others." As long as we tell our stories honestly, we can listen and learn and recover.

I do have a fear, however. It is summarized in another story. It's not mine; I heard a woman tell it on herself in a meeting. She (I'll call her Lucy) had finally gotten a friend she was concerned about (I'll call her Gilda) to go to meetings with her. They went to a meeting together, once a week, for a little over a month. Lucy would pick up Gilda before the meeting and drop her off afterward so they could talk on the way to and from the meeting and discuss their reactions to the meeting on the way home. Lucy had carefully chosen a lively intelligent group, prone to talk about issues such as stress and anger and nutrition, in touch with their feelings, taking ownership of their recovery, serious (but not grim!) about sobriety. This all seemed to be good sponsorship and a sensible arrangement.

One night the meeting's topic was "the first drink." It was a vibrant meeting: First Step, "back to basics," heartfelt, the hot core of it all. Lucy was charged up by it. On the way home, she realized Gilda was less talkative. She asked her how she liked the meeting. "Oh, it was fine," said Gilda. "I just don't understand why all those people are so worried about taking the first drink."

Lucy wondered if this were a pink cloud, but again, being the perfect sponsor, she decided to be supportive and draw Gilda out. She said, "Well I'm glad that's not a problem for you. What do you do when you feel like taking that first drink?"

Gilda shrugged. "I take it."

When she got to that part of the story, we laughed uneasily. Lucy went on to point out that, somehow, in all her eagerness to give the program a sophisticated veneer of psychological and therapeutic respectability, she had forgotten why it exists in the first place. She had not emphasized the physical reality of the disease we live with, its inexorable progression, the need for abstinence. "My public relations policy was promotion, not attraction; I was people-pleasing, not being honest. This is a program of surrender, not self-improvement."

I recently saw an interview in a magazine dedicated to "recovery." The substance-abuse counselor being interviewed, when asked about different kinds of therapy for people in recovery, said group therapy was not necessary if people were already in a "twelve-step program," because "you get the group effect from twelve-step meetings."

Now, I understand this is only that counselor's opinion, but it suddenly put me in touch with something that has troubled me for some time. Is AA "therapy"? Is that what all those people I felt uneasy about thought they were doing here?

The remainder of this article quotes some things I have heard in AA meetings recently. They are treated by some members as the equivalents of the older AA slogans, but the principles they encapsulate seem far from the fundamentals of recovery. Many of them come from therapists or New Age sources. I want to say very clearly that I have found therapy helpful myself, and that I believe each of us has a right to the spirituality that works for us, "as we understand" it. My quarrel is not with either of those.

The danger I perceive is that these slogans are treated as *program absolutes*. They are announced without qualification. They are used with little understanding of their role in the therapeutic process or their place in New Age theology. They are promoted with indifference to their possible misunderstanding by newcomers and with no apparent awareness of their possible conflict with AA principles. They may be true, but they are not radically true, like the heart of the AA program is. I do not trust them as I trust the Steps, for example, because these new slogans require careful reinterpretation, and I cannot trust what I feel I must qualify and modify.

"I'm here to get in touch with my feelings." I had a sponsee tell me once that he knew he wouldn't drink, as long as he was "in touch with his feelings." My feelings never kept me from drinking; more often they were the best excuses I had. I listened to a woman whose car had been broken into say, "I know I'm supposed to be in touch with my feelings, I ought to feel angry, but I just cleaned it up and called the police." She added that she hoped she wasn't setting herself up for a slip. I spent years in a smouldering rage while drinking; I'm grateful when I can meet a crisis with equanimity. One of the Promises is that we will know peace.

"This is a selfish program; I've got to take care of myself." No question about it: if I'm about to drink, selfishly avoiding that takes precedence over anything else. But how often am I really that close? How often are people thinking of the danger of a drink when they use this "slogan" to help them make a decision? I've heard people say this to justify calling in to work sick, in order to get a day off. What if the woman who first brought me to AA had felt that way? This cannot be a governing principle, because its unqualified application would mean the end of the Fellowship. In recovery, how can I make personal decisions based on a principle that radically eliminates others from consideration? One of the things I learned in these rooms is that my disease is characterized by isolation, by self-obsession, by the exclusion of others. I realize that even twelfth-step work is done "for my recovery," but it simply doesn't work if I do it as a part of my "selfish program" and focus only on myself, on whether or not I'm getting quick relief.

"It is actually all one systemic disease; we are all addicts and co-dependents." From what I remember of drinking, I'm the one who, on the morning after, couldn't remember the night before. I'm the one who shook and puked. It is a subtle denial to agree that my *real* problem was how I fit into the system, not what happened when I drank. This is by no means to say that co-dependents don't have legitimate recovery, some of which I also participate in. But it does not look or feel like the same disease at all to me.

"I make amends by not drinking; the only person I really damaged was myself." I've been on the receiving end of this: I've seen that, as far as my alcoholic friend was concerned, I was only incidentally in the way of his suffering self-will. He was "confused and doing the best he could," and therefore felt he did not owe me an amends. (Part of my recovery is to practice some forgiveness of my own at this point, of course, which I need to do.) However, his form of self-deception is not the sanity to which I hope my Higher Power will restore me. I know I received some exquisite bruises, but I had an impact on others as well. The amount of reality I turn my back on is the amount I lose. In my case, making face-to-face honest amends restored me into my life, and the fuller my amends, the more of my life I received in return.

"The Fourth Step is realizing things are perfect as they are." My Fourth Step showed me to be a liar, cheat, and thief; I was totally ruled by fear and resentment. I thought of others only in light of my goals and cared about them only as they affected me. It may be that my life was perfect from a transcendent perspective, but the contingencies were hell — and it was the contingencies that had my back to the wall. Perhaps this is a compassionate maneuver for people overwhelmed by guilt, who can forgive themselves only when they see their actions as part of a perfect cosmic design. However, as an alcoholic, I prefer to avoid accountability. "Perfection" to me would have meant things were fine and I was off the hook.

"Your opinion of me is none of my business." When I was drunk, I practiced this principle fully: your opinions didn't matter to me at all. In fact, while I was drinking I believed your opinions of me were none of *your* business either. I suppose this saying means that the opinions of others should not dominate and define me; but is it true to say that they are "none of my business"? In recovery, I first thought this was profound. My boss, had he been asked, probably would not have agreed: he had increasingly strong opinions of me — and my perfectionism. I thought I was being honest and offering creative solutions to the problems of our organization. He thought I was being hostile and arrogant. His opinion of me ought to have been at least part of my business: that is the only job from which I have ever been fired, and that was in recovery.

The foundation of our program is, by one definition, honesty, openmindedness, and willingness. I am frightened that AA is changing dangerously with half-understood therapeutic concepts and unexamined New Age philosophy. I listen to people and no longer feel that relief-filled sense of "yes, I'm like that, too." I hear someone share and wonder if we are working the same program on *any* level, not just that our "footwork" is different, but that we do not even share the same basic principles of recovery.

When I came into AA, I was always always impressed, challenged, and frightened by the statement "if you want what we have and are willing to go to any length" — but my answer was still yes. Today my answer often is "no." I don't want what you have, because it is not grounded in any reality I recognize or appreciate. I'm not willing to go to any length for something which doesn't stretch me; I'm not willing to probe myself for something that has no depth. It all seems so blunt-edged and self-excusing; those are the values I lived by while drinking.

I do want what the people who wrote the Big Book have, however. I want recovery. But, I wonder, what is my problem with accepting these new formulations? Can't I see it as an opportunity to practice "Live and Let Live"? Have I become a "bleeding deacon" so soon, a boring Big Book thumper, to be endured and ignored?

Alcoholism is deadly, ugly, and tough. It is also cunning, baffling, and powerful. It wants me to consider perfection attainable. It wants me to regard only myself, others being merely what reflects my recovery back to me. It wants me to try to fix myself with the right therapist or the right religion. It wants me to believe that self-indulgence is fine, as long as I call it self-forgiveness. It wants me to think of drinking as an option that "I choose not to actualize at the present." It wants me to forget that it is a snake in the brain, hoping to catch my eye, watching, waiting.

The gritty pain of alcoholism is the traction of recovery. I cannot afford to sell off the principles for an easier, softer way.

M. W., Atlanta, Georgia

MONKEY SEE, MONKEY DO
JANUARY 1990

Here is the scenario: your very dear friend, who happens to be a Buddhist (or a Muslim or a Jew) finally has agreed to attend an AA meeting with you. Nobody but a recovering alcoholic knows the joy that comes from helping another out of the darkness, the hell of active alcoholism. You love your friend so very much and you have watched him (or her) suffer over and over; now hangover after hangover has finally chipped a little hole in the wall of denial, fear, anger, and suspicion.

You say, "AA is not a religious organization." He's still not sure he can trust you, even though he knows you wouldn't lie. He says, "Surely not everybody is treated the same."

You say, "No one is treated any better or worse than anyone else."

Just in case you have any lingering doubts that your Higher Power is with you all the way on this one, there's a roundup going on in your city. It's the perfect place to take your newcomer. How about that — there's a miracle in the making.

Friday night's meeting at the roundup is just about perfect. The speaker is almost sobbing when she recalls her first AA meeting and how it changed her life. The emotion is heavy, and everyone who has ever suffered from alcoholism feels every feeling along with her. The joy of recovery fills the room, and prayers of thanks saturate the whole environment. This is so good! The applause is soft and gentle; those present are awestruck at this miracle sent to us through Bill W. and Dr. Bob.

And then, "Would you please form a circle and join hands for the saying of the Our Father."

The chairperson of this particular meeting feels very good about holding hands in a circle when the prayer is said. For some reason he doesn't know that his feeling good about hand-holding is not universal. He assumes that because *he* likes it, everyone should. But Sam doesn't. Nor do Joe, Blanche, or Doris. Many simply back out of the circle while others join in although it causes them some stress. All the time the chairperson polishes his halo: "Isn't this nice?"

No, it's not nice, not if it makes one recovering alcoholic uncomfortable.

Saturday dawns bright with hope because a roundup always renews your enthusiasm. Your friend was so impressed by the sincerity of last night's speaker he is going back for more. He was somewhat surprised by the chairperson's request to join hands. But you convinced him that holding hands is not a requirement for membership.

So off you go to hear a "big meeting speaker." (This is sometimes called the guest speaker, much to our shame. If he's an alcoholic, he's one of us, not a guest.) The speaker is hilarious, one of the great entertainers of our time. The applause is thunderous and everybody jumps to their feet — everybody but you and Sam, Joe, Blanche, and Doris. You believe what you read in the Big Book where it tells us that humility is the only prerequisite for recovery in AA. It would be an insult to the speaker to treat him as if he were different from Friday night's speaker, who sobbed (and probably did more to ignite recovery in your friend). On the way home your friend puts it into words: "I thought you said that no one is treated any better or worse than anyone else. It sure looked to me like that guy who spoke after supper was treated better than all the other speakers I've heard."

Sunday morning you were late getting back to the roundup because you had such a good time at the dance on Saturday night. This is so good! But what's this you hear? Music? Music! Wait a minute! This is no ordinary music. It sounds like church! Yes, it definitely sounds like church music, music of a particular sect! Your eyes behold the glory of people holding hands, swaying back and forth, singing gospel songs accompanied by a church group brought in for that purpose. How can this be? AA is not allied with any sect? Well, what do you call this? A river barge? What's going on here? Did not Bill and Bob do everything to insure that we would not be a society of people of a distinguishable religious sect? Just try to convince your non-Christian friend that AA is not a Fellowship for Christians. Try to convince him that he belongs here.

"Monkey see, monkey do" is a phrase my mother used when I blindly followed the lead of others without thinking, "Just what am I doing? What does this mean and what will be the consequences?" Surely there is some of this going on in AA today. Isn't anybody thinking? The last roundup I attended almost made me think I was in the wrong place, perhaps Toastmasters International or a concert hall or church. I have been to those places and they're great, but I don't need them like I need AA. What are you doing to my AA?

I am no "casual" AA member. I have loved AA from the very start. From my first meeting over fourteen years ago, I've been alive, born of AA. My thirteen years of service work (mostly public information) keep me, I trust, from being a bleeding deacon. I read everything I can get to help me keep on learning and growing, but this has me stopped dead in my tracks. I'm ashamed to be in a crowd that gives a standing ovation to another recovering alcoholic. If we are going to start giving standing ovations to everyone sharing experience, strength, and hope — fine, I'm all for it. But I think it is hideous to single out one member as being somehow special.

We have a responsibility, a sacred responsibility handed down to us, to keep AA safe. We cannot afford to be careless with this.

Religion is something to be reckoned with. Glorification of individuals is dangerous. Stars or circuit speakers are entertaining, but we must let the newcomer know that the stars aren't any better than the rest of us.

Ellen B., Hampton, New Brunswick

IS THERE A GRAPEVINE IN YOUR FUTURE?
APRIL 1995

How long will it be, I wonder, before we see AA meetings on TV? I'm not talking about television or movie depictions of AA meetings, as on *Hill Street Blues* or in *The Days of Wine and Roses* or *Clean and Sober*, which show fictional meetings and characters portrayed by actors. I'm talking about real live AA meetings with real AA members, shown full-face, and carried, I predict, over some cable public-access channel. Furthermore, this won't be the brainstorm of some recently rehabbed, three-month-sober show-biz type who wants to show his "gratitude" to AA; it'll be the thought-out product of five- and fifteen-year sober middle Americans who will believe that this is the most productive way of carrying the message of AA.

Is this so far-fetched? It is, I think, the nearly inevitable consequence of a trend — or actually several trends — well underway. We live in a culture that has a ravenous appetite for entertainment. We're also becoming accustomed to the fact that ever greater proportions of our contact with other people are transmitted through electronic media: regular phones, cellular phones, TV phones, computers, computer networks, radios, faxes, home videos, broadcast TV, cable TV, satellite TV — and Lord knows what else down the pike. We have for many years now been used to the fact that our public discourse is mediated by celebrities, that issues simply don't exist unless and until a famous talking head says they do. And more to the point of this article, we're far less informed by the written word.

You are engaged in this last medium right now. You are looking at a bunch of lines and dots that, amazingly, you have the ability to "see through," so that you hear a little voice in your head, which is really me talking to you. If I am a skillful enough writer and you're a skillful enough reader, you will come to understand my attitude toward and my beliefs about my subject. But my appearance and my personality — facets of what one might be tempted to call the real me — are virtually unknown to you. This is quite different from, say, viewing a videotape of me reading this article aloud. There, an enormous number of other factors emerge. Am I good-looking? Well-dressed? Overweight? Wearing glasses? Well-groomed? Bald? Is my voice pleasant? Do I have a Southern accent? Or a Brooklyn accent? Do I appear credible? Likable? Etc., etc. Any single element, if sufficiently distracting or unusual, can completely derail my communication with you, regardless of content. It's the nature of visual electronic media to present personalities before principles.

TO READ OR NOT TO READ

It may seem un-American to say it, but not everything is televisable. In fact, even setting aside the influence of electronic media, not everything that's important to us in AA can be handed down orally. I have little faith, for example, in the oral transmission of our Legacies. A solid understanding of the Steps, the Traditions, the Concepts, our history, our place in the world now, and our goals may possibly be handed down by long-time members simply talking to newer members, but I don't think it's at all likely. Some things, for all practical purposes, have to be read. When they are not read, they are either forgotten or distorted, and they may be supplanted by something different. So, somewhere along the line, the newer folks are going to have to do some reading. But ask yourself: how many people read these days? It has been claimed that, once out of school, nearly sixty percent of American adults never read another book, and most of the rest read only one book a year. Are we to claim that we in AA are the exceptions? That hasn't been my experience.

I'm in my mid-thirties and, as it happens, those I sponsor are on average ten years younger. I keep trying, but I've almost given up on passing along to them copies of articles, chapters from books, or even (torture!) *whole books,* for the simple reason that I have to beg and nag them to get them to read the stuff. It's not that they can't read; they simply won't. They aren't illiterate; they're post-literate. The overwhelming proportion of their knowledge of the world has come to them through television.

Consider a book like *Twelve Steps and Twelve Traditions.* The number of shaking heads and exasperated laughs when it's read aloud at meetings moves me to think that if such a book were submitted today to the General Service Conference, it would never make it past the Literature Committee, on the grounds that it was too difficult. The fact is, Bill wrote for an audience with literary skills that will have largely disappeared a generation from now.

'I WANT MY MTV'

For the post-literate generation, the aptitude required to absorb lengthy, detailed, or abstract information in written form is becoming a minority ability, perhaps comparable to the percentage of people who can read and play music — perhaps not an elitist group, but one small enough that its members are worthy of note. (We older Baby Boomers are admittedly only slightly better. We were, however, spared the numbing influence of MTV-type entertainment in our formative years.)

In light of these facts, the Big Book's idea (in chapter seven) that a Twelfth Step prospect ought to read the Big Book before coming to AA is almost laughable today. We'd never get new members. I'd go so far as to hazard a guess that not even fifty percent of those who celebrate a year of sobriety have read *even once* the first eleven chapters of the Big Book, let alone really studied the text. If I'm anywhere near correct, is it any wonder that distorted and non-AA messages are so common among us? I know I'm not alone in the experience of attending AA meetings that are utterly unrecognizable as AA meetings. They could be the Rotary Club or slumber-party bull sessions or divorce recovery workshops. This isn't to say that there must be an absolute wall of separation between AA stuff and all the rest of life. Of course not. But while our spiritual method of recovery may be broadly interpreted, AA isn't an anything-goes program either. We do have a singleness of purpose, and we do share only one common problem. In order to affirm that, we must first *know* that.

AA IN THE TWENTY-FIRST CENTURY

It's possible that twentieth-century AA will be so foreign to future AA members that they'll muse over the fuss we made about putting AA on TV, and reflect that Gutenberg's generation, too, couldn't see the benefits of its new technology. Perhaps there will evolve an AA canon expressing a new openness and tolerance, a more profound psychology of alcoholism which will be available on the twenty-first century equivalent of videotape, showing the personal testimonies (and faces) of individual AAs, augmented of course with exciting background music and rapid editing, à la

MTV. These people will express gratitude that they didn't have to endure the "deuteronomic" Big Book, with its sexist language and narrow pathway of relying on God. They will say that they encountered the AA program on their own terms and made of it what they wanted.

I hope I'm drawing a caricature here. But I fear that my prediction is more accurate than inaccurate. The trends don't look good to me. What makes them more troublesome is the fact that they're out of our control; these are outside, or cultural, forces. But we in AA have to depend on the broader culture to provide us with literate members potentially receptive to serious spiritual challenges. I think our culture is failing us on both counts: more and more, our society tells us that neither serious reading nor serious worship is worth our time.

Telling this to Grapevine readers is, I suspect, preaching to the choir. But perhaps that is the place to start. It's naive to think that AA can survive automatically in every single cultural and intellectual environment. The irony is not that the emerging culture is at all hostile to our mission, but that it is so friendly. It wants our Fellowship to be a welcome player on its stage and will all too gladly put us on TV and speak kindly of us. All we have to do is be entertaining.

I judge that my finest accomplishment in nine years of AA membership was being part of saving a meeting. I and others dug in our heels and, in effect, said: "We're not leaving. We're going to make this a place where AA can be heard and found. This ragtag meeting is going to become an AA *group."*

It took nearly four years, and it was sometimes lonesome, but what we have today is a group, and AA's message can be heard there. I'm thinking that perhaps this will be the model for the whole Fellowship: little platoons of informed, literate members, anonymously holding down selected territories, being there as God expresses himself.

Jim N., St. Paul, Minnesota

RULES OF THUMB

SEPTEMBER 1987

I think we should sometimes take an inventory of AA itself as well as an inventory of ourselves. We need to take a close look at what we are doing and thinking as groups, as well as what we are doing as individual members.

I'm not writing this in order to rewrite the Twelve Steps, nor the Big Book, but we alcoholics are human beings first, even before we are alcoholics. Because we are, we tend to have the same frailties and shortcomings that are common to other humans. Oh, I know that some of us sometimes act and talk as if we were a separate species, but we aren't.

Human institutions and organizations tend to become rigid, to gather rituals and make them permanent after they have served their original purpose, and even extend them to areas where they were never meant to fit.

When I came into AA over twenty-five years ago, there were many doctors who thought the answer to alcoholism was a pill. Usually it was a pill that tended to be addictive.

Many times we had to tell people to throw out those durned pills. And we were right. But over the years doctors have been moving forward, and we haven't.

Very few doctors today will lead their alcoholic patients into addiction if they are properly informed by them. But we are still handing down the rigid commandment, "Throw out those durned pills."

A man came into the Fellowship here recently. He suffered from severe depressions. He was told, "Throw out those durned pills." He did. In short order he went into a severe depression. He attempted suicide. Thank God it was a failed attempt.

What if he had succeeded? Would the people who handed out the advice have acknowledged their error? Or would they have fallen back on the cliche, "He wasn't working the program"?

When alcoholics who are using medication come into AA they should consult their sponsor and inform their doctor. The doctor might very well decide to change or curtail the medication in light of the new situation. In case of doubt the newcomer needs to get a second medical opinion. But we're not doctors. Nor are we gods. We shouldn't attempt to play either role.

Here's another example. Over twenty years ago, in counseling a new man, I formulated a rule of thumb. The problem then (and it's still one we run into frequently) was that he was freshly sober and his wife was not pleasing him enough. So he was ready to divorce her after years of a drunken marriage and two months of a sober one.

Other alcoholics after just a few months of sobriety are wanting to rush into long-term commitments or break other long-standing ones. New jobs, new marriage partners, moving: we've all come across these things.

What was the rule of thumb I suggested? "Do not get married, divorced, enlist in the French Foreign Legion, or make or break any long-term commitments until you have been sober for one year."

In a recent conversation with a lady in AA, I found that when she first came around she was married to a brutal wife beater. In the course of eleven years of marriage he had broken ten of her bones. The beatings he administered were too numerous to count.

She was told she shouldn't divorce him until she was sober for one year. What had started out as a rule of thumb had become a commandment — a commandment in a suggested program.

Fortunately someone with enough sense to recognize when to ignore rules of thumb told her that it was almost impossible to get and stay sober unless she brought some sanity into her life.

When I came into Alcoholics Anonymous we opened the meeting with a moment of silence, followed by the Preamble. Then someone added a reading from the Hazelden book, *Twenty-Four Hours a Day.* Someone else thought it a good idea to add "How It Works."

I spoke at an open meeting last week. In addition to the above, we had "The Promises of AA," "The Tools of AA," and one other whose name I forget. It took fifteen minutes. We then had forty-five minutes for the meeting.

What has happened is that our propensity for ritual and habit has gotten hold of us again. Because one thing helped one person, one time, in one place, we must all have it forever. Castor oil did wonders for me once. Should everyone, everywhere take castor oil forever?

With our habit of adding and never subtracting, I fear to see the day come when we have forty-five minutes of reading and other rituals, and fifteen minutes of meeting.

In all of the above I see a growth of ritual and habit. In some instances I see worse. I see arrogance and conceit. I see us drifting away from the principles of the program. I see us missing the point in such ideas as being friendly with our friends. What happened to sticking with sobering up alcoholics as our specialty and allowing others to practice theirs? Where is the humility and compassion that Bill W. had when he wrote the Big Book?

The compassion and humility exhibited in writing that book when nobody had even four years' sobriety exceeds what I've gained in over twenty-five years. It shames me.

P. E., Merrillville, Indiana

AA IS NOT GROUP THERAPY

FEBRUARY 1994

I have attended AA meetings for fifteen years, but in the past few years I've left many meetings with an uncomfortable feeling. Why did I feel disturbed? What had happened? I unearthed the answer to those questions at a popular lunch meeting I'd been urged to attend.

A woman at this standing-room-only meeting began to talk about her mother and the damage her mother had caused in her life. She wept and damned her mother and blamed her for all of her unhappiness. There was no talk of sobriety. No hint of gratitude. No reference to working the Steps. Then this woman left the meeting early. I wanted to stop her and bring her back and tell her to listen. She just might find the answer to her problems.

At that moment, I realized with disturbing clarity that this was group therapy, not an AA meeting. What I had just been part of was what I believe to be the subtle sabotage of the AA program. This woman was just one of many people who are misguidedly using meetings to dump all their feelings and resentments in the name of sharing.

My intention is not to minimize anyone's grief. I speak as one who grew up in an extremely abusive alcoholic family, as a man who is a Vietnam vet, a survivor of divorce and other traumatic losses. I have attended therapy at various times and found it quite useful. However, I don't confuse therapy with AA's Twelve Steps and am disturbed as I see people increasingly using AA meetings for free therapy, in order to "get in touch with their feelings." My own primary purpose at a meeting is to better learn to apply the AA Twelve Step philosophy to the problems of daily life.

This intrusion of therapy talk in meetings causes a loss of focus on what this program is all about. The basic principles of recovery, honesty, open-mindedness, and willingness are being replaced with self-absorption, attention-getting, and "getting in touch with feelings." Instead of enlisting the principles of gratitude and acceptance, many are focusing on blaming in the name of sharing feelings. One of the stories in the Big Book states, "Acceptance is the answer to all of my problems today." That simple principle, acceptance, is what we're neglecting when we allow meetings to become therapy.

I hear people who've been around the Fellowship for over a year still "working on" a problem and then blaming their unhappiness on this still-unresolved problem. People are blaming everything that's not going right in their lives on ex-spouses, lousy parents, the government, or their bosses. Less time needs to be spent on complaining about the problem and more time needs to be focused on solutions. The solutions live in the application of the Twelve Steps.

"Acceptance is the answer to all of my problems today." As long as people are blaming, I don't think they're working the Twelve Steps, and as long as they're not working the Twelve Steps they will continue to use meetings as therapy. They will continue to dilute the higher purpose of this program, which is to share our experience, strength, and hope. Let's work the Steps and keep the therapy talk out. We know it works.

Craig R., Carnation, Washington

TOO YOUNG?

OCTOBER 1989

Like many other AA members, I feel that my life truly began on the day I came into AA. Prior to March 7, 1969, my life seemed hopeless, and I felt desperately alone and afraid. My trips to jails and hospitals weren't the worst things that had happened to me. Losing complete control over my own life, never knowing where I would end up next or what I might do led me to the pitiful and incomprehensible demoralization the Big Book describes. I feared death and insanity. I was eighteen-years-old. I had no idea that I was an alcoholic or that there was any way out of my alcoholism.

Although I was familiar with AA and had been to meetings, I was unable to identify myself as an alcoholic. Had I not met another young person who was sober, I might never have gotten sober. This woman, who was to become my first sponsor, was also my next-door neighbor, and she was a wonderful attraction of the program. She seemed genuinely happy, and she really cared about me. Although she knew I was an alcoholic, she never tried to force AA on me. So when I hit my bottom, I called her for help and she took me to a young people's meeting.

Although I was made to feel welcome by most people in AA, it wasn't long before I was greeted with that all too familiar line, "It's good to see you young people here before you had to hurt." After a few more remarks like that from some of our over-forty members, I began to feel that maybe I didn't really belong in AA, maybe I hadn't hurt enough.

In 1969 there simply wasn't the knowledge or the awareness of our disease that there is today. The typical alcoholic had drunk for many years. It's possible that the old-timers who thought we were too young were just passing on what they knew. After all, when they came into AA, they were told that if they still had a wristwatch they weren't ready yet. Past experience had shown that unless the alcoholic had lost absolutely everything in life, he wouldn't be ready to grasp the AA program. Others who were envious that we had gotten sober at such a young age believed that we had been spared years of suffering. Yet our stories were horrendous. Just because we looked young didn't mean we hadn't suffered. True, most of us hadn't lost careers or families simply because we weren't old enough to have had them. We also hadn't acquired drunk driving offenses or served a lot of time in jail because as juveniles we were treated differently by the legal system. Some of us had never had a legal drink, but all of us had reached our bottoms and we needed help. So, faced with a desperate need and a desire to stay sober, I joined the group of young people who were fighting for their place in AA.

As I look back now, I don't know how we made it. I often think that God worked through our character defects of resentment and defiance to give us the determination we needed to fight for our right to stay. Once when an old-timer told one of our members, "Honey, I spilled more than you drank," she told him, "Yeah, well, I never spilled any."

As if we didn't have enough problems being young alcoholics, many of us also had drug problems which posed an even greater threat to the old-timers. They simply didn't want to hear about it and wouldn't let us talk about drugs. They insisted we attend other twelve-step groups, which we did, but those groups seemed to be based more on bragging about drug abuse than on genuine humility, which at the time could only be found in AA. With these issues at hand, we had no choice but to learn to use the principles of the program. Tradition Three stated that the only requirement for membership was a desire to stop drinking. We also found a paragraph in chapter three of the Big Book that mentioned young people and said, "To be gravely affected, one does not necessarily have to drink a long time nor take the quantities some of us have"; we incorporated this into our format. We learned the Big Book and practiced the principles. We lived them — we had to — for we never knew when an old-timer would verbally attack; quoting a line from the Big Book would stop him dead in his tracks. We quickly learned that no one would argue with the Traditions or the Big Book. We went on Twelfth Step calls early in our sobriety. We carried the message into institutions and we brought sick alcoholics into our homes. With our loud clothes, loud music, and long hair we may have had different interests and values but we proved that as alcoholics we were the same. And because of the principles and the Traditions we shared one common goal: to stay sober and carry the message, and that we did.

As time passed and we stayed sober, the old-timers slowly began to accept us. And though they would barely admit it, we had added a new dimension to their sobriety, for we had taught them about humility, tolerance, and love. Many of them had children of their own dying from the disease and often asked for our help. Eventually we began to work side by side, and I learned that this is what AA is all about.

As time passed, we began to branch out and start other meetings. Today there are a lot more young people in AA and more young people's meetings. We also have people coming into AA from hospital programs and through intervention. No longer do you have to lose everything before you are ready for sobriety. This proves that alcoholics can begin recovery at an earlier stage in the progression of the disease and it doesn't mean they don't hurt or aren't ready. Even though there have been so many positive changes since I got sober in 1969, I still encounter young people who have what I call the "young person's problem." They are constantly apologizing for their age and trying desperately to prove that they belong. Having gone through this experience myself, I would like to pass on some of my thoughts in hopes that someone may benefit from it.

First, I think that to be faced with a life-threatening illness when young creates an unusual crisis because this is a time when life should be moving forward, from childhood to adulthood. Unlike diseases that can be detected with medical tests, alcoholism is one where we diagnose for ourselves. That's why I think it is so important for young people to learn the facts: that they can be alcoholics even at a young age and that they can recover. Taking the "20 Questions" or being around other young recovering people are some of the best ways I know for someone to find out if she or he is an alcoholic or not.

Second, in order to recover in AA, young people are asked to practice self-honesty when they have no idea who they are and to be responsible when they don't yet know how. Young people must be responsible for their own recovery, but it's also important for them to remember that they're still adolescents and need to allow themselves to be. When we confuse spirituality with being good or grown-up, it causes a lot of problems. It's important for the young person to know that it's still possible to have fun and do the things young people do *and* stay sober.

Last, as I've grown older, I've realized that there is some ability to cope with life and its challenges that comes only with life experience. This is practically absent in the young person, so it's sometimes difficult for him to separate his recovery problems from the problems of just growing up. A lot of the problems I had were the same problems every eighteen-year-old had and had very little to do with my alcoholism or with my AA program.

It is very different to be a sober member of AA when you are young. If you doubt this, think back to when you were sixteen and try to imagine yourself working the Steps in your life then as you do today. Couple this with other people telling you that you are too young to be an alcoholic and you can see how hard it is.

I know one thing for certain: no young person ever needs to hear that she has gotten sober before she had to hurt: she has hurt plenty. She needs to hear what every newcomer does who comes into the Fellowship: "Welcome. This is AA, where the only requirement for membership is a desire to stop drinking."

Robin F., Los Angeles, California

The Twelve Steps

STEP ONE
ADMITTING POWERLESSNESS
JANUARY 1991

"But you've taken the First Step already," the man said. "You've admitted that you can't stop drinking, that you are compelled to carry on drinking once you've had a small quantity of booze, that somehow you always take that first drink against all better knowledge, that the fact you didn't complete your University course and are homeless and deeply in debt is a result of your drinking. You have just admitted that and in AA we call that 'taking the First Step'."

So it was said to me when I was twelfth-stepped years ago, and I remember it, like many other things that were said that evening.

I try to recall these words when I twelfth-step someone today, because it worked for me — the simplicity of the message, the hope the man gave me, the fact that he saw and expressed my willingness to recover before I did.

It was not until later that I felt the enormous relief that the admission of powerlessness — and I think that admission is the key word — brought. I had fought my alcoholism for ten years, sometimes with bizarre tactics. Once I locked myself up in a hut in the mountains, miles from anywhere, with the intention of not drinking for a week. It lasted twenty-four hours, after which time I walked for a whole day to the nearest village to get a drink, thus ending my drying-out holiday prematurely. And I tried all the other things described in the Big Book: drinking beer only, not drinking until eight P.M., staying sober for a month, and so on. And nothing had worked. The insane voice that came into my head and forced me to act in a way I'd sworn I never would again — that insane voice was greater than myself.

The worst result of my drinking was the way I treated other people. I was young, I had ideals, and coming from an unloving alcoholic family, I had definite ideas about how I wanted to relate to other human beings. And throughout the progression of my disease, all this went out of the window: people were there to help me get drunk, they were manipulated to cover up the mess of my life, they had become mere pawns. And when they became obstacles between me and the glass, they had to go.

And then of course there were all the other aspects of unmanageability: the shame and guilt of waking up in some stranger's bed after yet another blackout, the terrible hangovers, the headaches that no pills could cure, the thirst that gallons of water could not quench, the occasional realization of the filth I was living in, the increasing inability to hold down even menial jobs. In short, I lived my life in a way I didn't want to, and I couldn't help it; it was all because I had to drink.

Still it took me a while to see how bad it had been. I had simply gotten used to it over the years. My demise hadn't happened overnight, and I suppose that deep down inside I hated myself so much — the true spiritual malady as I see it now — that I unconsciously believed I didn't deserve better.

Listening to someone else's sharing in a meeting a few months into AA, having stayed away from the first drink a day at a time, it suddenly hit me how much pain I had suffered, how close to death I had been, what a nightmare these years had been.

And it was soon after that incident that the miracle happened. I became willing to face the pain of my life without a drink; the fear of drinking became bigger than the fear of life without drink. When I surrendered to the fact that alcohol was greater than myself, accepted life without ever drinking again, the compulsion was removed, left me, as if it had never been there.

Some people have choices, and I had lost the power to choose. From Day One of my drinking career I had known that alcohol didn't agree with my system, and that I didn't have the ability to exercise choice over drink. Lack of power had been my problem, and recovery to me has meant to regain power.

"So you don't consider yourself powerless over alcohol anymore?" one of my AA friends asked me in disbelief the other day. "What would happen if I offered you a drink?"

"I would say, No, thank you," I replied, "because I've been given the power not to drink. God has restored my right mind."

Equally I believe that manageability is the goal in recovery. I don't want my life to be unmanageable anymore, and I believe that as I work the Steps, God gives me the ability to manage my life, exactly in the proportion that I'm prepared to work for it.

And as little as I could make myself stop drinking, as little am I able to restore myself to sanity in other areas in my life. As with drink, I first have to admit that I have a problem. As long as I minimize whatever plagues me, as long as I try to reason myself to mental health, as long as I "handle" my problem, I am a long way from asking God's help.

I've been troubled with lots of afflictions that resulted in temporary unmanageability in my sober days: anger, resentments, self-pity, fear of life in general and people in particular, obsessions and compulsions of all kinds. I just see them as demons from the past, old coping mechanisms that have outlived their usefulness. They are all I have if I don't turn to God, and they are so strong and destructive that it takes God to remove them. It is these things that stand between me and a sober, happy, God-centered life. If I drew a line between active alcoholism on one side and life as God wants me to live it and has equipped me to on the other, then I'm somewhere in the middle, striving toward the ideal. If I allow my character defects to rule my life again and forget the AA program, forget where the power to change for the better comes from, I will, in the long run, inevitably drink again.

The most recent and quite harrowing experience of powerlessness I had was a four-month spell of compulsive working. I rationalized, I lied to myself. I wasn't going to give in. My body gave me warning signals: palpitations, severe headaches. I ignored them. Eventually, it got really bad.

After a weekend of being ill with exhaustion, having lied to a friend in order to get out of an arrangement so that I could work a bit more, I threw in the towel. I admitted that I was unable to stop my destructive behavior and asked God for help. Instantly, the compulsion was lifted.

Sometimes I find it easier to accept my limitations than fighting yet another battle: I turned down an invitation to some social gambling the other day. It may well be harmless fun for other people, but I had an encounter with slot machines a few years back, and I am pretty sure there is a gambler in me.

I don't have to prove my power over certain things. I don't have a television because I can't handle it. I get addicted to watching trash. Maybe the day will come when I have power over the television and will be able to manage the on/off switch. If the day never does come, however, I am quite prepared to enjoy my recovery anyway.

Eva M., London, England

STEP TWO
COLD SOBER

FEBRUARY 1991

For fifteen years almost every time I work or think about our Second Step, considering the Power greater than ourselves, I'm reminded of a large refrigerator in a ward at a Minnesota state hospital. It's not really idol worship, but it's a way for me to gratefully recall who I am and how amazing it is that I'm sober today by the grace of God. The Second Step is for me the Step of expecting good things and expecting them not from me but from a Power greater than myself.

I was sober just a couple of weeks in a sanitarium for alcoholic priests. After fighting tooth and nail against going into treatment, my head began to clear and I started to listen. The proposed stay in the sanitarium was three months, and like everything else in life, I thought I could speed things up if I went to as many meetings as they would allow. I signed up to be taken out to a meeting at the nearby state hospital. I was picked up by a man whom I've never seen before or since, but he reminded me of the traveling salesman in *The Music Man* or maybe a character out of *Main Street* by Sinclair Lewis.

He was giving the talk at the hospital meeting and was telling everyone about the Power greater than ourselves. He told everyone that the Power could be anything, even this refrigerator he was standing next to. And then he said: "Isn't that right, Father?"

It was many years ago, but I can still feel the anger rip through my insides. Here I was sitting quietly; nobody knew I was a priest. Here comes this traveling salesman pointing me out, me with my advanced theological degrees, asking me to say that a refrigerator could be used as a Power greater than myself to restore me to sanity. Oh, how mad I was as I gamely smiled at this man that I now considered a complete idiot. But something all of a sudden hit me.

I looked at this smiling speaker. He had the keys to his own car. He wasn't three hundred miles from where he lived. No one had to sign him out of an institution to travel a few miles to another institution. Something inside me said that I'd better listen to this guy and these other people. The fact was, that all my great knowledge about God, my retreats, years of prayer, my consultations with psychiatric experts and wonderful spiritual directors — none of it had gotten me sober and kept me sober.

And so I try to keep listening, one day at a time. I know now that once I accepted that First Step, there was hope in the Second Step. And the Power was not me nor mine.

I have confidence now that it is the God who loves me and all of us. But every once in a while when I get messed up and feel these surges of anger and superiority, I think of a big refrigerator in Rochester, Minnesota and say: St. Kenmore, or St. Frigidaire, or whatever you were, pray for me . . . help me to listen and do what these people are telling me to do. Amen.

Dan M., Chicago, Illinois

STEP THREE
A PROGRAM OF ACTION
MARCH 1989

As an atheist with long-term sobriety in Alcoholics Anonymous, I'm occasionally asked how I resolve my atheist philosophies with the program's strong reliance on belief in God's participation in recovery from alcoholism. I've been asked, for example, "How do you work the program when you don't believe in God? Do you just skip the God Steps? What do you turn your life over to? I can see how you could do Step One, and maybe even Two, but how does an atheist do Step Three?" I've asked myself all those questions and many more over the years as I've learned how to stay sober within AA.

Perhaps the key to remaining atheist and in AA is that I got permission for some flexibility early in my AA experience. The man who urged me into AA told me that other members would speak about God, but I could overlook that and listen to their advice on daily living. He said I could accept their friendship and assistance without buying all their ideas. The woman who took me to my first meeting told me to accept what would help me and reject what didn't — I could choose. She pointed out that chapter five in the Big Book says the Steps are "suggested," which implies the right to reject some of the directives.

Although I was given the permission for selection of ideas, I was also told by my early sponsors that the Steps and recovery go together. In other words, it would probably be necessary for me to find a way to incorporate into my life *all* the actions described in the Steps. I would reduce the likelihood of gaining a successful and happy sobriety if I simply omitted the Steps that refer to God. So, with the permission for flexibility, I also got the responsibility to find ways to view each of the Steps as compatible with my lack of belief in God. My job would be to interpret the program so I could live with it, literally.

I cannot say when I began thinking about AA's Steps and how I could apply them to my life. I know that my initial sobriety consisted of little more than not drinking and going to lots of meetings. When I did start to listen to others' advice to incorporate the suggested Steps into my decisions, Step Three seemed the most important one to address. First, that Step contains an absolute declaration for belief in God, and I recognized that reconciling my atheism with such a seemingly incompatible concept might very well determine whether I could remain in AA. Second, everyone told me they had gotten the most benefit from applying Step Three. And third, I kept hearing people say that Step Three was their stumbling block. If that were true for believers, I thought I was facing one heap of trouble. I've since realized I couldn't have been more mistaken — Step Three has been no more difficult than those which have nothing to do with God.

Step Three had been thrust at me almost immediately. It seemed that nearly every discussion meeting I attended during the first few weeks used Step Three as a topic. What a greeting for an atheist! If I hadn't been so desperate, I might have been too narrow-minded and arrogant to think I could learn anything from all those strong believers. Luckily, I was frightened, miserable, lonely, physically weak, and unable to argue about anything. Because I wanted and needed the safety of AA, I was forced to listen to dozens of people describe their experiences with turning it over, letting go and letting God, and trusting in higher powers. I stuck around because I had nowhere else to go. I didn't do anything about Step Three, of course, but I did find out that all that God talk had not injured me.

My approach to Step Three started with the willingness to listen to spiritual and religious perspectives I'd dismissed many years earlier. I didn't listen with the intent or hope of converting to a belief in God. I listened because I figured that each Step had a purpose for being and a route for acquiring some aspect of sober, sane living; I needed to find out just exactly what Step Three was meant to do and how I could achieve the purpose. Based mostly on what I heard from others about the effect of the Step, I decided its purpose must be to relieve self-generated conflict and fear. The method almost certainly is to relinquish the compulsive need to control and to do what is reasonable.

Having realized Step Three's purpose, I've spent the past sixteen years trying to hear what people *do* when they *say* they turn their will and life over to the care of God. The distinction between what people do and how they talk about and think about that action is very important for me. Someone would tell their method of doing Step Three and it would strike me that I could do that; I could do it without believing in God. I could not, however, think about my action as having anything to do with God as my friend might, because I don't recognize any form of God.

All of us in AA have heard many different methods of acting out belief. Most of the time the process of exercising belief seems to consist of an internal pep talk and then going about one's business. One woman said that she "turns it over" by repeating an old phrase: Hope for the best, expect the worst, and take what comes. And then she cleans house or goes to work or visits a friend or whatever else occupies normal living. She does what actually is the only reasonable thing she can do. I can do the same thing — repeat her phrase to remind me of the reality of chance and the absurdity of expecting to be able to control all aspects of my life, and then go about the business of living. Another member described Step Three as "going with the flow" of life. That advice helped me try to fit myself to circumstances rather than insist on creating them. These are words for helping me establish more rational views of my role in life's events.

Countless numbers of people have told me they recite the Serenity Prayer as a tool for engendering an attitude of turning it over. I now regard the statements in that prayer, except for the part about asking it to be a grant from God, as a description of a completely sensible way to approach life. Even atheists can learn to recognize the futility of nonacceptance, the value of risking changes, and the way to tell the difference between things we can affect and those we can't. When I begin to worry about things I can do nothing about, I tell myself to "accept what you can't change." Often I've used the ideas in the Serenity Prayer as a trigger for relinquishing my need to control and as a reminder to take action when some discontentment can be remedied.

I find I actually do very little that is different from the actions of those who believe in God. I just think about the actions in a different way. The words of the Serenity Prayer are a concise way to tell myself to do what makes sense because sane and sensible action has a track record of success. When I make a decision to quit trying to control, I don't expect anyone or anything will oversee events and take care of me. I make the decision because it is the reasonable action to take. I get relief from anxieties and fears the same way the believers do — I stop concentrating on what dismays me and direct my attention to activities that are productive. For the past year or so I've been using an observation from a Zen master as a guide to Step Three practice. The Zen master noted that peace and enlightenment come when you stop evaluating in terms of good or bad and merely accept all of life as it is and try to learn from it. No mention of God is there, but that idea conveys a noncombative principle that is quite similar to that of Step Three, and it is said in a way I understand.

Observing what people do, rather than simply listening to how they talk, has been crucial to my interpretation of all of the Twelve Steps. This allows me to get around the words about God that get in the way of my understanding of how various Steps work. The Steps work the same way for me as for someone who believes in God. Only the words get changed. My Step Three might say, "Made a decision to turn my will and my life over to the care of reasonable action."

J.L., El Granada, California

STEP FOUR
WE SET THEM ON PAPER
APRIL 1993

"In dealing with resentments, we set them on paper." That simple sentence in chapter five of the Big Book slowed my reading one evening as I sat with a blank pad in front of me, making no progress on my Fourth Step.

At that time I'd been coming to meetings for two years and had not had a drink during that time. My introduction to the Steps was at my first meeting where the Twelve Steps were printed on a yellowed shade that hung behind the speaker. I thought that if this was all there was to Alcoholics Anonymous, I'd have it down pat in four or five weeks, because everything that was on the wall had been included in my religious education. The Fourth Step was nothing more than an examination of conscience while the Fifth Step was the sacrament of confession. With that settled, I sat back to drink my coffee and the days passed.

I found hope in the Fellowship and moved forward like a horse with blinders on, never looking back. But the sharing, especially at Step meetings, brought reality to me as my head cleared. Like all who had gone before me in the Fellowship, I could not escape the past.

For the first year, the first three Steps held my attention. Every time I got to the Fourth Step, I proceeded to lose myself in the text of the "Twelve and Twelve." Why did I get lost there? Easy – just the mention of the seven deadly sins – pride, greed, lust, anger, gluttony, envy, and sloth – and guilt raises its head. Guilt did help me not pick up the first drink but it also kept me from understanding the rest of the text in the "Twelve and Twelve." Privately I wanted to finish all the Steps so fast I'd make the *Guiness Book of World Records*, but publicly I nodded my assent when people said, "You should do a Step a year." I found myself writing in circles every time I tried to list all my sins.

One day, anger became my companion. It stayed day and night. My sponsor said that his sponsor claimed the Fourth Step was the Step for anger. Why didn't I take another look at what the Big Book had to say about it?

That night I discovered the sentence, "In dealing with resentments, we set them on paper." Nothing about guilt or sin here. No examination of conscience or sacrament of confession, just resentments. The Big Book says that "resentment destroys more alcoholics than anything else. From it stem all forms of spiritual disease. . . ."

I began at my earliest memory and came forward through my life. My list was thorough. No one I knew well was left off, nor were institutions with which I had had contact. I was a walking resentment.

As I got to the middle of my list, my need to justify my resentment with a short postscript disappeared and I attempted simply to discover whether my anger was based on threatened self-esteem, money, ambition, or personal relationships.

When my list was complete I began to discover a startling truth — I had really been dependent on everyone. In this context the words "selfish," "dishonest," "self-seeking," and "frightened" took on new meaning. I appeared to be as powerless over the things I feared as I was over alcohol.

But I had only to turn the page of the Big Book for the instruction to make a list of my fears, ask my Higher Power to remove my fear, and direct my attention "to what He would have us be." The Big Book says that after completing the Fourth Step, we have "swallowed and digested some big chunks of truth" about ourselves. This was true. Yet these truths were not accompanied by guilt. Instead I felt a deep sadness at the desperation with which I had acted. It was the beginning of an acceptance of myself, shortcomings, wrongs, and all.

The Fifth Step stood ahead — the road to "perfect peace and ease." I called my sponsor and set the date for two weeks from then — I wanted to stay on the old, familiar road a little longer before sharing my inventory with him.

Bernie B., New York, New York

BUILDING AN ARCH
MARCH 1989

I first heard about Step Five from my sponsor. He had recently taken his, and it didn't sound like fun. His immediate reaction to his own "spiritual house cleaning" was to launch me upon a Fourth Step. He wanted to give away what he'd received. I thought, "What happened to 'This is a selfish program'?"

Step Four took a very long time. At all of it I balked. I thought I could find an easier, softer way, but I could not. With all the earnestness at his command, my sponsor became cunning, baffling, and powerful, constantly reminding me that half measures availed me nothing. I hated him.

The day finally came when even I had to admit that I'd completed Step Four to the best of my ability. That's what had me so upset. The best of my ability didn't look so hot in those days. I called my sponsor to tell him I'd finished, expecting to take a six-month to one-year sabbatical from the Steps after this arduous trek into my life. That's when he lowered the boom. "Great," he said. "The best time to take the Fifth Step is right after you finish the Fourth. Meet me at my home tomorrow at six."

Son of a gun! "Who do you think you are?" I thought, but aloud I said "Okay, I'll be there."

I hung up the phone and said to myself, "I bet Bill W. didn't have to go through this!" I used to think the Big Book referred to Step Five when it said, "What an order! I can't go through with it." I thought, how can talking about all this junk that I never wanted to write down in the first place make any difference?

By the time I finished Step Five, I knew that I was well on my way toward "building an arch" through which I would "walk a free man." What happened? Did God convert me into a religious AA dervish? Was I brainwashed by some mystical technique into an AA true believer? Did I go into permanent shock? None of these things happened. The truth is much simpler. Step Five simply accomplished exactly what I was promised, based on the tried and tested experience of Alcoholics Anonymous.

This is what happened. For starters, I had prepared for Step Five by making a beginning on the previous Steps. I had my Fourth Step inventory which had given me a new awareness, albeit a not completely objective one. Nevertheless, I had it. Though the temptation to avoid sharing with "another human being" was nearly overwhelming, my fear of not following my sponsor's instructions to the letter was even greater.

I arrived at my sponsor's home promptly at six. I didn't want to be late for my "funeral." He ushered me into the living room and I sat in what was obviously the condemned man's chair. Given to redundancies in times of hysteria, I commented on the weather at least twice, and God only knows how many times I mentioned the state of local AA affairs. Then my sponsor said those terrible words: "Why don't you get out your Fourth Step so we can get started."

I feared that doors automatically sealed themselves during Fifth Steps. But I prayed to God and "asked His protection and care with complete abandon." "Okay, where do you want to begin," I asked, hoping for mercy. "Why don't we begin with your grudge list," my sponsor said. "But before we begin," he added, "why don't we pray and ask our Higher Power for guidance. After all, this is a three-way deal. God is very much a part of this. It's his grace that brought you here."

Sometimes sponsors can really surprise you. This was one of those rare times. We prayed, then he became his old self again, indicating that it was time I began. We went over my grudge list, item by item. I read and explained. He listened and commented.

Before we were halfway through the list, I began to realize that the advice, counseling, and experience he shared was not only his, but that of others as well. It was the experience of one drunk talking to another, but it was also the resonating voices of countless men and women in AA who had shared their experience, strength, and hope with each other. Was this God-consciousness? I wondered, as I continued my disclosures.

Finishing the grudge list, we assailed my list of fears. To my surprise, I discovered my sponsor and I shared some of the same ones. By this time, occasional laughter interspersed the more serious portions of the unfolding panorama of my life. I was beginning to feel a sense of relief. It continued to grow even as we discussed pertinent aspects of my "list of major human failings — the Seven Deadly Sins."

It was incredible! As years of humiliation, pride, and fear fell away into harmless debris, my sense of isolation actually began to dissipate. I no longer felt like a freak, a pathetic caricature of humanity, incapable of integrating myself into the world about me. The existence of God's presence was no theory; it was fact. God was with us and my cup did indeed run over. It overflowed with his love as it was translated into the experience, strength, and hope of two twentieth-century alcoholics joined in the miracle of a spiritual awakening known as recovery.

Those secrets that I'd sworn to take to my grave were now dead and buried under the fertile soil of a new freedom nurtured by truth and sharing and laughter, moistened by tears of relief and joy, and warmed by the sunlight of the spirit. "Step Five works! It really does!" I marvelled. I knew now that the man who was leaving was not the same man who had fearfully entered this Fifth Step sanctuary just a few hours previously.

Today, after many revisits to Step Five, I know that my initial experience was no fluke, that "God does move in a mysterious way his wonders to perform," and that Step Five is one of those wonders.

I've also been privileged to share in the Fifth Step experiences of others. Since there is nothing like personal experience to qualify one for this extremely personal spiritual awakening, I would suggest having done a Fifth Step as a prerequisite for hearing someone else's. We must be prepared to share our own Fifth Step disclosures, laughter, and tears so that the experience of others might be as profound as our own. Being able to keep confidential the disclosures of others is also essential. This experience is only between God and ourselves.

Franklin D. Roosevelt said, in his first inaugural address, "The only thing we have to fear is fear itself." If we're willing to expose the pages of our lives to the love and understanding of our Higher Power and a fellow alcoholic, we'll surely know a new freedom and a new happiness. We'll discover that love is never having to feel alone again; that God's presence in our lives has become profound; and that the unity of the Fellowship of the spirit can be ours so long as we are willing to pass it on.

Chico C., West Palm Beach, Florida

~

STEP SIX

THE CHOICE

JUNE 1991

Bill W. points out in the chapter on Step Six in the "Twelve and Twelve": "Some people, of course, may conclude that they are indeed ready to have all these defects taken from them. But even these people, if they construct a list of still milder defects, will be obliged to admit that they prefer to hang on to some of them."

Several years ago I had a vivid personal example of what he was talking about. At that time I had a sponsor to whom I was devoted, one possible reason for which was that she and I shared some of the same characteristics or, as some would say, defects. One of them was a quick temper. Restraint of tongue and pen didn't come easily to either of us.

One day, after a brisk altercation on the phone, she hung up on me. Indignation swelled up inside me. That was absolutely no way for a sponsor of many years' sobriety to behave! Indignation was followed by a delicious sense of grievance, of having been profoundly wronged.

For the next twenty-four hours I fed and watered that delightful sense of victimhood. I would not, of course, have admitted for one moment to myself or anyone else how much I was enjoying it, or my discovery that being a victim was not far removed from (in the words of Hamlet, the Prince of Denmark) a consummation devoutly to be wished. In my own mind I replayed the incident on the phone over and over, brushing aside my recollection of what I might have said or done to bring on my sponsor's action. And each time her hanging up on me grew more heinous. I was innocent, and in a case like this, innocence is power.

The next afternoon, after being out of my apartment for several hours, I called my answering service to pick up messages. The young woman at the other end of the phone said, "Jean called to say she's sorry and would you please call her."

You would think, wouldn't you, that now, with my sense of grievance fully vindicated, I would be filled with joy and forgiveness? You would be wrong. My first feeling, and I remember it well, was dismay, followed quickly by a flattening sense of letdown.

I worried at that letdown for a full day before some glimmering of its real cause dawned on me: I knew that when I would call Jean she'd repeat her apology and I would have to forgive her. And by forgiving her, I would yield up the sense of power, of self-justification, that I had enjoyed so much.

It took me another several hours to define what my choice was: I could have my grievance or I could have my friend. Not both. I had to choose. And I saw further that choice is one of the fruits of sobriety that by putting down the bottle I now had, not only about this, but about other aspects of my life and other defects of character. It was the first time I understood a defect for what it was: something out of which I derived pleasure or power and was therefore not entirely willing to give up. Obviously, in this particular example, by relinquishing the pleasure I would get something better — the restoration of friendship.

But sometimes the sense of gratification and of power that a grievance can bring is hard to yield up. I once heard a well-known doctor, one of the first to recognize what AA could do, say: "Self-pity is followed by isolation is followed by a drink."

And I began, especially after the incident involving my sponsor, to understand why, when I first came into Alcoholics Anonymous, the most frequent warnings from some of the old-timers were against self-pity. All those sensations I'd been wallowing in with such enjoyment — of being aggrieved, of being wronged, of being victimized, of being (for once!) in the right — added up to the heady brew of self-pity. And I then comprehended fully why self-pity, leading to isolation (and wasn't I isolating myself from my sponsor?), was presented by that doctor and the old-timers as such a formidable enemy of sobriety.

P.S. I called Jean and we made up and the incident passed.

But I still think about it a lot.

Isabelle H., New York, New York

STEP SEVEN
THE PAIN WAS LIFTED
JULY 1989

After several years of enjoyable sobriety I was suddenly seized by negative thinking so devastating that it wiped out my peace of mind, undermined my ability to work, and might eventually have sent me back to drinking. Today, with thirty years of continuous abstinence, I am convinced that I was saved from relapse by applying Step Seven fervently and in desperation.

When I was only a few months sober in AA, I included Step Seven in my self-directed crash course in the entire Twelve. While my Step Four inventory and Step Five were as thorough and honest as I could make them at the time, and were repeated a year later, my treatment of Steps Six and Seven was superficial, little more than turns around the pylon without reducing speed. After a perfunctory, "Yes, God, I humbly ask you to remove whatever shortcomings I might happen to have," I moved on to the later Steps.

At that time I didn't feel it necessary to itemize for my Higher Power exactly what those defects and shortcomings actually were. After all, he should know. Wasn't he listening during my Fifth Step? I know now that I also skipped too lightly over Steps Eight and Nine. While I did make some difficult amends, I'm abashed today at how blind I was to the need to make certain others.

Lest this confession be seized upon by newcomers as evidence that an alcoholic can safely go easy on the Steps, I had other support. Members of my home group in North Hollywood, California, dragged me along on Twelfth Step calls and flung me into group assignments despite my touchingly modest protests that I didn't want my inexperience to embarrass AA as a whole. Working with other alcoholics and performing services for my group may have helped me reduce some of my defects even though I had not fully confronted them.

When I later applied Step Seven during a mental and emotional crisis in my seventh year in AA, it was not, like the first encounter, a casual ritual. After I describe my crisis you are apt to think, "Anybody who makes a big crippling issue out of such triviality is certainly neurotic!"

Good! You are now prepared to appreciate my difficulty. If

alcoholics or others become upset over a death, job loss, or a broken relationship, they can talk about it or cry about it with dignity. Their problem will be heard with respect and sympathy. But a neurotic's problem is based on an inner conflict that he is in some way ashamed of, and he knows no one will understand. I knew my problem was petty, yet it was overwhelmingly painful and paralyzing.

My "crisis" came at a time when everything was going well. I was then a television writer in Los Angeles, and had begun to sell scripts regularly to situation comedy programs, a new field for me. I was faithfully attending several AA meetings a week, was active in the local central office (intergroup), and was frequently invited to speak at meetings, including some out-of-state AA conferences.

The previous year I'd contributed sketches for a variety show to benefit a halfway house for male alcoholics. AAs and nonalcoholics in the entertainment industry had freely contributed their various talents to the production. It was successful, and now a show was planned to benefit a similar house for alcoholic women. I submitted several sketches for the new revue at the request of the production committee.

While busy at work on TV scripts for which I was being very well paid, I heard from an acquaintance that someone on the benefit show's production staff didn't think my sketches were funny.

There. That's the crisis. Big deal, huh?

I brooded over this reported verdict. I knew this one member of the script committee didn't have the final say on selecting material. Further, he was not in the industry, and could well lack the special ability to judge from a typewritten script whether the material would "play well" when performed on stage by skilled actors. His opinion, if in the minority, would be overruled by the other committee people, both laymen and professionals.

This knowledge in no way reduced my discomfort. To get my mind off this rejection, I tried logic. After all, it was only a benefit show, and all of us were donating our talent. On the other hand, my TV scripts were being readily approved by the producer and I was earning more money than at any other time in my life.

Logic didn't help. I was obsessed to the point that I could think of nothing else. I tried self-ridicule. Shakespeare and Hemingway had their detractors, even among literary scholars. So who was I to get upset over this third-party report that my work wasn't appreciated by a real estate agent or a bookkeeper?

I went on brooding.

Sitting alone in a restaurant one afternoon, I realized if I didn't rid myself of this obsession I would be unable to do the work I was being paid for. Also, a negative state like this was actually a dry drunk. Unless terminated it would result in the loss of writing assignments and a sense of failure, likely to get me back on booze.

This at last turned my mind to the Steps. I reviewed them one by one. Nothing in the first five offered a solution. None offered a visible handle that I might grasp to get out of my misery. Something was blocking me from being able to turn my will and my life over to the care of God, as Step Three suggests. Then I pondered Step Six. Was I ready to have God remove all my defects of character? A new thought arose.

Was it possible that my psychic pain came not from the situation *but from a defect of character?* If so, I definitely wanted it — or them — removed. But I had to know which ones were involved, lest like the demons in the New Testament they return after the empty house had been swept clean.

In a moment I was identifying resentment, the alcoholic's Number One offender: I *resented* my critic's unflattering opinion.

Only when illuminated by Step Six did I see that my problem involved resentment.

Like all TV writers I'd experienced many rejections of my story ideas and scripts by producers and story editors. After normal disappointment I quickly bounced back and returned with new ideas. So why this intense depression over this nonprofessional's viewpoint that did not in the least affect my livelihood? What character defect might I be demonstrating?

The reader of course has already spotted my difficulty: Pride!

My alcoholic ego, sufficiently smashed seven years before to permit me several years of comfortable sobriety, had returned during my recent good fortune in a difficult occupation. I had become intolerant of the slightest bit of criticism. My pride was now hurting so much that I was not only ready but almost frantic to have that defect removed.

At the restaurant table I bowed my head and silently, humbly asked God to remove that pride, referring to it by name. Head still bowed I reflected honestly that I had turned to God only because I was in pain. It was then that I added this to my prayer:

"If it is necessary for me to hurt in order to be rid of the defect, *then take the defect and leave the pain!*"

In a split second the pain was gone, and I was free of the crippling obsession that had tortured me for nearly two weeks. Step Seven, sincerely and intensely uttered in silent prayer, had done what my own reasoning, commonsense and self-ridicule were powerless to achieve.

My acquaintances will attest that my Higher Power did not completely and permanently remove my false pride. I'm sure it returns more often than I am aware. But so far, in the twenty-three years since my prayer in the restaurant, pride has not returned so overwhelmingly. Identified for what it is, it shrinks enough to prevent serious damage to myself and others.

Admittedly my problem was based on a triviality, but it was leading to disaster. My AA experience in four widely separated States of the Union teaches me that we alcoholics return to drink far more often because of petty difficulties than because of life's serious setbacks and tragedies. The big problems seem to bring out our virtues, petty ones our faults.

For God to remove our shortcomings, we need to identify the defect for what it is. Thus we attain the humility required by Step Seven. And certainly the most difficult fault to see in ourselves is pride, aptly termed the first deadly sin.

Lou H., Greensboro, North Carolina

STEP EIGHT

THE YEARS THAT THE LOCUST HATH EATEN
APRIL 1997

Neither our literature nor the most enlightened of old-timers can fully explain or define the meaning of "forgiveness," the powerful concept at the heart of the Eighth Step. Like everything else in our spiritual program of Alcoholics Anonymous, forgiveness has entered my life through my heart and not my mind. In my first year of sobriety I listened with a kind of puzzled yearning to meetings where it was being discussed. To this day, I find Eighth Step meetings particularly poignant. The men and women in my regular Friday night Step meeting are so simple and direct when they speak of how they have hurt others and how in almost all cases, relationships have healed. There's no room for posturing as we speak up about our recklessness, self-centeredness, dishonesty, lost or soured marriages and families, and violence of various kinds. More than a mere chronicle of bottles and blackouts, these stories of "twisted and tangled relations" with other people bring home the lonely tragedy of alcoholism and the miracle of our all sitting peaceably there on folding chairs with the Twelve Step shades on the wall above our heads. Sometimes as I sit listening to these tales told in the language of the heart, I remember a quotation from the Book of Joel: "And I will restore to you the years that the locust hath eaten." Individual pain and guilt has been alchemized into something very grand that makes us collectively well. As a group we are at our most human in those Eighth Step evenings. And we seem to be held most closely by the Higher Power.

My own drinking days were all mixed in with my marriage to a man who, when I met him, was only recently married to another of his several wives. I was young, scared, and thirsty; I can see now that I never would have fallen for him if I hadn't been an alcoholic and if I hadn't liked the way he fixed my glass of Scotch. The wife before me was a very nice person who worked in the same office as I did. As I got involved with her husband, I didn't stop to think about the pain I was causing her. I ducked into a doorway if I saw her coming down the hall. I had the worm of conscience, I'm sure of it, but I stilled it with another drink. After he and I had lived and drunk together for some years, he left me in turn for someone else. In a karmic way I felt just how the wife before me had suffered because now I suffered the same myself. She wasn't alcoholic; in the years of my own marriage she had absorbed the blow and moved on with her life. But for years and years after I was alone again, I got stuck in whiskey-soaked self-pity, tormented by an obsessive hatred of that man. This almost killed me; it made me hit my bottom, and I am eternally grateful to him for that.

I can see this story now, but for the first few years of my sobriety I was in an awful fog. I had smart feet, though. I was going to meetings, getting active, sponsoring and being sponsored — *doing* the right things. I had been brought up in England in a rather ladylike way. Without the Scotch inside me, at first I couldn't tell whether I was angry or not. I would study that yellow booklet called *Living Sober,* which had many interesting pointers in it, including "shapes and colors" that anger might possibly come in: cynicism, rigidity, snobbishness, and sarcasm were on a list that helped me to see that rage didn't necessarily mean shouting obscenities or knocking people down. I realized that I was mad at my poor little mother, and at my sister as well. (Honestly, I can't quite remember what that was all about, and I think today that I am very lucky to have these ladies in my life.) I did a Fourth and Fifth Step, and still I kept on getting upset. My skin was very thin, and I was tormented by the "bondage of self." I got mad at people in AA all the time. They rearranged "my" cookies; they would wound me to the quick by going off after the meeting arm in arm with some other friend. In meetings, it seemed there was always someone glaring at me or I was glaring at them. (I'm happy to report that this is also not a problem today at all.) The idea that for us alcoholics there can be no such thing as a "justifiable resentment" is a concept that has come home to me as slowly and through as much painful experience as the concept of forgiveness, its twin. "Where other people are concerned, we have to drop the word 'blame' from our speech and thought," it says in the "Twelve and Twelve." I was still at sea and ill at ease in my relations with other people when an old-timer, hearing me share, asked me whether I had got round to making my Eighth Step list.

Glad that there was an action that might relieve me of my discomfort, I dug out my index card of "cringes" — people who, for a variety of reasons, I would feel embarrassed to see again. Then I transferred some of the still-smoldering resentments from my Fourth Step. Since I had taken that inventory, I had run into my ex-husband on the street, after many years without a glimpse. Something told me to give him a hug, and I'm glad I did because he died not long after that. I put the name of the ex-wife on my list, as well. But it took several years for me to become willing to make amends to her. We had gone on working in the same office without speaking to each other. I was walking down the hall one day, carrying my briefcase, which contained my Eighth Step list — by now a rumpled and creased piece of paper I had often unfolded to cross off names of people I had made amends to in various ways. I had been asked to lead a meeting on the topic later that day, and I wanted to take the list along. I noticed that the door of the woman's office was open. I stepped over the threshold as if pushed from behind by an invisible hand. I told her I was sorry for the pain I had caused her; she was gentle and more than generous with me. We talked at length about the man who had betrayed each of us — and whose life was not improved by the way I hated him and drank at him for years. I understood things about my life with him that I could only have understood from talking to her. I felt profound compassion for his demon-haunted life. I went off to lead my meeting, and I spoke about that encounter. One of my woman friends was sitting nearby; she was nearing the end of a pregnancy and her belly was enormous. Soon she and her AA husband would be blessed with the arrival of a baby boy. Sitting next to her was another friend — a man who had gotten very thin. I was shocked to see him, for I could see that he had started to die of AIDS; in a month or so, we would be taking meetings to his hospital bed. I felt privileged to be at the meeting, to be alive, to be a sober member of Alcoholics Anonymous. At the end, I held the hands of these two friends as the group stood saying the Serenity Prayer. In my bones, I felt the promise of the Step: that it is the beginning of the end of isolation from our fellows and from God. As for that ex-wife, I am happy to count her among my friends today. The other night, she came over to my house. I cooked a nice dinner for a group of us; we laughed a lot.

K.F., New York, New York

STEP NINE

A BENCHMARK IN SOBRIETY

SEPTEMBER 1991

When I arrived at the Eighth and Ninth Steps, I found I had an unusual amend to make. I needed to make amends to the entire town I grew up in, for various acts of juvenile delinquency. There was no way of finding individual firemen, policemen, or citizens I may have involved or harmed twenty years before, but I wanted to make amends in some way.

I first tried writing a letter to the local newspaper, outlining my transgressions of the past, and declaring that I wanted to apologize to the town. The editor refused to publish my letter, saying that such a letter might actually encourage other young people to misbehave.

So I turned the whole thing over to my Higher Power and went on about the business of living in sobriety.

One day, after about a year in the program, I sat down on a park bench to rest. It occurred to me that someone ought to paint the bench, spruce it up. I thought about doing it myself, but I realized I would need a whole bagful of tools, besides the paint, to do a good job. It was too much for me to deal with. So I turned it over to my Higher Power.

Another year had gone by when I sat on another bench in another park and I thought, "Somebody ought to paint this bench!" I realized that over the preceding year I had acquired most of the tools I would need. All I needed to buy was some paint and some brushes.

I bought the needed supplies, assembled my tools, put them all in a large shopping bag, and I began to paint park benches. I took it one day at a time, painting one bench at a time.

Over a period of three years I painted about thirty benches in three parks. Some of the benches were getting tough use and those I painted twice. I used a rasp to smooth out coarse edges and sandpaper to roughen the surface of the smooth, weathered boards so they would take the paint. I did a priming coat and another day a finishing coat. It took about four hours' work altogether to do one bench.

I want to say right off that I enjoyed the work. It wasn't drudgery for me. I was outdoors, in the parks, out in the sun and the wind, listening to the birds, watching the squirrels, and sometimes interacting with people in the park.

I never told anyone, outside of AA, that I was doing this to make amends. I just said that it needed doing and I enjoyed doing it. Some people asked if this was required court-ordered community service, and I said, "No, I'm just a volunteer."

Then came a day, after about three years, when it occurred to me that I was done. I had made my amends to the town. I didn't have to do it anymore.

Several years have passed. I still use those parks as a place to sit and rest. Occasionally I see a bench that needs painting and I remember the work I did. But I don't do it anymore. Now the town does it.

If you can't figure out how to make amends, just turn it over to your Higher Power. In time, there will be an answer, there will be a way.

Jack A., Montclair, New Jersey

HOW TO LOSE 100 UGLY POUNDS

OCTOBER 1991

In the Altiplano (high plateau) of Peru and Bolivia live the descendants of Inca Indians. Over two miles up, the air is thin and the Indians have adapted to their harsh and difficult climate. Many are potato farmers, cultivating several varieties of potatoes which grow up there.

On market days, it is customary to see men trotting along the road with one hundred pounds or more of potatoes in sacks on their backs. At that altitude, carrying all that weight must be quite a job. When they sell their goods, they return to their distant homes. It is said that on the return trip they fill their backpacks with one hundred pounds of stones so as not to grow unaccustomed to carrying!

These images came back to me when I took my Fifth Step with Jim, my sponsor. We had gone to a diner after a meeting. With fear and trembling, I began what I thought was going to be a very painful exercise. Quite the contrary! Jim made it easy for me to unburden myself of the weight I'd been carrying around for years. In the course of the next several hours, little by little, I emptied that backpack. As weighty matter after weighty matter came spilling out, I felt my spirit soar.

Like a descendant of the Incas, I went to that diner with my one hundred pounds of wrongs. I admitted them to my sponsor who then assured me that through this process, I no longer needed to be concerned about them. Then and there, the burden of guilt, shame, and remorse was lifted.

But how often we begin to fill our newly emptied backpacks anew under fresh loads. It is as if we had become accustomed to carrying all that junk around, almost as if we had grown fond of the burden.

So we need to take an occasional look (every day?) into our backpacks to see if we haven't tossed in a stone every now and then. And when we discover some load of guilt or shame, some wrong we may have committed, we can toss it out. Otherwise, we spend all our lives struggling to walk, burdened by these impediments.

The word "impediment" comes from the Latin word *impedimenta* which means baggage. To me, it means whatever we carry around — guilt, wrongdoing, shame, remorse. Instead of trying to live our lives with that burden, we unload all of that weight through Step Five, and we drop off the occasional rock or two which we may have acquired through Step Ten. Unlike the Indians of the Altiplano, we don't need to continue our journey with a fresh load — "so as not to grow unaccustomed to carrying."

Dan J., Maryknoll, New York

STEP ELEVEN
TRUSTING THE SILENCE
NOVEMBER 1991

Sometimes my faith in a Higher Power slips. I look at the people, places, and things around me and ask, "Is this really what you had in mind for me? Is this what I sobered up for? Is this all there is?" And I sometimes get the silent treatment. That's only fair. My mouth has usually been running overtime, anyway.

Who is God? I don't need to know. I only need to have faith in a power greater than myself. What matters is what works, not my opinion of what works.

It took me years to figure that out, years in which I did mental and emotional battle with other people's conception of God, years in which I managed only to make myself miserable, cringing or scoffing whenever someone mentioned Step Three or Eleven. It took me a while sober to realize that it's a waste of time to take God's inventory.

So I don't pretend to know God well. And I really don't claim to pray respectably. I say the words "Thy will, not mine, be done" as if they were magic, as if they could help me stop yammering so much to have my will done. My prayers are usually brief and to the point. "Help!" is one I use often.

Sometimes in sobriety I've prayed when I needed to meditate. I've yammered at God so much that God can't get a word in edgewise. (What I practice with people, I cannot help but practice with God.) To me, meditation is simply being quiet and listening for a change. It is buttoning up my lip — and my mind that yaps even when my mouth is shut.

Meditation is the path by which I cease being caught up in my own mental "garbage in/garbage out" recycling. It is the path by which I walk out of the turmoil, trouble, pain, depression, and frustration that I create in and around me.

Meditation is when I learn to be a child again. Not a noisy brat, but a child of the sort I always admired but rarely was: quiet, serene, loving, trusting, teachable.

To meditate means I have to become willing to sit alone in silence — and endure silence patiently. It means trusting the silence around me for a while, as if it were an answer I had long sought. This is simple but not easy for me to do. I don't meditate to hear God's voice inside me, but merely to allow some space and time for the awareness of something higher than myself to grow more strongly within me.

I began doing meditation when I gave up my childish habit of expecting God to part the Red Sea and save me from myself once again, when I gave up my spoiled-brat routine of expecting God to show me a burning bush to prove that God really does care about me.

Practicing meditation means I open up for spiritual contact before disaster strikes, before even the need for prayer becomes desperately obvious. It's the brand of spiritual contact with God that I practice early enough in the day that I have nothing to tell God and nothing to ask God about in prayer.

Meditation is the only time when I can be absolutely sure that I am not running on self-will.

In the beginning, while admitting I didn't know the first thing about how to meditate, I turned my ignorance into a major case of self-confusion by reading various books on meditation and trying to follow all the guidelines they presented.

Then simplicity mercifully struck. I found I didn't need to learn how to meditate before meditating. It turned out to be one of those learn-as-you-go things — just as learning how to stay sober is part of staying sober a day at a time. Meditation is something like showing up on a new job I don't know how to do, only to find out that by merely showing up on a regular basis and doing what is placed before me, I'm automatically doing what at first I didn't know how to do and was sure I could never do.

When I practice listening in AA meetings, I am learning something I can use in private meditation practice. It took me a while to learn how to really listen to others in AA, to have my mind solely on what the speaker was saying, instead of hearing only the part that plugged me into my own preferred thinking. What I do in meetings is called listening. When I listen alone with God, it is called meditating. When I can listen completely to what you have to say without having to change or criticize it to meet my expectations, then I have a better chance of being able to do the same thing with God the next time I pray or meditate.

The hardest thing for me to do is listen honestly when I've asked God in prayer for direction regarding a particular person, place, or thing. I tend to put words in God's mouth — the ones I want to hear. After years of misunderstanding God, I've devised for myself a simple test for reliability in prayer: if the answer is the one I want to hear — or the one that lets me sit back amid my complacency, laziness, or fear and let someone else do all the work in solving my problem for me — it probably isn't God's answer. What God wants me to do is rarely what I want to do.

For instance, if I want to avoid or leave, God wants me to stay and handle. If I want to be understood or accepted by others, God wants me to try to understand or accept others a bit more. If I want to forget, God wants me to forgive. If I want to point the finger of blame at someone else, God wants me to see my part in creating the disaster. If I want to dislike someone because of a grating character defect he or she has, God wants me to see the same defect in myself.

Meditation not only helps me hear God and others better, it also helps me see how even the tiny things I do daily for others strengthen me in my ability to cooperate with God. For I am one of those hardheaded alcoholics who had to practice cooperating with others for a while to learn how to cooperate with God, so that "turning it over" could become almost as easy and often as automatic as not taking the first drink.

In the last year, I've heard more silence than messages from God while praying or meditating. At this stage in my development, I think God is trying to teach me something I could not learn otherwise about patience and trust. What I'm now learning is how to apply to myself a bit of Native American wisdom that my sponsor shared with me over a decade ago: "If someone comes to you who is hungry and you give that person a fish, that person will expect to get a fish from you every time hunger strikes. But if, when the person comes to you the first time, you teach her or him to fish, that person will never be hungry again." So the messages I receive during meditation or prayer aren't anything like a fish from God. Instead, the messages are like God's lessons in fishing.

Whatever I learn during meditation applies to me in my life, not necessarily to anyone else. The messages are usually what I need to hear at a particular time, whether I agree or not. For example:

Help yourself by helping someone else first.
When in doubt, be silent.
Grow where you are planted.

Anonymous, U.S.A.

STEP TWELVE
IN MY NATIVE TONGUE
MARCH 1996

When I was sober for two or three years, I went with my friends Ben G. and his wife, Rita, to Portland, Oregon for the Pacific Northwest Conference. Our excitement was understandable: it was going to be our first big AA convention. Ben had been asked to chair the opening meeting on Saturday morning and I'd been asked to read the Twelve Traditions. Rita was a member of Al-Anon and was along to give support.

When we arrived at Portland, the excitement I felt was almost unbearable. The hotel was a big one and there were AA people from all over the West Coast. I was surprised at how many people I already knew. My intention had been to go to my room to start rehearsing how to read the Twelve Traditions. (My Norwegian accent was still quite pronounced, and I'd never been good at reading aloud. I had mastered the reading of "How It Works" by repeatedly reading it in front of a mirror.) But that night we ended up going out for supper with a group of people we met in the Hospitality Room. After supper we attended the Friday Night Meeting and then discovered the Night Owl meetings. I don't remember going to bed. I was too tired to look over the Twelve Traditions. I decided I would practice reading them in the morning.

However, the next morning I overslept. It was nine o'clock before I stirred. I had to get dressed and eat breakfast and get to the meeting in less than an hour. As I left the room, I stuck a wallet-sized "Twelve and Twelve" card into my pocket. At least, I thought, I could read it over while having breakfast.

In the cafeteria I encountered several people I knew but had no time to chat with them. I wanted a table, alone, by the wall, where I'd be left in peace to practice my reading. Bill S. and his wife, Obie, had a big group at their table. They were having fun, laughing and talking to everyone who passed them. It had been arranged that I would drive home to Vancouver with Bill and Obie, while Ben and Rita continued on their holiday. Bill called me to join them. I declined. He insisted. I told him: "I have to learn to read before the meeting!" Finally, he left me alone. Time was getting short.

I finally got hold of a muffin and a coffee and found a quiet table in the corner. I had eighteen minutes left before the meeting. I pulled a card from my pocket. Oh no! I had, in my haste, taken the wrong card. It was the Twelve Steps and Twelve Traditions, all right, but it was in Norwegian! Bill came over again to ask me to join them. I told him what had happened. He thought it was funny! He couldn't understand that Ben wanted a perfect meeting and I was about to ruin the whole show. Bill said, "Just read the Norwegian version. Nobody listens to the Traditions, anyway."

I said, "I can't do that. Ben would be furious."

Bill said, "Why not? I dare you."

Then I remembered. I had arrived in AA on a dare that had not turned out too badly. I brought my coffee over to Bill's table and began to relax.

Ben opened the meeting. His attire was impeccable. His manner was that of a man who had complete control of a solemn occasion. Oh, he was good. His funny lines were delivered with precision. After the reading of the Twelve Steps, my name was called. I introduced myself, picked my card from my pocket and started to read — in Norwegian! The first two Traditions went fine. By the Third Tradition, someone started to snicker. I didn't dare look at Ben. I read on. By the end of the Fourth Tradition, there was a roar of laughter.

At first, Ben was so busy checking his notes that he didn't realize he was hearing a foreign language. I finally looked at him. He hadn't rehearsed for this event and he looked absolutely devastated. I had committed treason! That's when his wife Rita could no longer hold her laughter and everybody joined in. I said: "I was just checking to see if everyone was awake. I will now read the Traditions in the language of their origin." Somebody applauded and I read on in English from the book on the podium. I was told afterward that never had there been such attentive listening during a reading of the Traditions. When it was all over, Ben was quite pleased with the way things had turned out.

But that's not the real story. On that particular weekend, out on the Pacific Ocean, a fishing boat was homebound for Alaska. The skipper and his wife were Norwegian immigrants. The wife had been drinking for days. Something had to be done. The skipper told his wife he was altering course for Portland, the nearest large city, because this time he was going to get some help for her, whether she liked the idea or not. They came ashore and he phoned the AA central office, only to be told that no one was available because the local members were all attending the AA convention at a hotel downtown. So the skipper helped his wife get cleaned up as best he could and sent her to the hotel in a taxi. Someone led her into the meeting hall and sat her down. She looked at all the people. They looked so happy and so clean! Could they be alcoholics?

The meeting had started. Someone was called to read. A young woman began to read . . . but listen! Was it possible? She was reading in a familiar language, Norwegian. The woman heard the Third Tradition and she started to cry.

After the meeting, I was ushered out to the lobby where Marge H. was sitting with the woman from Alaska who was very shaky and still in tears. After a little while, we were able to settle down and talk about Alcoholics Anonymous in our own language. The woman stayed for the meetings all of that day. The next morning her boat sailed for Alaska.

Elisabeth G., Vancouver, British Columbia

The Twelve Traditions

THE BEST OF AN AWKWARD SITUATION
MAY 1988

Many AAs can tell horror stories of the egos of recovering alcoholics colliding with those of judges, doctors, and other professionals. Even though all involved are moved by good intentions, the results are often resentments on both sides. The ultimate victims are the unknown numbers of alcoholics who are not referred to our Fellowship by professionals whose AA contact has left a bitter aftertaste.

At a recent closed meeting in my community, the chairperson began the closed meeting with the usual preliminaries, then asked if there were any visitors. The group heard a visitor announce that he and his companion were counselors from a local university;

concerned about the increasing problem of alcohol and drug abuse among students, they had decided to visit an AA meeting to see how our Fellowship could help.

Uneasily, the chairperson made a polite expression of welcome and was about to proceed with the discussion, but another member — aware of the tension on some faces around the table — remarked that this was an established closed meeting for alcoholics only. Embarrassed, one of the visitors defensively said he had phoned AA and was directed to that meeting.

In this awkward moment, several turned toward "Clarence," the longest-sober member present, who was familiar with AA meetings in many parts of the country. Clarence explained to the visitors that the number they had reached was the intergroup answering service. The operator, a nonalcoholic, was accustomed to giving locations to AAs who didn't care whether meetings were open or closed, and had assumed the callers were members.

A possible solution, Clarence suggested, was to determine by a group conscience vote whether to declare that meeting an open one just for that night. As several heads nodded, Clarence added that it would only be fair to ask if any alcoholic present would find it uncomfortable to participate in an open meeting.

A woman broke the silence. Yes, she said quietly, she would find it difficult to express herself with nonmembers present.

The two visitors promptly stood up to leave, apologizing for causing this situation. Immediately, Clarence and others expressed regret for the misunderstanding, which certainly was not the fault of the visitors. They told the counselors their interest in AA was greatly appreciated, and gave them the location of an open meeting being held that same night.

The visitors departed and the meeting resumed.

In the aftermath, however, several members were troubled. How, they wondered, could such situations be prevented? Was there a better solution than choosing between offending visitors and compromising the integrity of AA closed meetings?

Members of that closed meeting learned later that they had made the best of an awkward situation. The next day one of the group was chatting with an AA friend who told about an open meeting he'd attended the previous night.

"At the end of it," he said, "a couple of people got up, said they were counselors from a local university, and were there because they were concerned about a big alcohol and drug problem on the campus. They said they'd gone to a closed meeting by mistake and described how courteous the members were in explaining the different types of meetings and referring them to our meeting."

Not all nonalcoholic professionals can be expected to be so patient and understanding of either our procedures or our explanations. Obvious preventive measures include AA phone services specifying which meetings are open or closed, and a clear announcement by the chairperson that a closed meeting is for self-described alcoholics only, along with an offer to direct nonalcoholics to an open AA meeting.

Most of all, members of our local group want to avoid forcing upon an alcoholic the Catch 22 dilemma: either revealing to an outsider that a deep personal problem exists, or enduring the pain of withholding its expression when nonalcoholic visitors are permitted to remain.

The presence of nonalcoholics in a closed discussion meeting can arouse in members fears of being recognized and gossiped about by those not bound by AA's code of anonymity and confidentiality. A cautious member may feel that outsiders will interpret his reluctance to speak as evidence of scandalous or degrading behavior by himself or his family. Whether well-founded or not, such fears result in maintaining resentful silence, or an awkward, unproductive tailoring of expression.

Years ago in the Grapevine, co-founder Bill W. suggested that we be "friendly with our friends." Surely we resourceful ex-drunks can do so without penalizing those AAs who, whether new or old-timers, need the security and comfortable intimacy of a closed meeting.

Anonymous, North Carolina

THE OTHER SIDE OF SELF-SUPPORT
AUGUST 1989

"Don't worry about paying rent; we're just happy to have an AA group in our church hall."

The two AAs, however, immediately declined the clergyman's generous offer. "Thank you, Reverend, but our Traditions tell us that our group ought to be fully self-supporting. We're grateful for your kindness, but we must pay our own way." And so began a verbal contract with my husband, who was the clergyman, and the founders of what was to become my home group, which met at my church for many, many years.

As time went on, I became more conscious of the full meaning of Tradition Seven, which tells us that every AA group ought to be fully self-supporting, declining outside contributions. From the beginning, my group declined outside contributions by insisting on paying a fee for the use of the hall, despite the tempting offer of a free ride. The two AAs might have rationalized: "Maybe we should let the church support us. After all, it may be rough getting this group off the ground. We may not be able to afford the fee." But they didn't.

It pleases me to know that my group didn't let the church support them in the beginning and this impressed the church. What many of us AAs do not realize, including me (until I "married into the church") is that many of our AA meeting halls are the property of poor, small parishes who struggle to stay open. When my church offered free rent to AA, they were offering the tremendous maintenance costs that a small working-class parish must pay. Like most unendowed churches, we exist from month to month waiting for the pledges to come in. The weekly ten dollar pledge from a church member is vital for paying the clergyman's salary, mortgages, utilities, water, janitor services, paper towels, light bulbs . . . well, you get the picture.

The words *fully* self-supporting" have new meaning for me, examined from both sides. I've been in some groups in the past in which it seemed reasonable to offer a "donation" instead of rent to a church. A charitable and well-intended pastor or institution would suggest a token payment and the group would readily accept the offer. We believed that we were observing the Seventh Tradition. But a token is not rent; a token is a partial payment. I've seen more than one AA group which paid token rents be asked to leave a facility; the group had become a financial liability. Other reasons to ask a group to leave might have been superseded if the group had been fully self-supporting.

There are numerous costs to maintaining a site that are not usually factored into even a "full" fee: the wear and tear and replacement of chairs and tables, plumbing, floors, and carpets; dirt and smoke damage to ceilings, walls, and windows; heating cost overruns when a group forgets to turn down thermostats and close windows; the cost of paper products, garbage bags, and collection; and the cost from damage, loss, and theft. To a group that feels comfortable in paying a token amount, the burden falls on the church members. My AA group was firm in its commitment, thank God, to be self-supporting.

I've heard it said at a business meeting that "we don't need to raise the amount of our donations toward the rent (after five years) because the church hasn't asked for more." Now is that the spirit of Tradition Seven? If we are fully self-supporting through our own contributions, as our Preamble reinforces, then should we put the church in the position of begging money from us? Or should we spare them that indignity and offer rent increases on a regular basis?

Long ago, Bill W. observed in the groups and in himself, the peculiar phenomenon of our tight-fisted approach when we pass the hat. Way back in the fifties, some groups would say, "Please, if you have it, dig in. The group needs the money to pay the rent. We don't want to hear any noise from loose change, so we won't object to any folding money you choose to drop in!"

Thirty-some years and a quadruple inflation rate later, we tight-fisted alcoholics — who squandered thousands — still see the one dollar bill as the upper limit of our contribution. Speaking for myself, I find no problem with paying a therapist $80 a week for my other mental health program. The AA program which saved my life and offers me every bit as much help and healing as my outside program gets the short end of the financial stick from me — a dollar at best. Translated into realistic terms that means: am I willing to spend the equivalent of a cup of coffee to save my life?

Well, all of these new perspectives on the meaning of our Twelve Traditions have come from two sources: my life as a clergyman's wife and my Step and Traditions meetings. My eyes are opening to these inspired and brilliant plans for living. The Steps ensure the mental and spiritual growth of the individual; the Traditions ensure the growth of the group.

I have learned another lesson about being a good AA tenant from my experience "on the other side." I learned what a nasty job it is to pick up discarded cigarette butts from lawns and walks, because I am a groundskeeper at my church. Guess who spent many years tossing away butts as I approached a church, a meeting hall, a movie theater? It never mattered that someone would have to pick up after me. Now that *someone is* me. Yes, it's been a valuable lesson being on the other side.

Anonymous, Oxford, Massachusetts

⌒

SERVICE: A FRAMEWORK FOR THE FUTURE
JANUARY 1991

For quite a number of years now I've been working in the service structure of our wonderful Fellowship of Alcoholics Anonymous. I've had the unique opportunity of traveling around the area, meeting and sharing with many dedicated and service-minded AA members, and I've often heard a particular phrase mentioned: "The Fellowship of Alcoholics Anonymous must change to keep up with modern times and the problems of our society today."

When I first entered the doors of Alcoholics Anonymous over nine years ago, I was sick, confused, negative, depressed, and lonely, and I needed and wanted help. Many hands reached out to me and made me feel wanted and comfortable in all the meetings I attended. For the first time in my life I felt part of something. In a short amount of time I had loads of friends, all with the same problem I had, coupled with a strong desire to do something about that problem. These recovering alcoholics were telling me how they got sober and how they stayed sober one day at a time, and I listened.

These same recovering alcoholics handed me two books: the Big Book and *Twelve Steps and Twelve Traditions*. The most important lesson I learned from these resources was that in order for me to enjoy a happy, peaceful, sober existence, I had to change — I had to change my attitudes, my way of thinking, my habits. As a matter of fact, I had to change everything about me. This I attempted to do very slowly through the use and practice of the Twelve Steps of Alcoholics Anonymous and the help of other recovering alcoholics. I learned that in order to like other people, I had to like myself; in order to receive all the benefits of the AA Fellowship, I had to give of myself. The original and only Twelve Steps of the Fellowship of Alcoholics Anonymous became the foundation for the new me.

All this restructuring of myself was not done overnight. However, to my amazement, after some time, I was able to notice changes in me and I liked the changes. What's even more miraculous is that the changing for the better is still going on. All this I owe to a "Society of nameless drunks."

About this "Society of nameless drunks": should their Fellowship change to keep up with modern times? I don't see why it should. It is my belief that our common disease of alcoholism and the symptoms of our disease (the way we drank, the things we did under the influence of alcohol, and our character defects) are no different in 1989 than in 1935. I still see the best medicine for arresting the disease of alcoholism is sharing with another alcoholic and thoroughly following the path of the first one hundred members of the Fellowship of Alcoholics Anonymous as outlined in the AA literature.

I do see problems or situations that have created some controversies among fellow AA members. Is our message of recovery from alcoholism becoming diluted? For instance, should nonalcoholics be allowed to attend closed AA meetings or should they seek help for their other addictions elsewhere? Should we as AA groups be signing proof of attendance papers at AA meetings? Should we as a Fellowship attempt to be a cure-all for all the problems of the world? Should we as AA groups be displaying and selling non-AA literature at group meetings which may possibly be implying affiliation with outside enterprises? Are we as AA group members each allowed to express our individual opinions at group conscience meetings on issues affecting our groups? Do we allow well-meaning AA members to be all-powerful in dictating how groups should be run? Do we protect our individual and group anonymity at the level of press, radio, TV, and films?

These are just some of the concerns I've heard expressed in the past few years. I believe all the answers to these questions can be found in our Twelve Traditions.

Practicing the Twelve Traditions to the best of my ability has become just as vital a part of my personal recovery program as practicing the Twelve Steps. The Steps teach me how to think and act. The Traditions keep my personal program of recovery simple, well-balanced, and healthy. Whenever I do a Twelve Step inventory of my personal recovery program, I also do a Twelve Traditions inventory, including questions such as the following:

Do I share any concerns I have for the group welfare with other members of my group?

Do I participate in group business and group conscience meetings whenever I can?

Am I a good leader, serving my group according to the group conscience, and not making decisions and rules based on what I personally feel is good for the group?

Do I encourage my group *not* to make decisions and carry out actions that may adversely affect other groups or AA as a whole?

Do I encourage my group to cooperate but not affiliate or imply affiliation with outside entities?

Do I notify the proper people when I observe an anonymity break at the level of press, radio, TV, and films?

Do I support my group by contributing money to help the group pay its expenses, thus enabling it to be self-supporting?

Do I encourage my group to contribute extra group funds to the service entities within AA?

Do I guide the people I sponsor in carrying the AA message of recovery as described in the AA literature?

Do I encourage my group to stick to our primary purpose of recovery from alcoholism?

When speaking at meetings, do I keep my personal story focused on alcoholism and my recovery from alcoholism?

Do I practice placing principles before personalities in everything I do?

If a nonalcoholic comes to a closed AA meeting, do I lovingly take that person aside and in a gentle and courteous manner explain that Alcoholics Anonymous is for recovery from alcoholism? Do I offer assistance in steering that individual to a program of recovery for his or her particular addiction?

Do I continue to practice humility in all that I do?

If I can honestly answer yes to these questions, I know that my personal program of recovery from alcoholism is on the right track today. If I have to debate any of these questions in my mind, I know there is something in my thinking that is causing turmoil within myself. Most of the time, the solution has been rereading and reapplying the Twelve Traditions to get my personal program of recovery strong and healthy again.

By equally combining the Twelve Steps and the Twelve Traditions, I'm able to work a *whole* program of recovery. Today I live a happy, healthy, well-meaning life filled with gratitude toward the Fellowship of Alcoholics Anonymous.

Anonymous, Fanwood, New Jersey

OUT OF THE HAT

FEBRUARY 1990

During the first year I was sober in AA, half a dozen regular members abandoned my home group over a dispute about the group conscience. The process was frightening; the outcome reassuring.

At issue was the fate of one of our members who had lost a considerable chunk of the group treasury on a slow pony. The group decided that he must pay the money back, but — as the weeks went by — he didn't.

Then followed a business meeting. Tempers flared, friends fought, order barely prevailed. Finally the group conscience followed the wisdom of those who said that it was not a requirement that our members stop gambling and pay their debts: we voted not to expel the liable one.

However, there were those who felt the group unity was threatened, that we were reneging on a responsibility to be self-supporting, that we were enabling a member to continue non-sober behavior. And some of them took their resentments and left the group. I was reassured by the fact that the gambler stayed sober, AA proved big enough to welcome the wanderers into other rooms, and the group survived.

Ours is a rambunctious group, not for everyone. We're one of our city's "intake" meetings and newcomers are encouraged to share there. We have a two-part plan to deal with disruptions, and both parts depend on a vote by the group. First, the group conscience decides whether or not to warn the person causing the disturbance. Then, if the disruption continues, the group conscience is called again to vote on temporary expulsion, usually for the length of the meeting.

And what is a disruption in a large meeting where business as usual includes people talking in the kitchen, at least one active drunk, and a couple of regulars who can't or won't sit still and be quiet? Well, throwing a coffeepot once merited expulsion. Refusing to stop yelling at the speaker did too. Of course the very few times one person laid a hand on another he or she got booted, but so did the person who launched a verbal attack.

Lest a reader get the idea that there is a free-for-all going on, I must say that — no matter how out of control the offender — rarely in ten years have I known of people who tried to stay after the group conscience decided they must leave. Most leave with no more than a parting word or two.

And it was at my home group that I learned to trust the experiences of the early groups. We have a Traditions meeting once a month, and when I was new and heard the Traditions read out loud, the experiences of the early AA meetings gave me the first notion that real people — drunks like me — had started this program.

In fact, it was easier at first to accept a higher power for my personal recovery in the form of a "Group of Drunks." Until very much later, turning over my individual will to a caring God was difficult (and often still is). But I knew that our coming together to stay sober was a spiritual act.

When I rotated into service beyond the group and became a district committee member, I was once present at a large meeting that expanded my understanding of "spiritual leadership." We fought through three ballots trying to agree on the person who would represent our area at the General Service Conference. All of the candidates had put in many years of service and had their champions. Tempers were getting warm. Then the secretary announced that it was time for the Higher Power to decide and the three names went into a hat. Some of us were flabbergasted. This really was too silly, we said to each other.

However, the name drawn out of the treasurer's fedora was accepted at once. And the huge hall hushed for a long moment before hundreds of us boomed out the Serenity Prayer. We modern folks were not even embarrassed to be moved by that process.

Angela D., New York, New York

THE COSTUME AND THE MASK
DECEMBER 1990

I am a celebrity — by no means a big one and far from being a household word — but I'm lucky enough to see that welcome little light which now and then brightens a stranger's face when he recognizes my name.

I was in AA a long time before it dawned on me that the notion of celebrity is exactly and precisely opposite from that of anonymity, and though conflict about anonymity is by no means peculiar to celebrities, it does seem to cluster around them in strange and peculiar ways, and it sure meant trouble for me.

We've all sewn together a mask and costume in order to have something respectable to introduce to others, but celebrities' public disguises are not only their livelihood, they are a large part of their beloved craft. It's understandable that celebrities can become more obsessed with these public presentations than most other folk.

I had occasion to work with a famous model during one project. She was, at the time, on the covers of three major magazines and featured in at least that many television commercials. Women would rush up to her on the street and it was touching to see the way their eyes searched her face and figure for the secret of her magic.

The model possessed in a spectacular degree a trait which I have noticed off and on in various celebrities, myself by no means excluded: a tendency to regard oneself from an observer's point of view. When she entered a room you could almost see the imaginary surrounding cameras with which she skillfully watched herself, knowing exactly how each movement looked from all directions, every getting up and sitting down, each smile and head toss. Occasionally you could see her quickly correct herself because she'd caught herself in some faulty pose from a bad angle.

I was fairly new to sobriety and to AA when I met this woman, and I've been grateful to her ever since for what I learned from the sight of her in action.

The first thing I realized was how much I'd used the same trick of viewing myself from a distance when I'd been an active drunk. I realized I'd been living outside myself for so long I'd almost become a walking vacancy. In my prized AA sobriety, I was still running a kind of circus which had numerous, highly believable posters plastered all over its outside — *See the Spectacular Non-Drinking Person! Watch How Movingly He Can Recite the Twelve Steps!* — but which had nothing much going on inside the tent. I've been working hard to shut that circus down ever since with varying degrees of success.

Obviously you don't have to be a celebrity to waste AA by reducing it to just another clever act; it's only that the scam's more spectacular and blatant when you turn all of it into a novel or a sitcom. And, sadly, the fraudulence is more generally observed and likely to be more destructive.

And of course only celebrities are brought on stage to work that dubious show-biz routine of topping one another publicly about how sober they've become. It's not just the obvious fact that they have feet of clay the same as everybody else and may end up by not setting such a grand example after all which makes the exercise so dangerous. It's that the whole thing has the effect of reducing their revelations (which may indeed be sincere) into nothing more than talk show gabble.

Perhaps the scariest part of turning recovery into just another celebrity act is that, even though it may well have the best intentions, it tends to glamorize drunkenness almost exactly as an ad does and make it seem that being a poor sot is somehow an especially interesting and possibly even superior condition. I can't speak for anyone else, but I can state without reservation that as far as this particular drunk is concerned, that foolish notion got me into a whole lot of trouble. Over and over.

Anonymous, New York, New York

INDELIBLE HUMILITY

DECEMBER 1990

As a newcomer in AA, I had a lot of ideas about needed changes. Even in 1970, I thought the Big Book was too sexist and I couldn't understand why none of the AA meetings served decaffeinated coffee. And I was absolutely certain that the biggest mistake was keeping Alcoholics Anonymous anonymous.

In fact, I made an emotional plea to that effect when I had six months sobriety under my belt, holding the Fellowship responsible for my father's death from cirrhosis of the liver. It embarrasses me to recall saying that if AA weren't so anonymous, my father would still be alive, which was, of course, an absurd statement. My father knew of AA and chose not to go.

Since then I have seen example after example proving why anonymity is so vital for our Fellowship. For instance, a few years ago I was in a country in the Caribbean when AA was celebrating its 25th anniversary there. At that time, it was their feeling that anonymity was fine for AA in the United States but not for them. The Fellowship was getting a great deal of publicity because of the anniversary convention. There was media coverage. One active member, a teacher by profession, was being interviewed live by a local talk show host. He was identified by full name as an AA member and was plainly recognizable. In the course of the interview, he was asked what percentage of the country's teachers were alcoholic. Not anticipating the question and being nervous in front of the cameras, our friend answered, "About fifty percent." The headline in the newspaper that evening shouted, "Half of

Country's Teachers Alcoholic According to AA." Our non-anonymous member had become an AA spokesman.

As expressed in a letter to Sam D., Bill W. had some thoughts on the subject of anonymity at the public level. Sam, an AA member who was also a minister, had written to Bill stating that he thought, in his case, it would be helpful to reveal his AA membership before the general public by name and picture. Here are excerpts from Bill's response, from a letter dated June 22, 1946. Our Fellowship was eleven years old: "As a fact, there are few principles or AA attitudes about which I have a more definite conviction than that of 'anonymity before the general public.' I find support for my conviction among the vast majority of AA members despite the fact that there seem to be a considerable number of AAs in our southeastern chapters who agree with you. But in discussing this matter I would rather not rely too much upon the numerical support my own view has. Which of our views is the better policy, the finer spirituality, that's the question, isn't it?

"Though less well schooled than you, I, too, regard myself a follower in the tradition of the Master. Perhaps as a layman, I have not much standing to interpret him. Yet my own observation is this: that sometimes Jesus advanced propositions seemingly contradictory. He lambasted money changers and people who stoned whores, yet I believe he said 'resist not evil.' He preached in public, and this to such great effect that millions wish they could see him and hear him today. Yet, did he not reprove those who made a public show of giving alms, and did he not say that a prayer in a closet was better than a prayer in public? What did he have in mind when he said such things? If, as one who doesn't know the Bible very well, I were asked to answer, I would say that he was trying to throw a heavy emphasis on modesty and humility; that he was deeply conscious of the human tendency to exhibitionism. So, if I hear him aright, he is now saying to us AAs 'go and preach these principles to all the world. But beware of parading yourselves in the process.'

"Just as you are now searching your soul about anonymity in public, so did I have to go through that very process in 1939, the year our book *Alcoholics Anonymous* went to print. I was then called upon to make a decision, perhaps the most far-reaching one I have ever taken. Had it not been for the wise counsel of my friends in AA I must humbly confess that I probably would have abandoned my anonymity before the general public. Two courses were then before me because two titles for the book had been proposed, and both were equally popular. Here they were:

"1. The Way Out by Wm. G. Wilson

"2. Alcoholics Anonymous

"I don't mind saying, Sam, that the first one looked mighty attractive to me. To justify myself I used to say 'Well, Bill, you have surely learned enough about humility by now. So the mere signing of this book will never go to your head. The leaders of every other movement are publicized. All movements have to be personalized. They have to have personal symbols to lend them power and character. So why shouldn't I sign this book? A good title too — *The Way Out!*

"I almost succumbed to these rationalizations but my friends tipped the scale the other way. 'What if you got drunk — and Bill, what kind of an example do you think you would be setting for the rest of us egocentrics? Even if you could stand a lot of newspaper publicity, *we couldn't*. Lots of us would get drunk and let our movement down. And anyhow, isn't the American public pretty well fed up on personal ballyhoo, however good.' Well,

Sam, my friends wouldn't let me do it, and how right — oh how very right — they were."

The spiritual value of anonymity has been recognized for a long time. The ancient Greeks had a word for it and Christ spoke in praise of the humility that fosters anonymity when he said, "Blessed are the meek for they shall inherit the earth."

We will now take a big jump in time and space and atmosphere from the Sermon on the Mount to the second day of April, 1840, and Chase's Tavern in Baltimore, Maryland. On that date, six drinking friends made a decision to stop their drinking and took a pledge to do so.

They called themselves the Washingtonians and in a year's time they had reformed 1,000 drunks and had 5,000 other members and supportive friends. On their second anniversary one of their groups in the Midwest was addressed by a young U.S. Congressman from Illinois named Abraham Lincoln.

So rapid was the group's rise that it soon had 600,000 members. Along the way, however, it became so involved — even concentrated — on promotion of its aims and success that its main original purpose began to evaporate. Many of its members became embroiled in public activities, giving voice to and taking sides in outside matters such as abolition and temperance.

By the end of 1847, just seven years after it began its original noble venture, the Washingtonians had faded out of existence and ceased activity except in Boston where, in all too brief a time, it vanished altogether.

About seventy years later, another movement surfaced that was to be remarkably effective for a couple of decades. This was the Oxford Group. Interestingly, its founder Frank Buchman saw great virtue in anonymity and there was a considerable length of time that he preferred to be known as Frank B. This was to change, however, along with the overall tone of the original Oxford Group movement. Before too long ordinary membership purposes were shunted aside and eventually overwhelmed by increasing cases of personal ambition, campaigns for funds, and eager public searches for support, endorsement and participation of well-known personalities.

AA's earliest members, chief among them Bill and Dr. Bob, were associated with the Oxford Group and were on hand, it is reported, for a gathering in New York City where Buchman revealed for the first time his personal hopes for dealing with the problem of alcoholism. "I'm all for alcoholics getting changed," he announced, "but we have drunken nations on our hands as well."

It was 1938 and before long the Oxford Group was transformed into what was called Moral Rearmament with Frank Buchman still at the head of it — with a purpose to bring the nations of the world together by strictly peaceful means.

By 1939, AA and the changing Oxford Group drifted apart. But in talking later about AA's infancy, Bill said of the Oxford Group: "They had clearly shown us what to do [and] we also learned from them what not to do so far as alcoholics were concerned — too authoritarian, aggressive evangelism, absolute concepts, which were frequently too much for drunks, dependence upon the use of prominent names (mighty hazardous for us). Because of the stigma (at that time) of alcoholism, most alcoholics wanted to be anonymous."

Commenting on this still further, Bill said: "Anonymity was not born of confidence: the bare hint of publicity shocked us . . . we were afraid of developing erratic public characters who. . . might get drunk in public and so destroy confidence in us. . . ."

No look at anonymity as practiced by AA can be truly complete without including the question: is it possible for an AA member to be *too* anonymous? Too anonymous for the good of the individual and the Fellowship? The answer is "yes." And there are more than a few examples of this: members who feel they must not tell their families or their friends or co-workers or doctors or ministers or lawyers that they are members of AA.

There have even been instances when members have sent requests for information to the General Service Office in New York and not included a last name or have sent checks to GSO — unsigned!

There is indeed such a thing as an AA member being too anonymous: where it can mean failure to extend the helping hand when the need arises; where it can mean failure to correct misconceptions about AA both inside and outside the Fellowship; and where it can stifle — even stop — the flow of AA knowledge and sobriety from one person to another.

This is anonymity at the personal level and can indeed be carried too far — in Bill's words — to "the point of real absurdity." Anonymity at the public level, however, is another matter and no member of the AA Fellowship has shown the genuine humility to practice anonymity at the public level more dramatically and in a more truly self-sacrificing manner than our co-founders, Bill and Dr. Bob.

I've quoted Bill a lot in this article because he was a prolific writer. Dr. Bob also provided us with many illustrations of living the Tradition of anonymity. The example I cite took place soon after his wife Anne had died and nearly a year after he learned he had terminal cancer. It is from his biography, *Dr. Bob and the Good Oldtimers.*

"This was at a time when AA members were thinking about a monument for Anne and Bob. In fact, a collection had been started. Hearing this, Dr. Bob promptly asked that the money be given back and declared against the Fellowship's erecting for Anne and himself any tangible memorials or monuments. He told Bill, 'Let's you and I get buried just like other folks.' Later, while shopping for a stone for Anne's grave, he was asked, 'Surely you're going to have something on it about AA?' He replied, 'Mercy, no!'' "

Another example: in his farewell to the Fellowship at AA's first International Convention in Cleveland, Ohio, in July 1950, Dr. Bob said: "I get a big thrill out of looking over a vast sea of faces like this with a feeling that possibly some small thing I did a number of years ago played an infinitely small part in making this meeting possible." This from a co-founder of what some have called the greatest social and spiritual movement, the most far-reaching crusade for health and mental well-being, of the twentieth century — an organization with a couple million alcoholics who have lived or died sober as a direct result of Dr. Bob's and Bill's determination and dedication. This is humility. This is anonymity.

Considering the size of today's AA population, the number of public anonymity breaks — discomforting when they do occur and sometimes potentially dangerous — are comparatively few and infrequent. This may be because as AA matures, its members more fully understand the value to themselves for anonymity at the public level. It may also be because of Bill's remarkably powerful example of personal sacrifice for the good of all. As a demonstration of anonymity in action, this is for all to follow:

Bill discouraged any Nobel Prize possibility for himself.

He declined awards from several colleges (suggesting they be offered instead to the Fellowship itself).

He turned down the inclusion of his name and a brief personal history in "Who's Who in America."

He said thanks but no thanks to an honorary degree from Yale University.

He rejected a *Time* magazine story that would have included his picture on the cover.

He refused the Lasker Award (which was given to AA instead).

And posthumously (through his wife Lois), he declined a degree from his old school, Vermont's Norwich University.

When Bill died, his anonymity was broken by the press (as was Dr. Bob's at the time of his earlier death). Yet both Bill and Dr. Bob were buried without fanfare and, as they wished, there is no mention on their tombstones of their great indelible contributions to Alcoholics Anonymous.

Anonymous, New York, New York

WHERE ARE THEY NOW?
FEBRUARY 1995

Maybe I should have known I was an alcoholic when I went to school so drunk that I couldn't make it to class, and instead passed out in my high school's boiler room for six hours. Or when I misjudged the amount of 150-proof rum it would take to make my senior class retreat tolerable, and vomited all over the retreat director. Perhaps the bare fact of my daily drinking and the associated lies and theft it took to maintain it should have clued me in to the fact that I had a problem with alcohol. It didn't: my denial was etched in granite, and the well-intentioned teachers, parents, and coaches trying to divert me from the disastrous path I was on were easily ignored.

After several turbulent, painful years, I came to realize that the immense loneliness and despair I felt were somehow related to my drinking. Hoping to learn to "drink like a gentleman" — I couldn't comprehend a life without alcohol — I made a phone call one night that led me to Alcoholics Anonymous, via a local detox center. In the rooms of AA I learned the fatal nature of my illness, and in the Big Book and fellowship found a power that enabled me to stay sober one day at a time. I had just turned twenty-one years old.

The power that I found in Alcoholics Anonymous has kept me sober for nearly five years now, and has given me a life beyond my wildest dreams. Marriage, a house, an interesting job, an education — all of these things have come my way as a result of being sober and applying the principles I've learned in AA to my daily affairs. Even more importantly, I've developed a deeply satisfying spiritual life as a result of working the Steps as directed by the Big Book and a loving, caring sponsor. The past five years, however, have had a few downs as well as plenty of ups and a recent one of those downs has reminded me of the importance of the concept of singleness of purpose, both to my personal recovery and to the survival of our Fellowship.

The phrase "singleness of purpose" can be found in the account of the Fifth Tradition in the "Twelve and Twelve." Tradition Five itself reads: "Each group has but one primary purpose — to carry its message to the alcoholic who still suffers." Our Preamble, printed in the Grapevine, also discusses singleness of purpose:

"Our primary purpose is to stay sober and help other alcoholics to achieve sobriety." The chapters on Traditions Five and Six in the "Twelve and Twelve" eloquently describe how absolutely essential this concept is to the survival of AA, stating that "the very life of our Fellowship requires the preservation of this principle."

The "Twelve and Twelve" goes on (in the chapter on Tradition Ten) to describe the Washingtonian Movement, a nineteenth-century movement among alcoholics that was, initially, similar to AA in many ways. Over one hundred thousand alcoholics sobered up with the Washingtonians, before the movement self-destructed in the chaos caused by involvement in a myriad of issues unrelated, or only remotely related, to alcoholism. Lacking singleness of purpose, the movement collapsed. The experience of the Washingtonians provides compelling evidence for the importance of AA focusing directly and exclusively on the issue of alcoholism.

My strong belief in the importance of the principle of singleness of purpose for the Fellowship of AA has some important consequences. It means that when I go to a meeting, I introduce myself as an alcoholic, period. Like many alcoholics (including Bill W. — see page 7 of the Big Book), my story includes drug use, ranging from pot to crack to LSD. I don't hesitate to share this at meetings when it is relevant, as it is part of the experience that brought me to AA, and a part of my story that many other young people, especially, can relate to. However, I think it is extremely important to emphasize that I am an alcoholic, and that in meetings of Alcoholics Anonymous we discuss the common solution to alcoholism that we share. If I'm "an alcoholic and an addict" and you're "an alcoholic and a compulsive overeater" and the person leading the meeting is "an alcoholic and a compulsive gambler," we begin to lose our commonality. I become slightly different from you — an attitude that I believe is potentially fatal. Moreover, we've started down the slippery slope that doomed the Washingtonians. Our program is no longer focused on the single purpose of recovery from alcoholism, but instead is tackling the issues of drug addiction, gambling, codependency, etc. — very serious problems, undoubtedly, but outside the scope of Alcoholics Anonymous. A careful reading of Traditions Five, Six, and Ten has convinced me of how dangerous this is to the continued existence of our Fellowship, and it is my responsibility as an AA member to ensure that the hand of Alcoholics Anonymous is always available in the future to reach out to the suffering alcoholic.

I've found that the concept of singleness of purpose applies to my life in an even more immediate, personal way as well. When I got sober at twenty-one, I didn't have an established career to return to, a family to reunite, or even that much wreckage of the past to clean up. The future was a blank slate, and the newly found freedom of sobriety made the possibilities overwhelming. I immediately jumped into school, work, and relationships — and suddenly didn't have time for meetings. Life would get chaotic and painful, and I'd make my way back to the Fellowship and principles just long enough to soak up a little bit of serenity by osmosis, then head back out into the fray. Fortunately, some AA members were able to point out to me the insanity of my actions, and I was able to alter my behavior before it led me to the inevitable drink. I discovered that in order to maintain any semblance of spirituality and serenity in my life, I needed to live by the principle of singleness of purpose. Like the Fellowship as a whole, I have but one primary purpose: to stay sober and help other alcoholics achieve sobriety. The same three reasons that support our group commitment to singleness of purpose underlie my personal commitment: 1) duty — I can repay those who have given me this gift by giving it away to others; 2) love — I've learned compassion for those still suffering and want to help others; and 3) self-preservation — I must help others in order to stay sober myself. I inevitably find that when I'm able to stay focused on my primary purpose, my "secondary purposes" (school, jobs, relationships) work themselves out quite satisfactorily. For me, the concept of singleness of purpose has become the bedrock of my personal program of recovery, just as it is the fundamental principle supporting the structure of our entire Fellowship.

Brad B., San Diego, California

Special Features

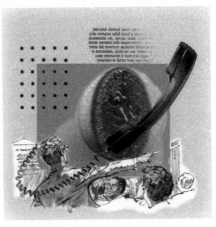

EXPERIENCE, STRENGTH, AND HOPE —
A VISIT TO THE SOVIET UNION

JULY 1989

The message of Alcoholics Anonymous knows no language barrier, nor do custom or cultural heritage have any meaning when it comes to our recovery process.

There were sixteen of us at the Moscow Beginners Group. We were there celebrating their first anniversary as an AA group. The meeting opened in Russian with the Preamble, then a reading of the Twelve Steps and the Twelve Traditions. The chairperson said, "This is a Second Step meeting," and they began to share.

One member spoke up. He was an enthusiastic Moscow businessman who was five months sober and beginning to work the

Steps. When he spoke, I heard my own alcoholism, I heard my own history of destruction and pain.

"I have no history of God in my life," he said. "But I began to do what they said to do here. And I have found a spiritual power within me. I think that might be God."

This man is now working with three other alcoholics in the group who also had no history of God in their lives, but who together have found a spiritual power they can rely on.

Inasmuch as AA can be official in any way, this was an "official" visit from the General Service Board of Alcoholics Anonymous in the United States and Canada to some very specific people in the Soviet Union. Over the previous year or so, there had been a number of communications back and forth between the Soviet and American governments concerning alcoholism; and AA, while not affiliated with these efforts in any way, had cooperated in full.

In September 1987, the general manager of the General Service Office in New York traveled by invitation to the Soviet Union with sixteen other individuals related to the field of alcoholism, as part of an exchange program between the two governments on the topic of alcoholism and drug abuse. Then, in May of 1988, a return visit was made by a group of Soviets.

Through the course of these exchanges, it became clear that there were quite a few people inside the Soviet Union who had a growing interest in Alcoholics Anonymous. We began corresponding with some of these people — Ministry of Health people, Temperance Promotion Society (TPS) people, psychologists, psychiatrists, narcologists, sobriety clubs — and in the course of this ongoing dialogue, another visit was set up which was to be independent of the previous trips.

The AA members picked for the trip were the two

trustees-at-large — myself from the United States and Webb J. from Canada — along with Sarah P., the GSO staff member assigned to the trustees' International Committee. In addition, since we'd be talking primarily with Soviet professionals and doctors, it seemed appropriate to have a doctor along with us. So Dr. John Hartley Smith, a nonalcoholic trustee from Canada, was added to the team. Of course it wouldn't have done much good to send us off without a voice, so we also added a nonalcoholic fellow who is a simultaneous translator.

Our first stop was Helsinki, Finland. We went there first for two reasons: first, we wanted to take care of jet lag and be fully adjusted to the time change; and second, the Finns have been carrying the AA message into Russia for some time and we wanted to coordinate our efforts so that each of us might be as effective as possible.

Now, I've been around drunks most of my life, but I've never seen quality drunkenness until I saw the Finns. They were big, they were like redwood trees, they were stoned, and they were moving. Finnish AA members are incredible, too. They give the same depth of love to AA that they gave to the bottle — and then some. One of the ways in which the Finns practice anonymity is by taking on a nickname. And so, in Helsinki, we met "Columbus," the fellow who first brought AA to Finland.

On November 13, we took the ferry from Helsinki to Tallinn, Estonia. Tallinn was one of the most beautiful cities I'd ever seen. There were buildings there which had been built in the 1400s and were still in use. Estonia was in the Soviet Republic, but it is a separate culture.

We'd carried with us a good-sized box of Russian-language AA literature, and though I knew we'd be stopped, I had no idea how this literature would be received. I've been through plenty of tough customs checks before — and after one of them, I ended up in prison — and I was getting a little nervous. I'd brought along a pocket knife to open up the box with, but I couldn't find it anywhere and ended up having to open up the box with a plastic pocket comb. The customs lady took out a piece of literature, looked at it, and walked off to show it to a fellow in a suit standing back in a corner. Our interpreter leaned over and whispered to me, "It's an ideology check."

In a short while, the customs lady returned with a smile on her face. She called over a uniformed guard. I thought, "There goes the box." As they talked together, the interpreter leaned over. "They like it," he said.

With another burst of conversation and a nod of the head, she waved me, the box, and the interpreter on through. On the other side of the check point, the interpreter translated her last comments to the uniformed guard for me.

"Look," she had said, "they are here to help us in our struggle with alcoholism." This seemed to set the tone for the entire trip, and we started handing out literature wherever we went.

Each one of us on this trip had a sense of the immensity of our task, and each one of us had a real desire not to promote anything but rather to share our experience, strength, and hope with the professionals we came in contact with so that they might better understand AA and perhaps allow AA to happen in the Soviet Union. At one of our meetings with the Sobriety Society of Estonia, the people involved in helping alcoholics there tended to dominate and tell us of their program and to slant the conversation politically, but eventually we got across to them that helping alcoholics was our only interest.

During one of our conversations, a girl spoke up in English and said, "I have read your book [the Big Book]. How am I going to work with these AA principles if I don't believe in God?"

"Well," I said, "that's no big deal. I didn't believe in God either when I came to AA. It's not a requirement, you know." With this, the girl visibly relaxed and I heard a sigh of relief.

We also met with a doctor there, a former government official, and he kept saying how the program would have to be changed to fit the Russian people, a people with no historical cultural background of God. "It won't work here" was something we heard a lot. I must admit that I did get a bit of a chuckle out of this. Quite a few times I heard people say, "We don't have any historical background of God," and then in the next breath would ask, "Would you like to see the cathedral?"

At first, many of the people we talked to were reserved. But because we talked so openly about alcoholism and about ourselves, they too began to share openly. We discovered that whatever else they might be doing in terms of treatment, they were already using some of the basic principles of Alcoholics Anonymous: admission of powerlessness, an honest belief that some sort of recovery is possible, and the importance of taking a personal inventory. It was rigorous, but they were doing it. They had a thirty-question inventory that had to be renewed every six months with a doctor and a peer group. Treatment was a three-year process, and if you slipped, you went to a labor camp for two years. The official position was that after six or eight weeks of effective treatment, the patient was no longer an alcoholic. There was a cure, they believed, and it took about six to eight weeks. The only catch was that they had to keep renewing this cure or they became alcoholics again. However, the drunks we talked to said, "We know it's important to understand that we're alcoholics forevermore." And they completely understood the need to pass this information on to the next person. This, then, was the foundation of whatever was going on in the Soviet Union, and it seemed like fertile ground for AA principles to flourish in.

I was looking forward to the trip from Estonia up to Leningrad because we were going to be traveling by train and I hoped it was going to be like the Orient Express. But it turned out to be more like the milk train instead. They put the four of us into one compartment with all our luggage, one bunk apiece, and gave us a cup of black Russian tea. It was an experience that I wouldn't have missed for the world, but I certainly wouldn't want to do it again.

In Leningrad, we met with a doctor who had alcoholic patients who were trying to use the AA method, but he didn't believe it would work because of the emphasis on God. Eventually this man brought some of his patients to see us and it is our hope that the sharing that went on will one day be of some use to them. One of the excercises this doctor has his group doing for therapy purposes is to translate the Big Book. "It's not a very good translation," he said, but they don't seem to mind.

The group that this doctor worked with has been using AA for about three years, and one of the group had three years sobriety, another had one year, and another had seven months. These people were allowed to come and visit with us in our hotel rooms, something unheard of just a few years back. On our end, we were not restricted in any way in our travels. We were allowed to just wander wherever we wanted.

The people of Leningrad had a pride and a spirit like I'd never seen. At one point during our stay in Leningrad, just prior to our scheduled meeting with the Temperance Promotion Society, an American movie was shown on Soviet TV — a movie about one woman's struggle with alcoholism and her eventual sobriety in Alcoholics Anonymous. The movie created quite a response from its Soviet viewers, and the newspaper *Komsomolskaya Pravda* printed a piece with some of the hundreds of requests it received asking for more information on AA. We had the article translated and were moved by the overriding tone of the responses. Here, translated from the Russian, is just one of the many responses:

"I have acquaintances but no friends. I have spent these last ten days at home. I have not gone anywhere and will invariably get drunk. And once I go on a binge, it lasts a long time.

"I don't work anywhere. I would love to go to heaven, but my sins won't let me. I'm twenty-four. My employment record is like an index of available jobs. Besides which, last summer I was released from incarceration.

"What should I do? I don't visit my neighborhood duty officer because I know his crowning remark: 'If you don't have a job in ten days, I'll send you to the Labor-Rehabilitation Camp.' Who wants to go there? So I hide. It was better in jail. I don't know how AA can help me, but I am writing nevertheless."

The newspaper article also carried the comments of the first deputy chairman of the Temperance Promotion Society (TPS), which had recently come under fire for what appeared to be a lack of effectiveness in supplying adequate answers to the huge problem of alcoholism facing the Soviet Union. Of AA, the first deputy had this to say: "We will not forge an alliance with them. Their method is interesting, but is only partially useful for us. And we will reject it primarily because certain interested parties from across the ocean are very clearly using it to promote the American way of life. The pretext is a good one; there is nothing to be said against it. But still I will block it."

With a note of uncertainty, then — and these conflicting messages in our minds — we went off to our scheduled meeting with the TPS. Of course, we got lost along the way, literally, and as things have a way of going in AA, it turned out to be one of the greatest days I've ever had.

Finally, after wandering around the city's back streets, we found our way. Unlike our dire predictions based on the newspaper article, the TPS people were very cordial, very kind, very open, very pro-AA. While we were there talking, a television producer showed up with her camera crew asking for permission to do some filming for a ten-minute documentary on Alcoholics Anonymous for Soviet television. We started to explain our Traditions, of course, and she cut us off; she understood them quite well, she assured us, and promised to maintain our anonymity. So, as we began to talk with the TPS people, the cameraman went to work. Rather than showing any faces, he focussed in on our hands as we were talking.

At the end of the meeting, the producer commented that she didn't think ten minutes was going to be nearly enough to give a sense of Alcoholics Anonymous to the Soviet public. So what they intended to do, at their own expense, was to travel to the United States in order to prepare a more in-depth documentary on AA. We made plans to send them copies of some of the films and video material that AA has already produced, such as "Young People and AA," "It Sure Beats Sitting in a Cell," and "AA — An Inside View," hoping that this material would add to their understanding of AA principles and practices.

Eventually, we headed up to Moscow, and on our first day there we met with the Moscow Beginners Group. There will be debates forevermore about which was the first AA group in Russia, but this group had as good a claim as the next. It was started by an Episcopal minister who was living and working in Moscow, and it now had a number of regular attendees. It was the first Soviet AA group registered with the General Service Office in New York.

Also in Moscow we had an appointment to meet with a doctor who had written a book about alcoholism and recovery, and a good part of it was about AA and its principles. The book, it seems, was a huge popular success and had already sold out. They were going to have a public debate about this book, and a big hall had been opened up at one of the cultural palaces where everyone — police, antagonists, proponents, everybody — showed up to debate the ideas in this book. We were invited to come. It turned into quite an afternoon—one we never could have planned.

The author of the book and several other narcologists fielded most of the questions about AA and were quite right in their understanding of anonymity and the purpose of Alcoholics Anonymous. These people proved to be great advocates of AA. And by the time the debate was over, a spokesman for TPS announced in public that they would now actively support Alcoholics Anonymous.

A woman stood up in the crowd and shouted out, "How do you think Alcoholics Anonymous will work in the Soviet Union?" My compatriots looked at me.

All I could really tell her was that it would be presumptuous of me to pretend to be an expert. I had been in her country only thirteen days. How could I possibly base anything on that? But I did say that we have the experience of 114 other cultures who have used AA quite effectively, and that the only purpose of our visit to her country was to share our experience with them if it could be of any help.

Finally, we were to have a meeting with the head of TPS, the man who had made the statement in *Komsomolskaya Pravda*. This fellow was a very short man with white hair — very charming, very cordial, and tough as nails. There was no question about who he was. The first thing he did was give us a cup of tea and say, "Now, here are the rules for this get-together." He laid out how the meeting was to be conducted and said, "Since you have requested this meeting, I have asked a number of people also to be here. They are alcoholics with another way of doing things." This was all done very graciously, however, and it was clear that he wasn't opposing us in any way.

So, off we went into another room, and sure enough there was this other bunch of people there. These were alcoholics from a sobriety club formed in 1978, and the founder of the club was there. He was now twelve years sober. The club was formed to give alcoholics something to do in their spare time. They were responsible for forming their own activities — staging plays, etc. Their charter stated that members couldn't drink until death, and they told us that only two people in the last nine years had slipped. They wanted to demonstrate the sober life. The trade union bosses had helped to organize this club. It was all done through the workplace. If you were an alcoholic, your name was on the wall at work. They knew who you were and lots of peer pressure was brought to bear. Their idea was to break the cycle of alcoholism. They wanted to have a whole generation of people who were living good, healthy lives without drinking alcohol.

One of the interesting things to come out of this meeting was our awareness of how little they really understood of the concept of anonymity. "How can you get well when you don't even know each other?" was the basic question the head of TPS asked us. He said that in these sobriety clubs, people weren't anonymous to each other — they got together frequently and were much like a family.

Our last really official meeting was with the chief deputy and chief narcologist of the Ministry of Health, the governmental agency that oversees all alcoholism treatment in the Soviet Union. This guy was tough — not in any antagonistic way, but he wanted "the facts, please." He wanted to know organizational things: how AA was set up, and how his agency could use AA. He voiced his biggest concern, however, by calling AA an "uncontrolled movement."

After we'd been talking with this man for an hour or so, he asked us pointblank, "What can we do to get this thing started here?" Our response was very simple: "Give them space. Give them rooms to meet in and a little bit of space to grow in." We told him we'd send him a lot of AA information, especially the organizational stuff he was interested in.

I believe that the purpose of our visit was accomplished. More and more professionals in the Soviet Union now know about and trust the process of Alcoholics Anonymous, and we've seen indications that they're willing to give it a try. We've also found that there are some necessities that the General Service Office can provide to these people, the greatest of which would be to provide portions of the pamphlet "The AA Group" in Russian so that some of the how-to questions might begin to be resolved. They also need the pamphlet on sponsorship, and of course the Big Book.

Like the businessman from the Moscow Beginners Group, I am a fellow who had no history of God in his life. I am a common, garden-variety drunk with all kinds of other problems, whose very best thinking got him into a penitentiary; a man completely without moral standards, a man you could not trust, a man for whom the ends always justified the means, a self-centered and domineering man. And yet, because of Alcoholics Anonymous and the grace of God I was able to participate in this trip because I was sober. It could happen to anybody reading this.

There are no Russian alcoholics, no Estonian or Siberian or American alcoholics. There are only alcoholics. Of this I am now certain.

Don P., Aurora, Colorado

AA: HOW CAN WE HELP YOU?
DECEMBER 1994

Monday afternoon, August, a large city: "Alcoholics Anonymous, how can we help you?" It's a man's voice. A woman says, "I'd like to go to a meeting near me tonight."

The man gives her some meeting times, and the woman says, with great casualness, "I wonder if you can tell me what the meetings are like? I've never been to one."

The man lets out a cheerful roar. "Why didn't you say so in the first place? Well, that's great! My name is Chuck and I'm an alcoholic." Chuck tells her about a nearby beginners meeting, encourages her to introduce herself to the chairperson, and reassures her that there's nothing to worry about. He says, "You'll be very welcome there." At the end of the conversation, he says in a quietly reassuring voice, "I haven't had a drink today and that's a miracle for me."

That night, the woman walks into a beginners meeting. The room is full of warm light and laughing people, and she is indeed welcome there. For her, as for thousands of people, the first extraordinary piece in the mosaic of a sober life began with a phone call to a local intergroup.

It wasn't always so, however. In AA's infancy, questions from alcoholics seeking help were directed to "Headquarters" in New York City, where co-founder Bill W. and a few others answered the mail. But as the Fellowship grew, so did the need for local offices to handle requests for information. As Bill later put it, "Goaded by the sheer necessity of the situation, responsible old-timers in such areas would often hire a small office and a paid secretary."

Cleveland formed one of the earliest intergroups. *Dr. Bob and the Good Oldtimers* reports that by October 1939 a committee of seven was meeting once a month "to coordinate efforts regarding hospitalizations and sponsorships." Another early intergroup was in Chicago, where an AA named Sylvia used her $700 alimony payments to rent a one-room office in the Loop and pay the (non-alcoholic) secretary. From there, Sylvia directed a stream of prospects to AA. Many groups within several hundred miles can trace their origins to the work of the Chicago Central Office — including those in Green Bay, Milwaukee, and Minneapolis.

The Los Angeles Central Office was established in 1944. In those days, AA wasn't easy to find — "and we kept it that way," one old-time member, sober since 1940, remembers. "A carefully selected group of priests, judges, and policemen knew about AA; our phone number wasn't listed, and could be gotten only from information; in that way, we knew that any newcomer who found us had generally made enough of an effort to guarantee the sincerity of his desire for sobriety." The Third Tradition changed all that by removing the subjective judgment of who was sincere and who wasn't.

Today there are over 400 intergroups or central offices in the

U.S. and Canada; ten new intergroups were formed in 1993. An intergroup acts as a clearinghouse for information about local groups and meetings, and is directly responsible to the groups it serves. In turn, these groups offer financial support, provide a volunteer base for Twelfth Step work, and — through their intergroup representatives — supervise policies and procedures.

RINGING OFF THE HOOK

Intergroups are on the front lines of carrying the message to the alcoholic who still suffers. Here, the vitality of AA's Traditions is renewed as fundamental questions are asked on a daily basis: "Do I have to sign something when I join?" "What are the rules and regulations?" "Do I pay a membership fee?" "Do I have to give my name?" "Don't you AAs have to believe in God?" "I've been in prison — does that matter?"

Intergroup phones are not only a direct link to the Fellowship for the still suffering alcoholic but also a lifeline for the traveler alone in a strange town and for those needing a meeting at an unforeseen time or place. How many phone calls does a large urban center get during a month? Lee D., office manager of the Washington Area Intergroup Association (WAIA), estimates 3,000 to 4,000 calls per month. Dick P. of the Intergroup Association of Houston says, "We quit trying to figure out how many a long time ago — the phone just rings off the hook."

In addition to telephone information, intergroups offer a complex fabric of services. They are a major source of Conference-approved materials for groups and individuals; half of all AAWS literature is sold to intergroups. Other services include publishing directories of local meetings; providing rides to meetings for newcomers or out-of-towners; maintaining Twelfth Step call lists; publishing newsletters and pamphlets; arranging community-wide "speaker swaps"; supporting signing for the hearing-impaired at meetings and workshops; setting up or housing archives; acting as a resource for the public, the professional community, and the media; supporting AA in institutions such as correctional facilities; and contacting people newly discharged from prison or from treatment centers.

For example, the St. Paul Central Office has set up a temporary-contact program which links an AA member with someone just out of a correctional facility. The new person is taken to four or five meetings, introduced to people in the group, taken out to coffee, and in general made to feel welcome in AA.

The Correctional Facilities Committee of the Intergroup Association of Houston covers the whole state of Texas and is in fact older than the intergroup itself. In 1993, it donated $15,000 worth of AA literature to correctional facilities. The intergroup's Grapevine committee recently collected enough money to send 240 magazine subscriptions into prisons; this amount was then matched by the intergroup.

KEEPING THE LINES OF COMMUNICATION OPEN

Like everything else in AA, intergroups manifest a great range in practice, policy, and procedure. What would be called inconsistency in a corporate entity is, in AA, a healthy diversity. Once a year, some of these diverse organizations rub elbows at the Central Office/Intergroup Seminars, instituted in 1986 by GSO and now sponsored by the intergroups themselves. Originally intended to be an information exchange about AAWS literature printing, pricing, and distribution policies, the seminar's function has expanded. Today, it gives participants a chance to swap information, ways of doing things, and solutions to problems. Seminars are attended by intergroup office managers (those who wish to go and those whose offices can afford to send them), as well as by some trustees, delegates, and intergroup representatives. GSO and Grapevine staff attend by invitation.

Susan K., administrator of the Baltimore Intergroup Council of AA, points out that the seminar is the largest gathering of special workers in the country. The hardest thing about being a special worker, Susan says, is that "you're a paid person among a lot of volunteers. The seminar gives everyone a better understanding of the Traditions and how they work. It pulls us together." Viki E. of the Vancouver Central Office says that the seminar gives her "confirmation and affirmation that while I am a member of Alcoholics Anonymous, there's a uniqueness about who I am and what I do."

Intergroup Seminars often help to open up lines of communication between intergroups and the area general service structure. In theory, the work of intergroups runs parallel to the AA area service structure and operates in a spirit of cooperation not competition. In practice, relations between the intergroup and the area service structure may be congenial, cordial, or strained, depending on the locale. At issue are responsibilities and territories — for example, of such standing committees as CPC, PI, or Corrections — though in most locales, an attempt is made not to duplicate the work of committees. One intergroup office manager said that sometimes "there's a them-versus-us mentality. The fear is: don't step on my territory. Fortunately, service work gives us the chance to work through our fears!" Viki E. points out that the seminars increase awareness of intergroups at the Conference level.

In some areas, a liaison from the intergroup attends district meetings and area assemblies; in a few places, intergroup has a vote at the assembly. But whether a voting member or not, the intergroup liaison can keep the assembly up to date on intergroup activities and can bring back news of the area to the intergroup representatives.

MIXING BUSINESS AND RECOVERY

Most intergroups are directed by a steering committee or executive board whose members serve on a rotational basis. Month to month, anything can be on the committee's agenda — from hiring practices, employee insurance, rent changes, and buying bookshelves to networking among AAs to find free or low-cost plumbing repair.

Mesa, Arizona's East Valley Intergroup (EVI) has a nine-member steering committee that meets monthly; intergroup representatives meet the following week. Office manager Dave F. explains, "The steering committee makes recommendations which are voted on by the intergroup reps. We focus on not making policy at the steering committee level. We believe the reps should be part of the process. And the bigger the group, the better the chance that we're doing God's will." In Vancouver, the operating committee is elected from the intergroup reps and makes recommendations to that body, which has the final say. In Baltimore, a personnel committee does the hiring and firing, and authorizes purchases under $1,000; purchases over $1,000 are authorized by the intergroup reps themselves.

Mixing business and recovery is not always easy. Intergroups have many of the responsibilities and problems of other small businesses: hiring and firing of personnel, paying bills, maintaining inventory, buying supplies, and caretaking of facilities and equipment. But while businesses can be guided by questions of profits and marketing, intergroups must be guided by the Twelve Traditions and the group conscience as expressed by intergroup representatives. An intergroup's nonprofit status is not just a legal category; it's a spiritual requirement for an organization whose primary goal is helping AAs carry the message.

One of the difficulties about running an intergroup, explains Peggy B-C. of the Middle Tennessee Central Office, is that the intergroup "can't generate income as an ordinary business does. We have to maintain self-support status but we're required by the Fellowship to fit within spiritual guidelines." Baltimore's Susan K. points out that other nonprofit organizations have the ability to raise money — an activity that alarms some AA members. Susan says, "Money is a dirty topic in AA. But it costs money to carry the message."

A work base that is primarily volunteer offers its own special problems. There is always the need to replenish the volunteer pool; recruitment and training are ongoing. WAIA's Lee D. says, "It's a constant challenge to find volunteers. Then it's mostly on-the-job training — volunteers work alongside somebody else until they're ready." However, Cheryl S., assistant executive director of the Boston Central Service Committee, says that finding volunteers is rarely a problem: "Somebody's always out of work!"

Many intergroups find themselves struggling to maintain financial solvency, much less stability. Intergroup budgets generally derive from two major sources: group contributions and literature sales. One much-debated issue is whether intergroups should sell non-Conference-approved materials — for example, medallions (which are popular in many groups as a way to celebrate time in the program), non-AA literature (such as that published by Al-Anon or Hazelden), or a wide variety of recovery items, such as jewelry, lapel pins, mugs, key chains, bumper stickers, and "birth-day" cards. Many intergroups say that without the income from these items, they couldn't continue to operate. An informal survey of those present at the most recent Intergroup Seminar showed that about half sold non–Conference-approved material.

The Washington Area Intergroup Association is one of the inter-groups that has chosen to sell a commercial item. Last year, although its prudent reserve was in good shape, its finances were "down." Manager Lee says: "We were afraid of a deficit. To earn more money, we decided to sell chips." The decision wasn't reached overnight; the issue had been in discussion for several years. Houston's Dick P. says that between sixty-five and seventy percent of his total sales are of non-AA items. "We would just close our doors if we did not sell these items. And the groups want them — they prefer one-stop shopping." Omaha Central Committee's office manager Bill S. estimates that one-half of his sales are from non-AA items; only one-tenth of the intergroup's income derives from contributions. "Without non-Conference-approved materi-als, I'd be operating in the red," Bill explains.

However, some intergroups with small budgets do manage to survive. The Flathead Valley Intergroup of Whitefish, Montana is an example. This intergroup is closely associated with the Whitefish Group, which has been meeting above a clothing store since its inception in 1953. The intergroup doesn't have a physi-cal facility but literature is available at the meeting. The group sells only Conference-approved literature; Dennis L. explains, "We did sell *Twenty-four Hours a Day* and *The Little Red Book* but enough of us didn't approve of it and it got changed. If you have a book that you cherish, that's fine, but I don't think we should sell everything." Dennis says that the twenty-three groups the intergroup serves "send a little bit once in a while." Valley Intergroup supports a twenty-four-hour answering service, produces a meeting list every six months, and publishes a monthly newsletter (a volunteer types it and runs it off). It also sponsors a campout; Dennis says, "We go to a lake for the weekend, take potluck, play horseshoes, play guitars, and sing." There's a fund-raising roundup every three years.

Mesa's EVI, which serves 330 meetings in its area, also sells only Conference-approved literature and Grapevine materials. At EVI, about $30,000 a year comes from contributions and $25,000 from literature sales. Manager Dave F. says, "I'm a vocal advocate of not carrying non-AA materials. Our own literature is confusing enough to the newcomer. And as somebody once said, 'You don't go to a Ford dealer to get GM parts.'"

REACHING OUT FOR HELP

Why should intergroups be struggling to keep in the black? Don't most groups contribute to their local intergroup?

The answer is no. Contributions are voluntary, and a contribution is not a requirement for being listed in an intergroup directory. Meanwhile, revenues to many branches of AA have decreased — from group contributions to Grapevine subscriptions — perhaps because of the economy.

In some areas, group contributions are down because the growth of new groups means smaller memberships which cannot support donations. Small groups may also have difficulty electing service workers — including intergroup reps — and this means the group doesn't get news about its local intergroup. Marlene S. of the Brevard (Florida) Intergroup says, "A lot of the meetings we list in the directory aren't actual groups — they aren't registered, and they don't support the service structure or donations to New York or intergroup." Marlene hopes that one answer to the problem is to encourage DCMs to get groups registered.

Sometimes intergroups are seen, as Peggy B-C. says, as "a stepchild — an unneeded stepchild. The perception is, 'Why should I give money to a central office when it doesn't have anything to do with me?' To be honest, I used to be one of the detractors. I thought intergroup was wasting my money. Then I was elected intergroup rep and got a very different view. I believe there has to be a central office where the alcoholic can call and connect to the Fellowship as a whole."

Lee of WAIA says: "There are many new people who don't realize how important their contributions to intergroup are. Some people have no idea who we are or what we do." In order to educate AA members, WAIA has an outreach program that goes into groups to explain what it does and to solicit support — not money, but volunteers. Sometimes WAIA intergroup representatives simply show up at a meeting and announce that they'll be available afterwards to answer questions. Lee says, "It's very important to keep the lines of communication open."

Baltimore Intergroup has launched a concerted effort to bring information to more groups in its area. It has published a pamphlet, "What is Our Intergroup?", initiated an outreach program which conducts workshops for group and meeting secretaries, formed a committee which makes personal contact with groups that have faded away, and visits new groups as well as groups that ask for support and groups celebrating their anniversaries. The stated aims for these activities are to strengthen groups, encourage adherence to the Traditions, discourage groups from indulging in discussion of outside issues, rekindle interest in service work and participation in intergroup activities, and encourage financial support for the local intergroup.

In 1993, staff members from the St. Paul Central Office went to AA meetings (eighty percent of the groups were reached) and asked for a few minutes to explain what intergroup was and what it did, to describe the Twelfth Step opportunities available in the office, and to make a soft pitch on contributions — especially the Faithful Fiver program, in which individual AAs pledge five dollars a month to intergroup.

Another source of income is the fund-raiser: the roundup, picnic, dinner, or other AA-related event. New York City Intergroup holds the annual Bill W. Dinner Dance, which celebrates Bill's sobriety date and raises money. The city of Defiance, Indiana hosts a hog roast. East Valley Intergroup sponsors a spring dinner dance, a fall old-timer's meeting, and a summer picnic. Baltimore's "Bull Roast" — a Sunday afternoon picnic with AA speakers and dancing — recently erased a $9,000 deficit.

NEW TECHNOLOGY HELPS CUT COSTS

All intergroups look for ways to economize. Increasingly, they are taking advantage of newer technology to cut costs. Computerization allows them to reduce staff, store data accurately and access it faster, and do their own printing. Computerized telephoning services provide cost-effective round-the-clock telephone answering by alcoholics: at EVI, for example, a "call diverter" forwards calls on nights and weekends to volunteers' homes. With EVI's system, the only continuing cost after the initial equipment cost is a second phone line for the outgoing "diverted" calls. Smaller intergroups have special problems: EVI's office manager plans ahead and puts in big orders so he can buy literature from GSO and the Grapevine at quantity discounts. Small intergroups also can pool orders with neighboring intergroups in order to get the discounts.

WHAT THE FUTURE HOLDS

Changes in the way medical services are paid for may mean a reduction of inpatient services in the future, and this may mean an increase in the Twelfth Step function of intergroups. In Tennessee, for example, the number of people who go through treatment facilities has been cut dramatically, and in the view of Peggy B-C., this isn't a bad thing. "I think this is going to save Alcoholics Anonymous. It seems to me that too many AAs have abdicated their responsibility — they depend on treatment to do Twelfth Step work. Twelfth Step work is what keeps us sober. It kept Bill W. sober." Twelfth Step work lies at the heart of every intergroup, as it does at the heart of the Fellowship. It's the wet drunk and the newcomer who renew AA's purpose.

This article began with the story of a woman, sober less than twenty-four hours, calling her local intergroup. The woman never found out who answered her call, though his kindness on the phone, his good cheer, and his gratitude were not forgotten. The man himself remained anonymous, a volunteer working the phones at intergroup on a summer afternoon.

COMING OF AGE

MAY 1995

The co-founder of Alcoholics Anonymous, Bill W. was what might be called a constructive worrier: he could easily imagine worst-case scenarios, but he could also imagine workable solutions to problems. By the mid-nineteen-forties, Bill looked around at the Fellowship, and this worrisome question came to him: What will happen to AA when the old-timers are gone? It was a question that most AAs didn't want to think about.

The Fellowship of Alcoholics Anonymous began as an organization of loosely associated entities — the AA groups — bound only by suggestions, "principles," and "traditions," not rules or regulations. The natural autonomy of the groups was balanced only by the need to have a centralized source for information, literature, and public relations. In the Fellowship's early years, this source was Headquarters: the New York office and the Alcoholic Foundation (a rather grand term for what was essentially a board of trustees consisting originally of five members — three nonalcoholics and two AAs). For a long time, the office was mostly Bill, his nonalcoholic secretary Ruth Hock, and an assorted staff of volunteers. The Alcoholic Foundation, which was set up in 1938, monitored the legal, business, and financial end of AA.

This arrangement was fine as long as AA was in its infancy. But as the AA population grew, thrived, and stabilized, it became apparent that this program for recovery was no mere experiment — it was going to endure — and Bill saw two problems for the future. First, there was no link between the AA members and

Headquarters. Second, AA's policy was being set by the trustees, who were not *directly* responsible to those they served.

Bill's worst-case scenario about the future went like this: "When death and disability finally took us few old-timers out of the picture, where would that leave the Trustees and the Headquarters? A single blunder on their part might cause a failure of confidence that could not be repaired. Lacking the moral and financial support of the groups, the whole Headquarters effort might collapse completely. Our services might never be reinstated because nobody could be authorized to do the job."

Bill knew that the Fellowship was used to relying on him and Dr. Bob and other old-timers, but he felt that eventually, AA members would want to run their own affairs. And whether they wanted to or not, they were going to have to face a growing-up process; after all, the old-timers were — as Bill put it — "perishable." Bill believed it was critical that the authority of AA should derive from AA itself — that is to say, from the broad spectrum of the membership. This authority, he came to believe, should be funneled through a practical body — an elected conference or an advisory council — which would be primarily representational and democratic. The AA membership, Bill wrote in a letter, should "assume some responsibility for its all too isolated Headquarters Services and, at the same time, afford our Trustees a real cross-section of AA opinion for their better guidance."

RENOUNCING AUTHORITY

In late 1945, Bill wrote a long memo to the board of trustees in which he introduced the possibility of holding a small yearly conference of "older members from all parts of the country for the purpose of meeting with the trustees, the Grapevine editor, and the national secretary." He went on to say that he and Dr. Bob had found "that the more we renounce our own claims to authority and power the more does group confidence in us rise" — perhaps tactfully laying the groundwork for the trustees to do the same kind of renouncing. He was trying to bring the grass-roots Fellowship into the decision-making arena.

The reaction of the trustees to what Bill was calling a "general service conference" was negative. They didn't share Bill's urgent sense that AA's future was in jeopardy, and they believed they could continue to handle AA's affairs with competence and fairness. A lot of AA old-timers around the country also felt that the status quo was just fine. But after Bill and Lois undertook a cross-country trip in 1948, Bill concluded that most AAs were behind the idea of a conference.

EASY DOES IT — BUT DO IT

When Bill was convinced that an idea was good for the Fellowship, he became tenacious. The conference became a near obsession for him, and his strong-arm tactics alienated many AAs and even some of his friends on the board. Dr. Bob was also unenthusiastic about the idea of a conference; he advised Bill in a letter to let the idea rest for a while: " 'Easy Does It' is the best course to follow. . . ."

"Easy does it" might have been good advice, but it wasn't always Bill's style. He continued to try to talk Dr. Bob into the idea of a conference, and he finally succeeded in the summer of 1950. Several weeks after the 1950 International Convention in Cleveland — where Dr. Bob had given his last, brief talk — Bill went to Akron and got Dr. Bob's go-ahead. (Dr. Bob died on November 16, 1950.) Meanwhile, Bernard Smith, the nonalcoholic chairman of the Board of Trustees, persuaded the board that the conference was a good idea.

So the General Service Conference was born, with a certain

amount of dissension and personality clashes, for the course of AA's history did not always run smooth in those early years. Bill called the Conference "a coming of age," and indeed, growing-up isn't always easy. He wrote to an AA friend in December 1950 that "the organization and functioning of the Conference is no world-shaking matter," adding hopefully, "Sunday school teachers and bartenders alike seem to bring off such events without undue harm. Maybe we can, too." The Conference was adopted on an experimental or provisional basis for five years, from 1951 to 1955.

"THE HOUR IS COME"

As he often did on important matters, Bill turned to the pages of the Grapevine to communicate with the Fellowship about the Conference. In the November 1950 issue, he wrote: "So the hour is come when you must take these things into your own keeping. We ask that you guard them well, for the future of Alcoholics Anonymous may much depend on how you maintain and support these lifegiving Arms of Service. Anticipating that you will happily accept this new responsibility, the Trustees, Dr. Bob and I propose the General Service Conference of Alcoholics Anonymous; a body of state and provincial representatives who will sit yearly with our Foundation trustees as their traditional guide. We have long considered and will soon present a detailed plan designed to bring this great change about."

The first General Service Conference convened in New York for four days in April 1951. Attendees included members of the Alcoholic Foundation (renamed the General Service Board), staffers from the Headquarters Office and the Grapevine, and, most importantly, delegates from the Fellowship. Delegates from half the areas attended; these were called the First Panel; the

Second Panel joined the first one the following year. Thus every Conference has two overlapping panels of delegates — one set of "veterans" and one of "newcomers."

In the June 1951 Grapevine, the delegate from California summed up the importance of the Conference. The delegate wrote: "I know how frightening it is to all of us to think of Bill ever leaving; I know also he can never be replaced. But Bill believes, and I gather Dr. Bob also believed, that he and Bill can be replaced by a principle, that being the collective conscience of AA speaking through the delegates of the General Service Conference."

The collective conscience of AA made several important decisions during that first Conference:

• The temporary Conference charter should be approved for the following three years.

• All AA "textbooks" should have Conference approval.

• All AA groups should be informed as to the 1951 Headquarters budget [which was $107,000].

• It should be suggested that AA groups wishing to contribute to AA general services give a minimum of two dollars per member for the year.

• Nonalcoholic trustees should continue to serve on the board of trustees.

COLLECTIVE AND EVOLVING PRINCIPLES

A GSO staffer who served on the Conference assignment in 1995, Valerie O'N., points out what a radical idea the Conference was when it was first conceived. In most human institutions, a leader who's stepping down arranges to hand over his power to one or two people he's personally selected. But, as Valerie says, "Bill didn't groom a successor to be 'Bill Jr.' — he chose a concept over people." The Conference replaced the guiding forces of the old-timers (personalities) with the collective and evolving principles of AA. It was based on rotation of power, and it elevated principles over personalities.

In this system, every member has a voice. Any AA member or group may participate directly in the Conference by writing GSO or by giving their input to their GSR, DCM, or area representative. Valerie explains, "Not every request or idea will reach the Conference floor, but every one is treated with dignity, honor, and respect."

In 1955, at the end of the provisional period, the Conference met in St. Louis just before the International Convention was held there. At the Convention, the Fellowship as a whole ratified the idea of the Conference and thus made it a permanent arm of AA. Bill offered a resolution, adopted by the Convention, which said in part that the Conference "should now become the permanent successor to the founders of Alcoholics Anonymous, inheriting from them all their former duties and special responsibilities, thus avoiding in future time all possible strivings for individual prestige or personal power, and also providing our Society with the means of functioning on a permanent basis."

HOW IT WORKS

The present-day Conference meets for a week every April. The voting members of the Conference are the delegates, the General Service Board of trustees, the AAWS Board, the Corporate Board of the Grapevine, and the AA staff members at the General Service Office and the Grapevine. The work of the Conference truly begins when the committees meet. There are conference committees for agenda, finance, treatment facilities, correctional facilities, literature, trustees, cooperation with the professional community, public information, policy and admissions, report and charter, and the Grapevine. Committees examine issues received from a variety of sources — groups, individuals, delegates, DCMs, GSRs, GvRs, area assemblies, and the trustees' committees. After two days of discussion, the committee decides whether to table an idea, make a suggestion, or make a recommendation. Later in the week, the entire body convenes to hear the committee reports and to vote on recommendations.

After each committee makes its report, those who want to speak on the issue go to the nearest of six microphones. Sometimes the lines at the microphones can get pretty long, and those who are chairing the meeting try to keep things rolling by calling on people in order of their arrival. To make speakers stay focused, there's a two-minute limit on speaking; after two minutes, a light goes off and the speaker must retire.

For the vote, hands are raised and counted by volunteer delegates or staff. Recommendations that are passed by two-thirds of the Conference become Advisory Actions. For those recommendations that pass, the minority opinion is allowed to be heard: that is, after the vote, those who are in opposition may speak once again to the issue. An interesting possibility then proposes itself: if someone *who voted with the majority* has now changed her or his mind, possibly as a result of hearing the minority opinion, they may call for a re-vote. Charles M., delegate from Tennessee, explains that he heard a minority opinion and changed his vote: "I got up at one of the microphones and I said, 'I apologize. I didn't do my job as a delegate. I was a sheep, just going along with somebody else's opinion.' "

Conference voting can become a marathon event, going from Wednesday night, all day Thursday, through Friday morning, with brief times out for meals. Out in the hall where the big coffee urns are always on, the debate may continue one on one.

The Conference coordinator made a point about the responsibility of the General Service Conference: "We aren't the only general service structure in the world. But because we've been around longer, our Conference does set an example. It provides a sober reference. We have an historical obligation not just to our U.S. and Canadian membership but to the Fellowship worldwide."

This responsibility is felt in a very personal way by the delegates — those who have been given "delegated responsibility" by the Fellowship. The Conference represents the intersection of business and spirituality, where the business practices and policies of AA are reviewed in light of the fundamental principles of the program. Robert P., a delegate from Quebec from 1991 to 1992, said for him the biggest fear was that in attending to business, "we would lose track of the simple AA spirit." However, the AA spirit always seems to prevail. Sandy C., a delegate from Southwest Texas, said she was impressed that the Conference was "structured but not rigid. It was flexible enough to work with real human beings. There was an openness there."

SPIRITUAL PREPARATION

Robert said the best advice he could give a new delegate is to be prepared spiritually and to know the Concepts and the Traditions. What does spiritual preparation provide? "It helped me realize I was powerless. Sometimes at the Conference, I was overwhelmed. I thought: I'm not prepared! I'm not good enough! On the first day of voting, I went into a corner and I meditated for a few minutes. I realized I wasn't a boss, I was just an instrument. I had to rely on the trust my area had put in me. I didn't have to be perfect. Understanding that, I saw that the Conference wasn't so overwhelming."

Sandy said, "It's scary because it's a responsibility. I feel inadequate sometimes." She added, laughing, "I think, I'm just a drunk! What am I doing here?" Did she feel any tension between what her area wanted and how her conscience directed her to vote? "No," she said. "My area is wonderful. They sent me up there with no agenda — just to do the best that I could. I was truly a trusted servant."

The purpose of the Conference is to reach an informed group conscience decision — a coming together of opinion, thought, feeling. The process by which it does this is a changing dance of talking and listening: sometimes lengthy and intricate, sometimes brief and to the point. Participants learn by listening — and since they sometimes change their minds, a discussion can go on for a long time, as issues are thrashed out and understood and language is revised. Delegates need willingness and patience. Susan C., a past delegate from Virginia, described the way one group conscience was achieved: "Someone made a comment, and I could feel the whole room shift: 'Oh yeah — oops, we forgot about that!' And the vote changed."

Shaaron J., who had just rotated as delegate from Central Southeast Ohio, described how she felt before her first Conference: "I came to the first Conference with preconceived ideas. Negative. Defensive. Looking for problems. But now I have a totally different viewpoint. I believe in the system itself. Mistakes are made, there are problems, but overall, the process works." What suggestions would she give to the delegate who became her successor? "Keep an open mind. I was very against the pocket edition of the Big Book, but after I sat there and listened to delegates from other areas, I changed my mind. One delegate made it clear for me: What are we doing for the still-suffering alcoholic? That's the bottom line."

REACHING A CONSENSUS

Debate, disagreement, even downright controversy may be inevitable components of decision making at the Conference. Charles M. believed that controversy was necessary, and that in fact it was part of the learning process for the individual AA: "With my head stuck in a jug, I didn't have to face pain or discomfort; I never had to learn anything. But I think that's why we're here, that's our primary purpose in living — to learn our lessons. Through service — through the pains and trials and tribulations — I'm kind of catching up. I'm learning." But he added: "It took me a long, long time to get to this point. Now I can sit quietly and listen to somebody rave and really listen and keep an open mind and see if there's anything to learn."

Susan said that the Conference "tested my patience and tolerance, but it also gave me a great deal of love and trust. It gave me the sense of being connected to something much greater."

Sometimes it isn't possible for the Conference to reach a consensus. In 1993 and 1994, for example, the Conference considered whether the Grapevine should continue to produce the Wall Calendar and Pocket Planner. After much intelligent debate, a vote was taken on the question, but in neither year was there a two-thirds majority, so no recommendation was made. (Instead, the 1994 Conference recommended that: All AA members be strongly urged to work toward the goal that the AA Grapevine magazine be self-supporting through the sale of magazine subscriptions.)

Not every Conference will deal with life and death issues: the Conference tends to respond rather than to initiate. It's in place to deal with the regular business matters of AA, and should a crisis ever arise, it will be there and ready to respond.

BRINGING IT ALL BACK HOME

The Conference week may be intense and challenging, but it's only one part of the delegate's job. When the Conference is over, delegates go back to their home areas and report on the Conference. Robert explained, "At the June assembly, I recounted my week in New York as I had lived it. I tried to give the spirit of the week — this is at least as important as the decisions that were made. I tried to be honest, I told when things were difficult." Last year, Susan C. spent twenty vacation and personal-leave days from her job, going to the districts in her area to tell them about the Conference.

How does the Conference affect those who participate in it? Susan said, "There's a subtle change in delegates between their first and second Conference. They become *stiller*. They quiet down. They watch and listen more. They step out of their own way."

For Sandy C., the Conference was a "life-changing experience." Sandy comes from a town of 1,000 inhabitants — "a little bitty town where I can count the cars that go by on one hand. The people in my town can't figure out why I'm always putting suitcases in the car and leaving my husband for days at a time!" Her very first plane ride was to a regional forum in St. Louis; she said, "And I'm a person who doesn't make left turns!" Like many other delegates, Sandy discovered that New York City doesn't live up to its unpleasant reputation. "I thought that everybody in New York was going to be mean and ugly and awful, but they were great. They were as nice as they are here in Little River." Charles M. agreed: "I fell in love with New York when I was up there. I loved the variety, the colorful characters, the street performers, even the scents and the sounds."

The first Saturday after Sandy returned from the Conference, she flew to South Padre Island (from the nearest airport in Austin, seventy miles away) to bring them the news of the Conference. Then she set out to visit all parts of her area, travelling 10,000 miles in four months; she was gone every weekend from May through November. "Before I stood for delegate," Sandy said, "I talked to my family about this. I said, you're important and I won't do this if you don't want me to." Sandy's kids were grown and she had a sympathetic husband. "But for six months my kids had to make an appointment if they wanted to see me!"

Like many other delegates, Sandy's Conference experience — as she put it — "reaffirmed my faith in the Fellowship." Forty-four Conferences have come and gone since the first panel was convened in 1951; there is a new generation of old-timers and newcomers. AA has survived and prospered for many reasons — including the success of the Conference structure.

Bill W. once wrote that the General Service Conference could never be "a policeman or a law-giver for AA." Rather, it is a source of guidance and a reflection of our common purpose. Valerie O'N. says, "Self-support doesn't always mean money — it also means personal responsibility"; the Conference is one of the ways we take responsibility for AA.

As Charles M. said: "I knew why I was at the Conference. I was there as a representative of AA — to perpetuate our existence and to find new and better ways to carry the message." Because of the

Conference, we, like our founders, can help protect the Fellowship — its present policies and its future survival.

$\approx$

CORPORATE POVERTY

MARCH 1997

This article is adapted from a presentation given by Gary A. Glynn, Class A (nonalcoholic) trustee at a general sharing session of the General Service Board, October 1994.

The subtitle for this sharing session on corporate poverty is: "spiritual and practical principles that assure AA's future." That got me thinking. I think in AA, spiritual and practical are the same thing. Imagine someone coming into service who wanted to have some influence in AA and promoted some practical-sounding idea that had no spiritual merit. The Fellowship would quickly put a stop to that. Such a person would have to find some idea with a spiritual basis — even if he didn't believe it. So anything that is going to be of any practical use to us has to be spiritual as well.

At the same time, it looks to me as if AA, beginning with Bill W., has quickly dropped any spiritual-sounding ideas that don't pass the practical tests of keeping alcoholics sober or keeping AA together.

So, is corporate poverty a spiritual and practical principle that will assure AA's future? Of course it is.

In the Seventh Tradition, when talking about how AA acted when it found out about the bequests that were coming its way, Bill wrote, "The pressure of that fat treasury would surely tempt the board to invent all kinds of schemes to do good with such funds, and so divert AA from its primary purpose. The moment that happened, our Fellowship's confidence would be shaken. The board would be isolated, and would fall under heavy attack of criticism from both AA and the public. Then our trustees wrote a bright page in AA history. They declared for the principle that AA must always stay poor. Bare running expenses plus a prudent reserve would henceforth be the Foundation's financial policy." He went on to say, "At that moment, we believe, the principle of corporate poverty was firmly and finally embedded in AA tradition."

That sounds pretty simple: avoid schemes that divert us from our primary purpose and only have enough money around to meet bare running expenses and maintain a prudent reserve. I don't think anyone in this room would object to those statements, so why are we sharing about them? The reason is that they mean different things to different people.

The Concepts try to help us a little more in making these principles concrete, but the Concepts can be confusing, especially about the power of the purse and our prudent reserve, which usually are at the center of debates about corporate poverty. In the first warranty, Bill tells us why a dictator wouldn't last a year: "And in the brief time he did last, what would he use for money? Our Delegates, directly representing the groups, control the ultimate supply of our service funds." Sounds here like the power of the purse is supposed to be immediate, doesn't it? That's on page 63 [of *Twelve Concepts for World Service*]. On page 65, in the second warranty, writing about what hard times might do to AA, Bill says, "Our present reserve and its book income could see us through several years of hard times without the slightest diminution in the strength and quality of our world effort." Sounds here as if immediate wasn't what he had in mind after all.

Throughout Bill's writings, there's the sense of his recognizing the balancing act he was asking us to take on. Too much, and we argue over perilous wealth and power and lose sight of our primary purpose of carrying the message. Too little, and we risk losing the ability to carry the message at all. So he spoke for both sides in different places.

What are the issues here? AA groups are formed and dissolved all the time, and a reserve of one or two months for a group seems adequate to a lot of people. I've been asked, "If one or two month's reserve is okay for a group, why do we need ten or twelve at GSO?" For one thing, it is probably easier to form a new group than it is to form a new GSO. There is no alternative GSO to turn to if ours goes under. The services we provide have been built up out of many years' collective experience and would be hard to recreate. Also, despite the eagerness of others to publish some of our literature, GSO needs to continue to publish regularly without the threat of interruption so the message of sobriety will continuously be available, both through the written message itself and the services supported in part by literature profits. Many of our projects extend over a considerable period of time, like financing new translations or planning a convention. I think the Fellowship takes the financial stability of GSO for granted and assumes it will always stay that way.

Bill wrote about how Alcoholics Anonymous got the outside world's attention when the world realized AA was going to be self-supporting. He pointed out that most people viewed alcoholics as financially irresponsible. When I tell people who don't know much about AA that we accept no outside contributions, and are self-supporting and solvent, the reaction is amazement and admiration. AA has such a solid reputation with the public.

When we discuss the idea that it might be sound to lower our Reserve Fund to come closer to some supposedly more spiritual level of corporate poverty, we should recognize that we would also be coming closer to the point of running out of money if we run into hard times or if some of those "possible demands on the Reserve Fund" occur at inconvenient intervals. The lower our Reserve Fund, the higher the risk of some financial accident where we run out of money. What would we do if we ran out of money? A financial failure of AA would do incalculable harm to our reputation with the public, the Fellowship, and with some poor drunk who's looking for a reason to believe AA doesn't work.

If we ran out of money, we might have to borrow from a bank temporarily to keep the doors open. If we did that, we would lose some measure of financial independence. A strong Reserve Fund is one of the prices we have to pay to assure that no one but the Fellowship sets our financial policies. And continually debating whether the Reserve Fund is perilously large is part of the price.

One counter to that argument is that if there ever was a real emergency, AA groups would increase their contributions and rescue GSO. This argument says, in effect, that we should rely on our Higher Power operating through the groups to save us from our own imprudence. Maybe that would work. If we rely on that, we wouldn't have to worry about the accuracy of our budgets, our accounting, or much of anything really. This may be the place to invoke Bill's comment in the Ninth Concept about casting the whole idea of planning for tomorrow onto a fatuous idea of Providence. I don't believe that because God looks after AA, it doesn't matter what we do in the practical realm. It's risky to ask our Higher Power to bail us out of trouble when we can avoid it ourselves by budgeting solidly, running GSO and the Grapevine in a businesslike manner, and keeping at least ten months' expenses in our Reserve Fund. I know that some responsible people in service think nine or even eight months might be okay. The treasurer probably should be a bit more conservative than most of you.

I also think that if we ever had to go to the groups and say, for example, "If you don't send us $500,000 of contributions within the next three months we'll have to lay off half of our staff and cancel the Conference," the reaction probably wouldn't be, "Oh, aren't they spiritual at GSO, practicing corporate poverty. Well, anyone can make a mistake. Let's send them more money." I think the actual and proper response from the groups would be that GSO didn't know what it was doing and shouldn't be trusted with any money at all.

But it is true that some groups are reluctant to contribute to GSO when they see a $9 million Reserve Fund. The problem with focusing on this amount is that the dollar amount low enough to counter that reluctance is so low that we would be running severe risks if we got to that level. That's the main reason we've been displaying our financial numbers on a per-group basis as well as in total, like $156 per group for the amount in the Reserve Fund. This is not a trick; it's a way to point out to the Fellowship how large we are. A large Fellowship will show large absolute dollar numbers.

Bill W. solved the question of whether a prudent reserve inhibited contributions. He wrote, "It is said that the impression is created that AA Headquarters is already well off and that hence there is no need for more money. This is not at all the general attitude, however, and its effect on contributions is probably small." I wish I could get away with simply asserting that conclusion the way Bill did, but I don't think I can.

I think the keys here are, first, we must be true stewards with AA's money, acting as if we were poor even if we have a prudent Reserve Fund. No one is going to send us contributions if we are perceived as wasting money or spending it in marginally effective ways. I have said elsewhere that there were two ways to avoid going over the twelve-month limit on the Reserve Fund: spend more money or reduce literature income. I said, "We will not increase spending above ordinary amounts unless the Fellowship clearly indicates a desire for new services. We must control spending, despite the presence of a large Reserve Fund, with the same sense of stewardship that we would exercise if the Reserve Fund were small." I believe that truly and think it's a reasonable description of corporate poverty in practice. And in fact that's what we did, reducing pamphlet and other literature prices in a way that makes it easier to carry the message and helps groups' finances.

The other two keys to more contributions, and what I think is much more important — the number of groups contributing — are, first, explaining what the money is spent on, which we are now able to do with our new reports, and second, emphasizing the spiritual benefits of making contributions. Contributions are as important to the contributor as they are to the recipient. Contributions are very important for AA unity because making contributions gives the groups an opportunity to know that they are part of carrying the message of AA around the world.

Group contributions are important to us and they must always be at a high enough level so we hear the Fellowship directly, but I've never understood the equation that group contributions equals self-support but literature sales do not. I agree completely with Bill W. that book profits are "actually the sum of a great many contributions which book buyers make to the general welfare of Alcoholics Anonymous. The certain and continuous solvency of our world service rests squarely upon these contributions. Looked at in this way, our Reserve Fund is actually the aggregate of many small sacrifices made by the book buyers."

What I'm trying to say is that corporate poverty is more a state of mind than the size of our bank account. We all know people and organizations that extravagantly spend money they don't have, living beyond their means either by ignoring the facts of their finances or by assuming a rosy tomorrow. So you can in fact be poor and not practice corporate poverty. It happens to museums and opera companies all the time. The opposite is also possible, that we can maintain a prudent reserve without falling into the temptation of spending it just because it's there. One fear I hear expressed is that GSO might ignore the will of the Fellowship because we have a prudent reserve. My experience at board weekends, the Conference, and AAWS and Grapevine corporate board meetings is that there is no danger of that. First of all, group contributions pay for three-quarters of services spending. But even more important, we listen because we know we should and must.

One advantage of having a sound prudent reserve is that it makes it easier for us to sign a lease for office space on good terms. A reserve fund is one of the few ways a nonprofit has to show a landlord that it is creditworthy. Another big advantage is that it lets us plan with better budgets. The year 1994 is a good example. We used best estimates throughout the budget. If we had had only five or six months' expenses in reserve, we would have had to use more conservative budget estimates, which would have meant either cutting expenses or raising literature prices to balance our budget, which we never had to contemplate. I wouldn't have been able to support reducing literature prices at mid-year, even though it was the right thing to do from a service point of view, if we had only had a six months' Reserve Fund.

I started out by saying that if it wasn't spiritual it wouldn't work in AA and if it wasn't practical, it wasn't spiritual. A solid, prudent Reserve Fund and good business management skills are both spiritual and practical. It is neither practical nor spiritual to accumulate more or spend more than we need to. It is also neither practical nor spiritual to run out of money. As usual Bill has a good phrase for what we need. He called it fiscal common sense.

Old-Timers Corner

LOVE

SEPTEMBER 1988

The spiritual growth we enjoy in Alcoholics Anonymous is a product of the never-ending school for living which our Fellowship provides. The subject in that school that opened my eyes most quickly and filled my heart most fully was love.

I never knew what true love was until I began my recovery in AA. My schooling in that emotion began early and led me to the conclusion that love is what creates in a sober AA member the outer show of an inner glow.

I misunderstood the mutuality of love so much that when I heard a husky guy at a men's stag meeting say, "You can just feel the love that fills this room," I leaned over to whisper to my sponsor, "I think I've got to go outside and throw up." He whispered right back, "Go ahead, then rush back and start learning about love." I did and I've kept learning ever since.

Discoveries about love started when someone explained that AA love is basically wishing someone well. We wish those who share our disease and solutions "the very best," which is continued sobriety. No one will ever wish a fellow alcoholic a return to the bottle, even one whom he may dislike. I was told, "Getting sober means you don't have to like someone to love him."

I came to AA from forty years in a cutthroat business where it was considered stupidity to do a favor for someone who would never be in a position to return that favor. So it was a revelation to find it easy and rewarding to care and share, to know that it is impossible to lovingly give without receiving or to get without giving with love.

I was moved deeply when I read and accepted the reality of Dr. Bob's statement that our Twelve Steps simmered down to two words: love and service. And I became aware how well those two words blend, for love without service is sentimentality and service without love is an empty gesture.

The role played by love in our program emerged even more clearly when I was told, "Let us love you until you can learn to love yourself" and "Live in our hearts and pay no rent." How well I knew then that I belonged in AA, that I was at last *home*, that I would never again be alone, that I would, as our Big Book tells us, make lifelong friends in an atmosphere where there is always love.

My class in love continued. I learned that love is the motivating force behind the attitude of gratitude and the emotion that makes true the shortest paragraph in our book: "It works. It really does." It is the force behind the reality in another sentence from the book: "The age of miracles is still with us."

The love I found in AA assured me that there are no strangers in our Fellowship, only friends we haven't yet met.

The truths came surely and rapidly in the class on love. In AA there's no recrimination and no lecturing of those who drink and then return. They are lovingly told, "There is no disgrace in falling. The only shame is not getting back on your feet and trying again."

Our love is both the result of, and the motivation for, such emotions as humility, gratitude, honesty, faith, hope, tolerance, and trust. It produces togetherness and friendship. We find in our book that "patience, tolerance, understanding and love are the watchwords of our recovery."

How easy it was to find love in the words, "*We* can do what I can't" and "We alcoholics are people who need people."

Long-timers suggested I do an act of love each day without boasting about it. That brought a lesson in humility for a guy who always wanted credit for things done — even some things I had little to do with.

Loving people have reminded me to "pray for the SOB" who angers me. I am told to live life with love for myself, love for others, and love for life.

We really do learn much about love in AA. Love encourages us to count our blessings when we feel rejections, failures, inadequacies, and unworthiness. And life in AA is full of blessings.

We learn to love the naturally lovable, but when we concentrate on loving those we think are unlovable we find out how expansive love is.

As time passes in AA, we hear or read much about love: love is as simple as becoming always available. Love is a sincere interest in others. Love is a desire to be of service. Love is an ability to understand others and their problems. Giving love is more important than being loved.

Love is always positive and constructive. It does not tolerate negativism. It must be given and received unconditionally, without reservations, with no strings attached. When we love, we will see in others what we wish to have in ourselves. We will know that love is a privilege given to us by God. When we love, we will never be bored with life or our program. It is what impels us to be active and to get involved in service.

Love will teach us values in life. It shows us that the things that count are never held in the hand but always in the heart. And people who are loving always live in the now. They cannot afford to live in the past or project into tomorrow. People who love laugh more and believe that a day without laughter is a lost day. Love is the cement for the unity we need in AA. It joins the power of the mind and the heart for emotional growth. It promotes lasting attachments, never divisive controversy.

The love we find in AA is always warm, never cold. It is firm, not loose. Companionship is a result of love. And love cannot be taught but is developed naturally.

If we ever doubt that love in AA does not bring unity, we can remind ourselves that most meetings end with a firm joining of hands and recital of the Lord's Prayer or the Serenity Prayer.

One of my favorite stories is about two men who, on an evening stroll along a street, came upon an open door through which they stopped to look. Inside, an AA meeting was about to start. One man asked, "What do you suppose is going on in there?" The second man shrugged. "Must be a big family reunion.

Everybody's hugging and kissing each other." Obviously with love.

C. C., North Hollywood, California

⤸

CONFESSIONS OF A BIG BOOK THUMPER
APRIL 1989

A close friend from Texas, where I got sober, told me once, "Nobody can stand a walking Big Book." It is true that there are those of us who tend to cling a bit tightly to those precious first 164 pages and many of us refuse to listen or even argue when the conversation tends to drift into non-Conference approved ways of looking at life, the universe, and sobriety. I am writing this in part to promote an understanding on the less-reactionary side, and partly to explain one alcoholic's reasons – or, if you prefer, excuses – for my hard-hat attitude on this sensitive subject.

In the old days, back before John Barleycorn became my constant companion, I was quite the bookworm. I read everything from science fiction to Plato, sure that the answers were on paper somewhere. I eventually gave up this idea and found workable solutions in my shot glass. From my present perspective it doesn't surprise me that having given up on any definite, workable way of life, I found one when I got sober via the medium I had first searched in — the printed word. That first night I went back to my pup tent (such were my lodgings at the time) and proceeded to gobble down every word of the Big Book. Every line rang as clear and true as the smile on the chairman's face that first meeting night, and not one whit of it was anything I'd ever seriously considered before. In my state of mind at the time, anything that wasn't my idea was probably a good idea. The phrases were full not just of information but of joy. I was free to be wrong, and maybe this God fellow might not be so bad after all.

It was as if I opened up my mind, cleared the shelves of all previous material, installed a Big Book and a "Twelve and Twelve," and then sealed it up tight. Having found an answer that had worked for so many others, I became unwilling to tamper with it in any way. I had messed up every gift I'd ever received, and I wasn't willing to do that with this precious thing I had so graciously been given. The Book (to me, the term included both pieces of literature) was not to be trifled with. Most Big Book Thumpers (BBTs) have similar stories to relate in regard to their extreme bias. We seem to share many other traits, also.

In my trials as a BBT, I have found many recurring themes which it is entirely possible are not conducive to AA unity. Yet, I cannot help but harp on them to the annoyance, no doubt, of my fellow members. I am sure this tendency goes back to my old need to be right, but I forget this and assume I am merely "viewing with alarm for the good of the movement" — and I have Bill's own printed Word right here to back me up, helped along by the swift cut and accurate aim of my interpretation.

For instance, I am perfectly capable of running down a women's group that has been helping drunks for twenty years because the Tradition says "the only requirement for membership," etc. I will glance askance at some drunk advising another drunk to slow down on some Step he is working, interrupting their seditious little session (uninvited, of course) with some comment like: "The only pause mentioned in the Book is on page 75, third paragraph, for one hour between Steps Five and Six." I am then free to return to my corner and recover, certain that justice has been served.

But this Big Book Thumping is not a form of hypocrisy. We BBTs are nothing if not honest Pharisees. We turn our perfectionist eyes ever inward. For instance, I am unable to watch television. I will start to turn on the tube, pick up the Book, check the first 164 pages . . . nope, doesn't mention TV. Never mind that TV hadn't been invented when the Book was written. If Bill and Dr. Bob didn't do it, then I had better steer clear. If I am asked to go water skiing — I'm sorry, it doesn't say a thing about water skiing in the Book. I can get away with golf (Bill played golf), but I can't comfortably go to even AA dances (doesn't mention dancing).

This preoccupation with a dogmatic view of the Book seems to be based on the belief that the human intellect is of no value at all. Given my record before AA, such a belief makes sense. However, where I make my mistake is in applying this judgment to you. I've assumed "you wanted perfection, just as I did" (page 449). My tolerance is based, not on the certainty that you are wrong, but on the fear that you might not be — and that would mean that there is more than one valid way of seeing things. The Book leaves many questions open, so I assume that means there are no answers meant for mortal drunks.

A week before this writing I was in conversation with an alcoholic who had some five times my length of sobriety, when the man made an obvious error. I responded with — my favorite line! — "That's not what the Book says." His response startled me. He said, "This program is not about the Book. It's about people. I'm telling you what I have learned." Well! That's a fine how-de-do! After all, I was only trying to help (forgetting that *I* had called *him*, asking his help on a medical problem we share which is only briefly mentioned in the Book).

It is denial, or something like it, that makes me want to gloss over the fact that there are certain phrases in the Book that I tend to ignore or even protest against. Ideas such as "Our book is meant to be suggested only" are obvious balderdash. Same thing goes for "More will be revealed," and "Here no specific rules can be given." These sentences leave one with the distinct impression that there is leeway involved in working this program — and leeway is something I cannot afford. Give me an inch and I'll take the interstate. And so I go my merry, rigid way, refusing any advice that doesn't have a page number attached, closing my ears if I hear something that sounds "tainted" by pop psychology or spiritual hedonism. "Straight is the way and narrow is the gate." Sobriety is the "eye of the needle."

It is not my intention to portray BBTs as unfeeling automatons, spouting truisms they've never experienced, harping at those around them to do things their way, and running training camps for bleeding deacons. The truth is that BBTs stay sober. They are emphatic about the Book because it works and has worked for them consistently. I see this around me and have for some time.

I, of course, had role models (having never had an original thought) and picked those who had what I lacked. I was inconsistent, undependable, given to intellectual and emotional flights of fancy, and totally without a conception of a God who could help me. The people I saw who seemed to have solved these problems were those people who began sentences with the phrase, "The Book says. . . ." So I talked to them at length, and they told me that I, too, could recover, just as they had.

It may be that you have someone like me in your group. If that's the case, there is no need to fear him or pick up a resentment. If such a person corners you and patiently tries to explain how something you said at a meeting was wrong, or some opinion you expressed is sure to get you drunk, it isn't necessary to choose between running and fighting as your only viable options. Just quietly say "Thank you, but I don't have to be perfect today." If he's like I am, this response is sure to put his tail firmly in between his legs, forcing him to retreat and lick his wounds until he musters the gumption to apologize. And remember — he is a valuable asset to the group, for should anyone need to know where to find something in the Book, he is there, ready, willing and anxious, with page numbers on tap, to fulfill his function as a Big Book Thumper.

Anonymous, Athens, Alabama

DROPOUT

DECEMBER 1987

Complacency, in my opinion, is as cunning, baffling, and powerful — and patient — as alcoholism.

At one time, I was very active in my home group, somewhat active with another; I was an intergroup rep, a group secretary, and a GSR. I sold raffle tickets for the anniversary and finance committees, performed in our annual variety show, twelfth-stepped active alcoholics and took newcomers into my home, lead meetings, transported hospital patients, and even tried my hand at giving public information presentations in schools.

Gradually, however, I became an inactive member, to the point where I would laughingly (while hurting on the inside) refer to myself as an inactive member-at-large. I became resentful of new-comers fresh out of treatment centers trying to tell us old-timers how to work our AA program. I became resentful of others telling frequent slippers to come see me, that I would make them a good sponsor, because "She understands . . . she's open-minded." I was tired of pretending to be nice to people I didn't know, or care to know. My health eventually prohibited me from attending smoky meetings. I quit reading the books and quit corresponding with my friends in the *Loners-Internationalists Meeting*.

I married a man in AA, with every intention of hiding in his shadow as only the wife of an alcoholic. That lasted less than two years, because, as I said, "His character defects are more than I can handle." The truth was that he'd confided in me and I turned on him, accusing him with every move he made until he fell back into his old ways. I then blamed him when my worst character defects surfaced.

Eventually, my physical limitations prohibited me from climbing stairs to and from meetings. For years I had chanted, "You don't need to attend AA meetings to maintain sobriety. We have Loners all around the world." So I began to practice being a Loner by not drinking and not going to meetings.

And then the thought began creeping back into my mind, "I could drink socially. . . if I go back out, I can always return to AA. Others do it all the time." Then it began to happen: the mental obsession began to take over. One cold winter night someone mentioned stopping for a drink after work, I said I could be per-suaded, and the next thing I heard was me ordering some kind of a mixed drink in hot coffee. I played around with it and sipped at it, and later I tried convincing myself and others that I had not actually drunk any.

That happened not long after a close friend in AA wrote me that she was no longer a member of AA, that she had accepted Christ into her life through the church. A short-but-sweet AA relationship had just ended. And I was working two jobs at the time.

A few months later I found myself playing head games again. Whenever a certain brand of wine advertised their new cute little bottles, I thought, "I could handle that." Before long, I found myself picking a fight at home, only to head straight to the nearest store to buy one of those cute little bottles. When I got home I wasn't so brave. I poured about a third of the bottle into a glass of orange drink, and the next day the rest went down the drain.

But by then the physical compulsion was beginning to take control — and the *fear.* All my old anxieties were back. But out of pain comes growth, and I was about to take another step in my recovery.

It wasn't easy, as the senior member with eleven years of sobriety, to sit in a small closed meeting and share my experiences. They were all supportive. It seemed ironic – a few years ago an ex-spouse spread the rumor that I was drinking when I wasn't, and people believed him. Now I was drinking and "confessing" it, and no one had even suspected. I'd been through so much in my sobriety — deaths, divorces, illnesses, poverty — that somewhere along the way I had begun to *assume* that I could, and would, survive anything without picking up that first drink. I'd forgotten to include God and the Fellowship of AA — or had just plain chosen not to.

It isn't easy to start over again, to try to remain teachable after being one of the teachers, to try to become humble after being (by self-proclamation) successful in AA and in a career. I dug out my AA books, the ones I nearly threw out the last time I moved. I consider one particular person my sponsor, because we've shared so much and I know she won't betray a confidence. I joined a new home group, one close to home and scheduled for a weekend night so I won't be too exhausted from work to attend. It looks like a slow, uphill process. But at least I no longer feel as if I'm going down hill on a greased slide.

L. S., Toledo, Ohio

PH. DRUNK

FEBRUARY 1987

"The alcoholic has an infantile ego." That's what the man told me. I cringed inwardly, knowing he meant me personally, even though I was one among several thousand people at the convention. It was the 25th International AA Convention in Long Beach, California, in July 1960. I'd been sober more than two years, a miraculous circumstance considering that I had remained ignorant of the true depth and scope of AA.

The speaker who had branded my ego "infantile" was Dr. Harry Tiebout, whom co-founder Bill W. called AA's first friend in psychiatry. At the time I didn't know Dr. Tiebout's credentials, but his words somehow penetrated my own hardshelled alcoholic ego. But couldn't he use a kinder adjective than infantile? Like "juvenile" or "adolescent"?

Dr. Tiebout described the characteristics we alcoholics shared with infants. First, there was the illusion of omnipotence — having all power. The baby controls his environment, his universe, by his cries and his cooing. The alcoholic, like the baby, is self-centered. His feelings, his wishes, are all-important. The baby doesn't *intend* to keep people awake, or inconvenience them. Those side effects of his needs and demands simply do not intrude upon his awareness. In the alcoholic's case, if others manage to make him aware of his unpleasant impact on their lives, he frowns briefly and shrugs off their trifling quibbles.

Both the baby and the boozer are impatient. We want what we want when we want it — and we always want it *now!* We will not tolerate procrastination other than our own. The world should respond immediately to our wishes or suffer the consequences of our resentment, defiance, and self-pity.

Dr. Tiebout's message was that if the alcoholic merely stops drinking he or she still has those infantile personality traits. It takes the Twelve Steps to bring about maturity. I waited for him to divide us alcoholics into classifications. My motive, as you have guessed, was obvious. If there were a special kind of *intellectual* alcoholic, I would belong in that category and would not have an infantile ego!

I didn't see that feeling superior was part of my infantile ego. Dr. Tiebout never opened the escape hatch. I remained lumped together with all of you other alcoholics — the dumb, the average, and the brilliant.

After the Convention I became more aware of a phenomenon in AA. Many very intelligent people were staying drunk: men and women with advanced degrees — doctors, lawyers, engineers, members of the clergy. On the other hand, a lot of virtual illiterates and those to whom English was a difficult second language were happily sober.

One of our beloved, long-sober AA members in California used to say in his talks, "If I had been two percent smarter, I'd be dead!" I first thought he meant intelligence was a handicap to sobriety. Had I been as keen as my ego told me I was, I would have perceived that *pride* in my intelligence blinded me to how much I did *not* know.

A medical doctor, sober six years, described his early difficulty in stopping drinking. After two years around AA he had never exceeded five weeks' abstinence. One night he heard a Mexican member accept his sixteenth anniversary cake with this humble response:

"I don't speak English so good, so I just want to thank all of you in AA and my Higher Power for this program."

The doctor marveled that this man, poorly educated even in his native language, had picked up enough serenity and wisdom in AA to keep him sober sixteen years. Yet the doctor, with all his education, training, and cultural advantages, couldn't avoid booze for much more than a month. The physician resolved to stop analyzing AA and its members for flaws and instead to apply the program as the Mexican had done.

A man with a Ph.D. in engineering told how he had attended AA for six months, drinking between meetings, anxiously waiting to hear our big secret of how we now drank without getting into trouble. He never heard the plain message which is voiced in every meeting and in our literature that our suggested Twelve Steps, if practiced, will keep us comfortably abstinent one day at a time.

One college professor, sober fourteen years in AA, told me he always wore his Phi Beta Kappa key when he talked at or chaired meetings. This was not to impress the general membership. He knew us noncollege types wouldn't notice the small emblem or know what it represented if we did. He wore it so college-educated persons who recognized it or who had one might see that academic achievement gave no immunity to alcoholism or raised one above the helpfulness of AA.

In my Twelfth Step work and talking to many intelligent, competent men and women who could not stay sober, I noted a common denominator. They were unable to grasp the simple concept that their mental ability was unrelated to their alcoholism. I've known professional athletes who eventually acknowledged that their physical prowess was not related to their ability to handle alcohol. But those who were hung up on pride of intellect were not even able to recognize they were being confronted with their denial.

Show such a person the statement, "A chief symptom of alcoholism is denial that one has it." If pride were absent, simple logic would tell him that mere denial of an alcohol problem, when family and friends are concerned about it, is futile and even ridiculous. It is the person's self-recognition of the problem that is in question!

This same person, if he doesn't understand your concept of a political issue or nuclear physics, will bombard you with probing questions, perhaps even get angry at you or himself for not comprehending. But the intellectual Narcissus doesn't get angry when you attempt to disclose his potentially fatal denial of alcoholism. He is above the issue, so far above it that it escapes his mental vision.

The writer Stanislaw Lem once said, "The first obligation of intelligence is to distrust itself." The pride-filled alcoholic, however analytical and perceptive on other subjects, is unable to distrust his own thinking about his drinking. He will distrust *your* thinking, even though your experience is much vaster than his. He will distrust the latest research on the subject by respected scientists. He will cling without self-doubt to his most absurd and unfounded assumptions.

Is there no hope for the very intelligent alcoholic who cannot see that it's his ego, not his IQ, that is the issue in his drinking?

Yes, there is indeed hope. By a paradox he will later rejoice in, but cannot recognize today, his progressive illness will save him. If it doesn't kill him first, alcoholism will beat him to his knees. Pain will be his educator, his mentor. He will topple from the throne from which he has looked down with condescension upon "those alcoholics." He will echo the words at the end of chapter two of the Big Book: "Yes, I am one of them; I must have this thing."

L. H., Greensboro, North Carolina

LEARNING TO FLY

FEBRUARY 1992

My name is Sybil, and I'm an alcoholic. I got to AA in 1941, and I want to reminisce with you a little bit about the old days, what I call the covered wagon days.

A couple of weeks ago, my husband asked me if I could recall my last drunk, and I said, "Yes, I can." I was driving along one day, wanting to go home but afraid to because I couldn't face anyone, and I ended up in San Francisco — the next day. Now I couldn't go home for sure. What was I going to do? Shaking, sweating, eyes bloodshot, face puffed up, I knew that even if I went home right away, it was going to be too late. I'd run out of lies. I couldn't think of a lie that would wash.

I parked the car, and I walked, and I saw this sign, "Sultan Turkish Baths." I decided I could sweat it out there and get myself in shape, but I thought I'd better have something to read. So I stopped at the newsstand and bought a *Saturday Evening Post* — five cents. It was dated March 1, 1941, and on the cover it said, "Alcoholics Anonymous, by Jack Alexander." I was stunned because I had read about AA in 1939, in the *Liberty Magazine, I* believe, one little paragraph about an inch long. Even that had impressed me and I intended to cut it out and save it but I hadn't. So I took the *Post* with me, had the Turkish bath, and even though I was just too sick to think, I knew there was hope.

I somehow got the impression that there was an AA hospital or clinic or something, but at the bottom of the article it said if you need help, write to Box such-and-such in New York. I rang the bell for the bath attendant and asked for pencil, paper, an envelope, and a stamp, and I think I wrote a rather pitiful letter to New York. I said, I am a desperate alcoholic and I'll take the next plane back there and take your cure.

The answer came a few days later, airmail special delivery, from Ruth Hock, God bless her. She was Bill W.'s nonalcoholic stenographer and had been for many years when Bill was in Wall Street. And now she was still working for him, and she answered all the mail from that *Saturday Evening Post* article. She answered my letter and said, You needn't come back to New York, there's one group in Los Angeles. That's for all of California. It's very small and it has been a struggle for them. They have met in a couple of hotel lobbies but they are now meeting in the Elks Temple every Friday night at 8:30. And she said, You'll be very welcome, I'm sure. They have no women alcoholics in California.

I seemed to have unbounded faith that it was going to be okay. It was Friday. I got dressed, but I couldn't comb my hair so I tied a turban thing on my head and I poked my hair all up under it, and down I went. When I got to the Elks Temple they directed me into a small dining room, and seated around the table were ten or twelve men, and a couple of women. I made myself invisible, if that's possible, because they all looked so happy and were laughing and talking. I thought, well, they're the doctors and the nurses and so forth, and I thought, They'll be giving me a pill any minute now — the magic pill, the cure-all.

Eventually a man got up and rapped on the table for order. And he said, "This is a regular meeting of Alcoholics Anonymous in California. We are a band of ex-drunks who gather to obtain and maintain our sobriety on an all-time basis with no mental reservations whatsoever." I thought to myself, What an order; I can't go through with it. Well, I didn't have to go through with it that night. I didn't get a chance because he continued with, "But as is our custom before this meeting starts, all you women leave." And these two women that I hadn't even noticed particularly because I was so desperately frightened, they just strolled out into the lobby. I later found out they were the wives — there was no Al-Anon then, and the women were quite used to leaving the meeting and waiting in the lobby; they came back later for coffee and donuts. But I thought this had been cooked up to throw me out. And it worked, because I put my hands over my face and I ran out into the lobby. I lurked around in the ladies' room awhile and then I went into hysterics and I got in my car and I headed for a bar and I got very drunk.

I thought, How exclusive can you get! To kick me out like that. And as I drank and got more livid, I turned to the people beside me at the bar and I said, "I'm a member of Alcoholics Anonymous." And they said, "So what!" Then at two in the morning, when the bartender was trying to get me out of there, I called Cliff, who's in the book *AA Comes of Age*. Cliff and Dorothy had been taking care of all the Twelfth Step calls for California since the group started in 1939. I was very indignant. I said, "Well, I went down to your group tonight and they threw me out." He said, "Oh no, no, I'm sure they did not do that. Did you tell them you were an alcoholic?" I said, "Of course not. No, they threw me out all right." He said, "Well, we need you, we need you. Please come back. We haven't had a woman alcoholic." When I heard the words "we need you," I thought, well, I am a good typist and maybe I should volunteer my services. Then I said, "All right, now, I've had about enough of this and I want you to send your AA ambulance." He said, "We don't have any such thing. You go back next Friday night and tell them you're an alcoholic. You'll be as welcome as the flowers in May."

I don't know what I did that week. Probably I was drunk and sober and drunk and sober, but I know this: it was a miracle I ever went back, and thank God I did. But I didn't go back alone. Because during that week my brother Tex came to see me. He came in the house and he picked up the pamphlet Ruth had mailed me from New York, the only one that AA had. It was a thin pamphlet and gave a few basic facts on the Steps, and as he read it he had a pint bottle in his hip pocket, as usual. He was reading and saying, "That's good stuff, Syb. They really know what they're doing there. So you're going Friday, huh?" And I said, "That's right, Tex." So he says, "Well, I'm going with you." He said, "I'll tell you the truth — the reason I want to go there. Those guys that are working for me down on Skid Row. I can't get a regular crew together." He was a vegetable peddler then, with a truck run around four in the morning, and the winos sometimes didn't show up. He said, "If I can sober them up, I'll make a lot of money. So what I'm going to do is take them all down there and get them all fixed."

So it was with fear and trembling that I looked forward to that Friday night, because Tex pulled up in front of my house in his vegetable truck and standing in the back were eleven winos. I crawled up in the cab of the truck with Tex, and down we go to the meeting. There were a few more people there that week, but the full impact of the *Saturday Evening Post* hadn't hit. But I got to hear the Twelve Steps read, and also the fifth chapter.

At the conclusion of that meeting, Frank R., God bless him — he was my sponsor and so was Cliff — reached over and got a bushel of mail that had come because of the article. Hundreds of letters from alcoholics. He looked at that skinny little crowd that was there that night — Tex and his winos and me and about fifteen others — and he said, "Well now, we got to get all these drunks down here by next Friday night. So we're going to have to cut this crowd up in sections. And if there's anyone here from Riverside County, come down and get these Twelfth Step calls." Tex went down in front and Frank gave him forty or fifty of the letters to read and answer from alcoholics who asked for help. Then he said, "Anyone from the beaches?" This guy raised his hand, Curly from Long Beach, and he went down and got forty or fifty letters. And this went on — Pasadena, Santa Monica, and one guy from Fresno, one from Santa Barbara and so forth, until there was one remaining stack of letters, about a fifth of them.

And he said, "I've been saving this stack up for the last because we now have a woman alcoholic. Her name is Sybil. Come up here, Sybil. I'm putting you in charge of all the women." I had to be honest. I went up there and I said, "Well, I'll probably be drunk next Friday. I always have been." And then I said, "What are you going to do tonight? What are you going to say to me that is going to make it different? So that when I walk out that door tonight, and during the week that I'm out there by myself, I won't get those butterflies and the sweating palms?" I said, "What's going to be different? You've got to do something tonight. How can I stay sober for a week? I'd like to be able to go and ring door-bells and bring all those drunks down here. But I haven't read the Big Book." He said, "I know that."

I said, "Truthfully, I haven't read your pamphlet. I haven't felt well enough to read." He said, "I know that. You're not expected to know very much." But he said, "You asked me how you could stay sober until next Friday. Now I'll tell you it's in that Big Book that you haven't read. Somewhere in that Big Book it says that when all other measures fail, working with another alcoholic will save the day. Now I'm going to tell you what to do quite simply. You take this basket of mail and tomorrow morning you start ringing the doorbells, and when the girl answers the door you say to her, 'Did you write this letter asking for help with a drinking problem?' And when she says, 'Well yes I did,' you say, 'Well, I wrote one like that last week and it was answered. I went down there and I looked them over. I didn't find out how they're doing it but they're doing it, and they look good. So if you want to quit drinking as badly as I want to quit drinking, you come with me and we'll find out together.' "

"Oh" I said, "I think I can do that all right." So I took the mail and I went home with it, and I was getting ready the next morning to get in my car and start ringing doorbells when my brother Tex came over. He said, "I'm going to ride around with you for laughs." Well, it wasn't for laughs. We made all those calls and out of fifty we may have gotten a dozen or more. Some of the letters were from landladies who wanted the guy upstairs not to make so much noise on a Saturday night, and sometimes it turned out the wife had written in for a husband who was an alcoholic, and Tex came in handy there. And some of them were from women who wanted help.

We did take a number of women down and a few men. The meeting grew — and I mean it mushroomed. But here's what happened. Frank had said, "I'm putting you in charge of the women." Well, to me that was like a neon sign that was going on and off, "charge, charge, charge." And I could be real big because Frank and Mort gave me a notebook and they said, "Now you write down all the names of women and then you get them a sponsor. And you have the sponsor report back to you. Then, when you look in your notebook, you will know who you gave the call to. You'll have the report on it. That's a good system." And I took it oh so seriously because I'd go down to the mother group — now we had two, three, four hundred people possibly, and a microphone and everything — and as the forty or fifty women came in and they were seated, I could think, "There's Eva. She called on Bonnie. Bonnie called on so-and-so, and Fran, and yeah, yeah." And it checked out perfectly. Then I would tell Frank and Mort it was working fine. They'd say, "That's nice. You're doing a good job."

But one night I went to the mother group and a gal came down the aisle and she had six strangers with her and they hadn't been cleared through me. And I walked up to her and I said, "Where did you get these women? You know what Frank and Mort are going to say about the system." She said, "To hell with the system! I have friends who have a drinking problem same as I do, and they found out that I was getting sober and staying sober. They asked me how I was doing it. I told them I joined AA. They said, 'Can I go with you?' I said, 'Yes.' " She said, "It's as simple as that and anytime anybody wants to come to an AA meeting with me for a drinking problem that's the way it's going to be, and I'll never report to you again."

When she told me that, tears came to my eyes and I couldn't get out of there fast enough. I wanted to run up to Huntington Park and tell my brother Tex all about it. But he wasn't there, and you want to know why? He had been excommunicated. Because he had started a group. The powers that be, the boys downtown, called Tex on the carpet and said, "Tex, fold the group up. Where's your loyalty to the mother group?" He said, "I'm loyal to the mother group. I'm just sick of picking up guys in Long Beach and driving them thirty-five miles to Los Angeles, so I started a group at the halfway point. Some of my boys are down here tonight. You come out to our group next Friday night and we'll just kind of visit back and forth." And they said, "No, you're excommunicated," and he laughed and laughed and laughed.

About a month later they called him down. They had a committee meeting and they asked him if he'd decided to fold up the group and he said, "Nope. Doing fine. Got a lot of the boys down here with me tonight and you're welcome to come to my meeting. It's a participation meeting where alcoholics all talk." Well, at the mother group, we'd had two speakers, Frank and Mort, for two years. So they said, "We thought you'd say that, so we have incorporated Alcoholics Anonymous in California." And they had. Those that are still around down there will tell you. It took us about a year to laugh that one off, until Tex began to visit the mother group and the mother group members began to visit the Hole in the Ground Group — it was called that because they met in the basement.

Tex advised me to resign my job of being in charge of the women. He said, "Tell them you're too busy helping your brother with his group and suggest that they have a secretary of their very own." I did that, but how it hurt. But it had been good for me at the time, because I had no ego. My ego had been smashed for so many years, and it was good to feel that I was wanted and needed and that I had this little job to do. It was good for me at the time and it was good that I gave it up.

Several years later, they called me up and told me to come down and be the executive secretary for the Central Office of Alcoholics Anonymous in Los Angeles, and I was, for twelve glorious years. So you see in AA you turn a new page and it's all new again. I want to be a newcomer — this seniority bit is a lot of baloney. We're all fledglings, learning to fly.

Sybil C., Los Angeles, California

MENDED BY AA

JUNE 1993

As I sit here recalling my childhood days before I was seven, I remember my parents being happy. We were an Indian family and there was always a lot of laughter in our home — wherever it happened to be. We used to travel all summer by canoe along Lake Winnipegosis. I was never afraid, even if we were in the middle of the lake with a big storm going on. The canoe would rock like crazy, but I was never scared because my mom and dad were there.

My parents did not booze. They were hard-working people, but they loved music and laughter and jokes. We had an accordion, a guitar, and a violin in our home. And I remember my dad doing pushups on the floor with my mom sitting on him. My dad was about 180 pounds and my mom must have been at least 250! My dad would beg her to get off but she would just sit there and laugh. My mom was a good cook and she could can anything — berries, meat, fish — and make maple sugar in the spring. We always had lots to eat. We never knew what hunger was.

Then my world came crashing down when I was seven and a half years old. That's when the priest put my brother and me in a boarding school where they broke my spirit and I found out what hunger was. Stealing and lying became a way to survive.

The way I understood their way was to be bad in order to be good. I could never figure that out. It was very confusing. I also picked up that you had to be white to go to heaven. So I used to pray to be white so I could go to heaven too.

Eventually I came home, a broken girl. But by then even my mom and dad were not the same. Mom was cranky, always yelling at someone, mostly my dad. She was crippled with arthritis, and only now can I understand the kind of pain she was in. Yet there still was no booze in their home, and never was till their dying day.

At the age of seventeen I was raped, and booze came into my life in a big way, bringing with it the seeds of a wrecked marriage and the pain of having to give my sons and daughter away. I ended up on skid row trying to drink myself to death. But then I got pregnant for the fifth time. I decided against abortion, thought of adoption, but in the end I kept her. But five years later, my baby was taken away from me.

That's when I decided to quit drinking for three months — just to get her back. Besides, I was broken in spirit, body, mind, and soul. But AA put me back together, and that three months is now fourteen years.

I no longer pray to be white. I like me just the way I am, and I am proud of my heritage. AA has helped me be the kind of person I always wanted to be.

I have that peace back that I once possessed as a child on Lake Winnipegosis. I feel the Great Spirit's presence and I'm not scared anymore.

Violet G., Edmonton, Alberta

⤳

LIFE IS MEANT TO BE LIVED
SEPTEMBER 1995

When some of my foggy thinking began to clear in the early days of my sobriety, I realized how often I had drunk to escape the realities of life. As a result, I worked hard at facing my alcoholism head-on, practicing the Steps, and convincing myself that I was, at long last, on a journey of discovery. It was exciting to think I could become a learning, growing, changing person, accepting my limitations, somehow finding the courage to seek a personal honesty for the first time. I naively assumed the escapist in me would just automatically disappear the moment I joined Alcoholics Anonymous. Now I realize how cunning, baffling, and powerful are the old ways of thinking and behaving.

In fact, I allowed the old escape act to seep into my family life in matters that were most important to me. At home, I refused to take an honest stand on issues or ask the questions that might have led to a deeper understanding of my loved ones, or my own role as wife, mother, or grandmother. What honesty I had was confined to the rooms of AA and talks with my sponsor. (Then I wondered why I struggled with depression so often.)

Very gradually I became a champion people-pleaser, a kind of emotional jellyfish who discovered that the silent martyr role at home was an "easier, softer way." At work I avoided additional responsibilities and treated myself like a fragile person to be protected from stress at all cost. I even gave some room in my head to the idea that I was now an AA old-timer and didn't have the energy for very much Twelfth Step work.

I was at a dead halt — spiritually, mentally, and physically. Depression smothered my muffled thinking even more. Serious illness came along, and it took me awhile to understand what was happening. Thank God I never gave up on meetings, so my Higher Power finally got through to me. I realized I'd been playing the great escape act all this time.

I know now I have a lot of work to do. There are more amends to be made, letters to be sent, Twelfth Step work to be done, responsibilities to be assumed, and honest talks to be had with loved ones. Life is meant to be lived by facing the challenges it brings. Otherwise, I'm not living, just existing. God didn't give me this gift of sobriety to sit in a rocking chair, imagining myself as some wise old woman who has arrived somewhere.

There is no easier, softer way. To bring the great escape act into sobriety is to travel with a companion that led me to despair long ago. The teaching I receive in Alcoholics Anonymous about courage and love helps me to continue to grapple with the challenges of life as they are given to me, one day at a time.

Louise A., Spring Hill, Florida